A-Z Handbook
for
Veterinary Nurses

PasTest
Dedicated to your success

A-Z Handbook
for
Veterinary Nurses

Alison Lomas BVetMed MRCVS

Annaliese Magee VN AVN Dip (Surgical)

Claire Wilson BA PGCE VN

© 2006 PASTEST LTD
Egerton Court
Parkgate Estate
Knutsford
Cheshire
WA16 8DX

Telephone: 01565 752000

First Published 2006

ISBN: 1904627994
        9781904627999
A catalogue record for this book is available from the British Library.

The information contained within this book was obtained by the author from
reliable sources. However, while every effort has been made to ensure its
accuracy, no responsibility for loss, damage or injury occasioned to any person
acting or refraining from action as a result of information contained herein can
be accepted by the publishers or author.

Text prepared by Keytec Typesetting Ltd, Bridport, Dorset
Printed and bound in the UK by Athenaeum Press, Gateshead

Contents

Preface

Welcome to the *A-Z Handbook for Veterinary Nurses*. This practical, pocket-sized, reference guide provides quick access to the essential information veterinary nurses need whilst in practice. Covering the whole of the veterinary nursing syllabus, it is a portable, easy-to-use source of information for both trainees and qualified veterinary nurses. This handbook features definitions of key concepts and terms relating to small animal health and disease and information on veterinary equipment and surgical instruments. The appendices contain additional essential information making this handbook an invaluable reference source for veterinary nurses at all stages of their training and career.

Claire Wilson BA PGCE VN

How to use this book

This book is designed to allow the reader to check the definitions of terms which may be encountered when working in veterinary practice. It is aimed at anybody who works with small animals in the field of veterinary medicine – particularly trainee and qualified veterinary nurses, but also veterinary receptionists and kennel staff.

To make the book easy to use:

- Words within the main text which appear in *italics* are defined elsewhere in the handbook.
- Words which are related to or which are similar to the word being defined are listed at the end of the definition.
- At the end of the book you will find a list of prefixes and suffixes making up many common veterinary words, together with relevant examples.
- There is also a section containing useful reference ranges for the veterinary nurse to have to hand during the working day.

Abaxial – away from the axial skeleton, ie away from the trunk and the head.

Abdomen – the cavity located between the *diaphragm* and the *pelvis*. The *abdominal viscera* are found here (*small* and *large intestines, liver, spleen, kidneys* and *bladder*, and the *uterus* and *ovaries* in the female animal); the cavity is lined by a *serous membrane* (the *peritoneum*). See also Abdominal breathing.

Abdominal – relating to the *abdomen*.

Abdominal breathing – respiration is performed primarily by the abdominal muscles rather than by the intercostal muscles. Conditions such as asthma can cause this.

Abdominocentesis – the procedure of aseptically obtaining a sample of abdominal fluid by inserting a needle through the body wall into the abdominal cavity.

Abducens nerve – sixth (VI) *cranial nerve* which controls the muscles of the eyeball.

Abduction – describes the direction of movement of a limb; the limb in question is being moved away from the *midline* or *medial* axis of the body. See also *Adduction*.

Abrasion – wound caused by friction, removing the epidermis and superficial dermis. There is often a very small amount of haemorrhage. It is usually painful and prone to infection.

Abscess – a *pus*-filled area of tissue which has developed as a result of localised *inflammation*. Abscesses commonly occur at the site of a bacterial *infection*, eg following a cat bite (cat-bite abscess), from *bacteria* entering a *wound* or from the presence of a *foreign body* irritating the surrounding tissues. Treatment involves lancing (puncturing) the abscess, allowing the accumulated pus to drain away, removing the foreign body (if present), then flushing out the area with *sterile* saline or *antiseptic* solution.

Absorption – the process of transfer of a molecule or chemical across a membrane. Examples include absorption of digested material across the lining of the gut, or absorption of molecules from filtered fluid in the kidney.

Acaricide – a substance which is used to kill *mites*. Examples include fipronil, ivermectin, selamectin and moxidectin.

Accelerator – contains potassium carbonate or sodium carbonate. Increases the efficiency of x-ray *developer* by increasing the pH.

Accessory nerve – eleventh (XI) *cranial nerve* which controls the muscles to the *pharynx*, *larynx* and *palate*.

Accident book – a record book approved by the *Health and Safety Executive* (HSE) in which the practice is legally required to report in full all accidents occurring on the premises to members of staff or members of the public during working hours. The name and address of the injured person must be entered, along with the date, details of the accident and extent of injuries. See also *Health and Safety at Work Act* and *Reporting of Injuries, Diseases and Dangerous Occurrences Regulations* (RIDDOR).

Accommodation – the process by which the *lens* in the *eye* changes shape to focus on both near and far objects to produce an image on the *retina*. The muscles of the *ciliary body* contract and relax to change the shape of the lens. When the muscles contract, the lens becomes more spherical in shape which allows light from close objects to be focused onto the retina. Relaxation of the muscles pulls the lens into a more flattened shape which focuses the light from further away objects.

Angiotensin - converting enzyme (ACE) – angiotensin-converting enzyme is an *enzyme* produced in the *kidney* which converts *angiotensin I* to the active form *angiotensin II*.

ACE-inhibitor – a drug used to stop the actions of *angiotensin-converting enzyme* (*ACE*). It is commonly used to treat *congestive heart failure* or *renal failure* by reducing *blood pressure*.

Acetabular plate – specially designed curved plate used in repairing fractures of the *acetabulum*.

Acetabulum – a cup-like structure in the pelvic bone in which the head of the *femur* sits. Together, the acetabulum and the femur form a *ball and socket joint*. See also *Hip dysplasia*.

Acetylcholine (ACh) – a *neurotransmitter* which travels from one *neurone* across the *synapse*, attaching to receptors on the second neurone to create an *action potential*. See also *Noradrenaline*.

Achilles tendon – a group of *tendons* running down the back of the leg, connecting the hamstring muscles (*biceps femoris*, *semimembranosus* and *semitendinosus*) and the *gastrocnemius* muscle to the point of the *hock* (calcaneum).

Acid – a chemical substance having a *pH* lower than 7. An acid will release hydrogen ions (H^+) when in solution. See also *Alkali*.

Acid citrate dextrose (ACD) collection bags – a prepared blood collection bag used to collect blood from the donor patient during blood transfusions. May be stored at 1–6 °C for 21 days.

Acid-fast bacteria – bacteria which resist decoloration by acid once they have been stained. The mycobacteria (such as *Mycobacterium bovis*, which causes tuberculosis) are acid-fast and this feature may be used to identify them.

Acidifier – neutralises any alkaline developer carried over to the fixer tank in the x-ray processor and accelerates the action of other chemicals.

Acidosis – the build-up of *acid* within the body. It can be caused by failure to breathe out enough *carbon dioxide* (respiratory acidosis), or by a build-up of acids in the blood in conditions such as *kidney failure* or *diabetic ketoacidosis* (metabolic acidosis).

Acquired – a condition which occurs after birth (ie is not congenital or inherited) and is produced by external influences. A broken bone is an acquired injury, as is a virus caught from another animal.

Acral lick granuloma – a condition affecting the skin caused by prolonged licking of the same area. The term acral relates to the extremities – usually the paws. The causes vary and include pruritic (itchy) skin disease, joint pain and boredom.

Acromegaly – an *endocrine* disorder in which there is over-secretion of *growth hormone*, usually from the pituitary gland in cats or mammary tissue in dogs. Clinical signs include gain in body weight and size; in particular the size of the head and feet increases. Most animals also develop diabetes mellitus and cardiovascular disease.

ACTH stimulation test – a diagnostic test used to check the reserves of *cortisol* (steroid) in the *adrenal glands*. It is used to diagnose *hypoadrenocorticism* (Addison's disease) and *hyperadrenocorticism* (Cushing's disease), or to check the effects of drugs on the adrenal glands. The test involves measuring cortisol levels in the blood before and after injection of synthetic *adrenocorticotrophic hormone* (*ACTH*).

Actin – one of two *proteins* found in muscle fibres (see also Myosin) which play an important role in muscle contraction. The release of a *neurotransmitter* at the *neuromuscular junction* causes an *action potential* which stimulates the actin and myosin fibres to shorten, causing the muscle to contract. See also *Muscle tone*.

Action potential – an electrical impulse conducted by a nerve cell (*neurone*). The action potential is carried along the length of the neurone as a *nervous impulse*, jumping from one *node of Ranvier* to another in myelinated nerve fibres (see also Myelin sheath), making the conduction along the *axon* much quicker than in non-myelinated neurones.

Activated charcoal – a substance known as an *adsorbent* which is administered to animals that are suspected of having ingested a poisonous substance. It works by binding to the toxin, preventing it from being absorbed through the intestine wall. It will pass through the digestive tract and eventually be excreted in the faeces.

Active drain – used when there is extensive fluid or air that needs to be removed. Examples include Heimlich valve and sump drain. Drainage is provided by using pressure, either continuously using a suction device or intermittently with a syringe. The tube has to be rigid so that it does not collapse under pressure.

Active immunity – the ability of an animal's *immune system* to resist infection by *pathogens*. This is achieved by the action of *antibodies*, which are formed in response to exposure to a specific *antigen*. The antibodies have learnt to recognise and destroy specific invading pathogens. This type of immunity is acquired during the animal's lifetime, either by natural exposure to a pathogen or by *vaccination*.

Active scavenging system – removes waste gas from the expiratory limb of the anaesthetic circuit. Comprises a piece of tubing attached to the expiratory valve on the circuit at one end, while the other end is attached to an extractor fan. Several anaesthetic systems can be scavenged using the same system.

Active transport – movement of molecules across a membrane *against* the concentration gradient. This process requires energy in the form of adenosine triphosphate (ATP). An example is the pumping of sodium and potassium across cell membranes.

Acupuncture – an ancient Chinese technique, involves fine needles being inserted through the skin at specific locations on the body, to help treat certain conditions and control pain. Acupuncture is a complementary therapy which can be used alongside conventional treatment or used alone.

Acute – describes a condition or disease that has a rapid onset and that may have severe symptoms. It may be immediately life threatening, but it may also subside rapidly once treatment is administered. See also *Chronic*.

Acute-phase proteins – a group of *proteins* which are produced by the *liver* in response to *inflammation*. *Fibrinogen* is an example of an acute-phase protein.

Acute renal failure – a rapid deterioration of *renal* function with sudden development of *azotaemia*. It may be reversible if diagnosed and treated promptly and if the cause can be identified and removed. Renal failure may be pre-renal (eg *dehydration* or *hypovolaemia*), renal (eg *pyelonephritis*, *toxicity*) or post-renal (eg urinary tract obstruction). See also *Chronic renal failure*.

Addison's disease – see Hypoadrenocorticism.

Adduction – describes the direction of movement of a limb; the limb in question is brought in medially, towards the *midline* of the body. See also *Abduction*.

Adenitis – *inflammation* of a *gland* or *lymph node*. For example, lymphadenitis describes inflammation of a lymph node, sebaceous adenitis describes inflammation of a *sebaceous gland*.

Adenocarcinoma – *malignant tumour* of a *gland*, eg *mammary* adenocarcinoma which is fairly common in unspayed older female animals.

Adenohypophysis (anterior hypophysis) – the anterior lobe of the *pituitary gland*. It secretes hormones such as *ACTH, growth hormone, follicle-stimulating hormone, luteinising hormone, thyroid-stimulating hormone* and *prolactin*.

Adenoma – *benign tumour* of a *gland*. An example is sebaceous adenoma – a benign tumour of the *sebaceous gland*.

Adenosine triphosphate (ATP) – a molecule which is found in the *mitochondria* of the *cell* and which stores energy. ATP is broken down into adenosine diphosphate (ADP) in a process that releases energy; ADP is then used to carry out many functions in the cell.

Adenovirus – the causal agent of *infectious canine hepatitis* (adenovirus I), while adenovirus II makes up part of the *kennel cough* complex, along with *parainfluenza virus* and *Bordetella bronchiseptica*.

Adhesion – when structures within the body (commonly the abdomen) have grown or 'stuck' together. Adhesions can be repaired surgically if necessary. Adhesions are usually caused by inflammation or injury.

Adhesive dressings – used to cover a wound, may have absorbent properties. When applied, these dressings will 'stick' to the skin.

Adipocyte – a fat cell. See also *Adipose tissue*.

Adipose tissue – *loose connective tissue* made up of many fat cells (*adipocytes*) found in the *subcutaneous* layer of the *skin*. The tissue acts as a fat store and also as a protective and insulating layer for any delicate organs or structures beneath.

Adjuvant – a substance (usually aluminium hydroxide) contained in *inactivated vaccines*. Its purpose is to enhance the animal's immune response, as inactivated vaccines tend to cause a more short-lived immune response than that of a *live vaccine*.

Ad libitum (ad lib) – the patient is given as much as it wants, eg water.

Admission (of patients) – the patient is formally admitted into the hospital/practice to enable monitoring and investigative work to be carried out.

Adnexa – the accessory or adjoining parts of an organ. The adnexa of the eye include *lacrimal* glands, eyelids, lacrimal ducts, etc and the adnexa of the skin include hairs, *sebaceous* and *sweat* glands, etc.

Adrenal glands – a pair of *endocrine* glands which are located just outside the *peritoneum* (*retroperitoneal*) in the abdomen and *cranial* to the *kidneys*. Each gland consists of an outer *cortex* and an inner *medulla*. The adrenal medulla produces two *hormones*, *adrenaline* and *noradrenaline*. Both these hormones act in similar ways and are involved with the functioning of the *sympathetic nervous system*. The adrenal cortex produces steroid hormones – *glucocorticoids*, *mineralocorticoids* and *sex hormones*. Glucocorticoids (eg cortisol) are released when the animal is under stress because they stimulate the production of glucose from glycogen. Mineralocorticoids (eg *aldosterone*) regulate the concentration of *sodium* (Na^+) and *potassium* (K^+) ions in the body.

Adrenaline – one of two hormones secreted by the *adrenal medulla* to prolong the actions of the *sympathetic nervous system*. Adrenaline prepares the body for the 'fight or flight' response in times of danger or threat. It causes an increase in heart rate and causes the *pupils* of the *eye* to dilate. It also causes an increase in respiration rate and depth and dilates the arteries supplying skeletal muscle. It also stimulates an increase in blood glucose level by increasing the rate of *glycogen* breakdown. This ensures that the muscles have a ready energy source if required. Adrenaline is also known as epinephrine. See also *Noradrenaline.*

Adrenocorticotrophic hormone (ACTH) – a *hormone* produced by the *pituitary gland* which stimulates the production and secretion of *cortisol* and *aldosterone* from the *adrenal gland.*

Adsorbent – a substance, eg *activated charcoal*, which is given to animals that are suspected of having eaten a poisonous substance. The adsorbent binds to the toxin, preventing it from being absorbed through the intestine wall.

Adverse reaction – an unwanted or unexpected reaction following administration of a drug. Symptoms may be sudden or may develop over a longer period of time.

Aelurostrongylus abstrusus – a nematode lungworm which affects cats and is often asymptomatic but may cause respiratory disease in animals with suppressed immune systems. The life cycle involves snails or slugs.

Aerobic – a process or organism that requires air (or more specifically oxygen). See also *Anaerobic*.

Aerobic bacteria (obligate aerobes) – aerobic bacteria require oxygen to survive.

Aerobic respiration – a process where energy is produced (in the form of *ATP*) from glucose breakdown products by the *Kreb's cycle*. The process requires oxygen to proceed. Aerobic respiration occurs in the mitochondria of the cell.

Aerophagy – ingestion of air.

Aerosol – an airborne suspension of potentially *infectious micro-organisms* (eg from a sneeze). In densely populated areas, for example in kennels or a cattery, precautions should ideally be taken to prevent airborne transmission of diseases from one animal to another through the presence of 'sneeze barriers' between cages.

Afferent – usually used to describe *nerves* or vessels, meaning conducting towards, or inwards, eg an afferent nerve fibre carries *nervous impulses* from the sensory receptors towards the *brain* and *spinal cord*. See also Efferent.

Afterbirth – see *Placenta*.

Agar – a solid medium (usually a gelatinous substance) used to allow a bacterial colony growth. Used in culture and sensitivity testing.

Agonist – a *muscle* responsible for producing a certain movement. Muscles are usually found in opposing groups so that when they work together, they produce a range of movement around a joint. The opposing muscle to the agonist is called the *antagonist*. For example, the muscles around the elbow act to *flex* and *extend* the joint; the *biceps brachii* acts as the agonist while the *triceps brachii* opposes its action and is therefore the antagonist.

Agranulocyte – a division within the group of white blood cells known as *leukocytes* that includes *lymphocytes* and *monocytes*. The name comes from the fact that the *cytoplasm* of these cells appears agranular (no granules) following staining. See also *Granulocyte*.

Air sac – thin walled structures which are an important part of the respiratory system in birds. No gaseous exchange occurs in the air sacs. The air sacs act like bellows to move air in and out of the lungs.

Alanine aminotransferase (ALT) – a liver enzyme which is usually measured during a biochemistry blood profile. It is increased when there is damage to the liver cells. It may also be increased by some drugs, such as steroids or phenobarbitone, or by severe muscle damage (eg road traffic accident).

Albumin – a *protein* found in *plasma*, along with *globulin*. Albumin and globulin combined are known as *total protein*. Albumin is synthesised from *amino acids* in the *liver* and is mainly responsible for maintaining *osmotic pressure* in the *blood*. Increased plasma albumin levels can be caused by *dehydration*; decreased levels can indicate heart failure, *haemorrhage* or kidney disease.

Alcohol – used as an ingredient for some skin disinfectants, eg surgical spirit is 70% isopropyl alcohol.

Aldehydes – used as an ingredient for some environmental disinfectants, eg glutaraldehyde in Cidex®.

Aldosterone – a steroid hormone produced in the *adrenal gland* which is important for maintining *electrolyte* balance. It is known as a mineralocorticoid. It acts on the kidney stimulating excretion of potassium (K^+) and hydrogen (H^+) ions, and retention of sodium (Na^+) and chloride (Cl^-).

Alkali – a chemical substance having a *pH* higher than 7. An alkali has the ability to neutralise an *acid*.

Alkaline phosphatase (ALKP) – an enzyme which is usually measured during a biochemistry blood profile. It is produced by hepatocytes and biliary epithelium or by bone. ALKP is increased when there is *cholestasis*. It may also be increased by some drugs such as phenobarbitone (and steroids in dogs), in young animals as a result of bone growth, or following bone disease or injury.

Alkalosis – the build-up of *alkali* within the body. It can be caused by loss of acid in conditions such as vomiting (*metabolic alkalosis*), or by increased loss of carbon dioxide from the lungs (*respiratory alkalosis*) which may occur during hyperventilation.

Allantois – part of the fetal membrane system which provides protection and nourishment for the developing fetus.

Allele – a sequence of *DNA* in a *chromosome* which codes for a *gene*. Each gene is composed of two alleles, one from each parent.

Allergen – any substance which causes an allergic reaction by the immune system. Most allergens are inhaled (eg pollens) or ingested (eg some drugs such as penicillin, gluten, peanuts) although contact allergy may also occur (eg nickel allergy).

Allergy – a reaction of the *immune system* to an *allergen* which can have *symptoms* varying from mild irritation through to *anaphylactic shock* and death. Treatment may involve allergen avoidance; use of drugs such as *anti-histamines* and *corticosteroids*; and immunotherapy (vaccines designed to reduce the scale of the reaction).

Allis tissue forceps – surgical instrument designed for handling soft tissue. They have rounded tips with tooth-edged grippers and ratchet handles.

Allograft – a type of skin graft. Skin is taken from another patient but of the same species.

Alopecia – lack or loss of hair. Common causes include *endocrine* diseases, such as *hypothyroidism* or *hyperadrenocorticism*, and skin diseases such as *atopy* or *mange*.

Alphadolone/alphaxolone – a steroid general anaesthetic. Can be administered to cats but is dangerous to administer to dogs and therefore must be avoided. Can cause histamine release in cats, demonstrated as oedema of the ear pinna and paws; more severely, oedema can occur in the larynx or present as pulmonary oedema.

Alpha-2 adrenoceptor agonist – a potent sedative for both cats and dogs, can be used alone or alongside other drugs such as analgesics. Causes side-effects such as vomiting, bradycardia and hypotension. Examples include medetomidine (Domitor®) and xylazine (Rompun®).

Alpha-2 adrenoceptor antagonist – reverses the effects of alpha-2 adrenoceptor agonists. An example is atipamezole (Antisedan®).

Alpha-linolenic acid – one of the three essential fatty acids.

Alternative medicine – treatment without the use of drugs and outside conventional methods. Examples: *acupuncture*, *homeopathy*.

Altricial – adjective used to describe a *neonate* meaning being born blind, hairless and helpless. Eg puppies and kittens are altricial.

Aluminium filter – a piece of aluminium placed between the X-ray tube and the collimator. It acts as a filter, absorbing the 'soft' X-rays such as alpha and beta radiation.

Aluminium splint – a pliable splint made of aluminium providing dressings/bandages with some rigidity.

Alveolar sac – each alveolar duct found at the end of the *bronchioles* in the *lungs* terminates in an alveolar sac, each containing many *alveoli*.

Alveolus (pl. **alveoli) – 1.** a pocket within the lungs, at the end of the *bronchioles*. The alveoli lie in close proximity to an extensive network of *capillaries* to allow *gaseous exchange* to take place. Each alveolus is formed from a single layer of simple squamous *epithelium* that allows for the rapid diffusion of gases across it. **2.** the bony socket in which the tooth sits, held in place by the *periodontal ligament*.

A-mode – a type of image display used in ultrasound, it is not often used. Shows only the position of tissue interfaces.

American Society of Anesthesiologists (ASA) – founded in 1905, its main aim is to maintain the standards of anaesthesia and improve patient care. They are responsible for developing the physical status classification system which enables you to classify patients according to their health status, before anaesthesia.

Amino acid – a nitrogen-containing molecule which is a building block for *protein* synthesis. Amino acids join into chains called *polypeptides*, which then fold up to make proteins.

Ammonia – a toxic nitrogen-containing molecule (NH_3) which is produced during protein breakdown and converted to less harmful *urea* in the liver. Ammonia levels may increase during severe liver disease causing *hepatic encephalopathy*.

Ammonium thiosulphate – a clearing or fixing agent used in fixer. It dissolves and removes unexposed silver halide crystals from the film.

Amnion – part of the fetal membrane system. The amnion is the inner membranous sac that contains the embryo/fetus and *amniotic fluid* during development within the uterus.

Amniotic fluid – the fluid contained within the amniotic sac that protects the fetus during development. It is sometimes known as the 'waters'.

Amphibian – member of a class of cold-blooded animals; most species live in a semi-aquatic environment. Examples include frogs, toads, newts, salamanders and *axolotls*.

Ampoule – a small glass bottle containing drugs. The glass around the neck of the bottle is usually scored to make it easier and safer to break by hand.

Ampulla – a widening of a tube; specific examples include:

❖ the dilated part of the *semi-circular canals* in the ear which is involved with detecting movement of the head
❖ the end of the *vas deferens* in which some spermatozoa are stored in species such as the rabbit
❖ the expanded end of the *semi-circular canal* of the *inner ear*.

Amylase – digestive enzyme produced in the *pancreas* which breaks *polysaccharides* down into *monosaccharides*. It is often measured in biochemical blood profiles and may be increased in animals with *pancreatitis*.

Anabolism – the process of building complex molecules from simple ones. Anabolism is the opposite of *catabolism*. Examples of anabolism are the creation of proteins from amino acids, or starch from simple sugars. Anabolic steroids are used to build up muscle proteins.

Anaemia – a condition in which there is a drop in the number and/or size of circulating *red blood cells* below the normal range for the species in question. Anaemia can be described as regenerative or non-regenerative. *Regenerative anaemia* is where the *bone marrow* is able to respond to the reduction in circulating *erythrocytes* by releasing immature erythrocytes (*reticulocytes*) into the bloodstream. *Non-regenerative anaemia* describes a situation where there is no response from the bone marrow. Anaemia can have three primary causes:

❖ increased loss of erythrocytes (usually regenerative)
❖ increased destruction of erythrocytes (usually regenerative)
❖ decreased production of erythrocytes (usually non-regenerative).

Anaerobic – describes a process or organism which does not require air (or more specifically oxygen). See also *Aerobic*.

Anaerobic bacteria – anaerobic bacteria do not require oxygen to survive. Some are obligate anaerobes (where the presence of oxygen actually inhibits growth and division) and some are facultative anaerobes (which can function with or without the presence of oxygen).

Anaerobic respiration – the process by which energy is produced in the form of ATP through the incomplete breakdown of sugars in the absence of oxygen. *Glycolysis* and *fermentation* are examples of anaerobic respiration.

Anaesthesia – a lack of sensation and pain as a result of the administration of drugs. Anaesthesia may be general, local, regional or topical.

Anaesthetic chamber – a clear (see-through) plastic box with inlet and outlet limbs (for the attachment of an anaesthetic circuit). Used for anaesthetising or oxygenating exotics.

Anaesthetic machine – a piece of equipment with either three or four wheels used to support the equipment needed to maintain general anaesthesia.

Anagen – first stage of the hair cycle, when the hair grows from the follicle. See also *Catagen, Telogen*.

Anal furunculosis – a condition which mainly affects German shepherd dogs associated with deep-seated skin infection in the perianal area. Clinical signs include *dyschezia*, *haematochezia* and perianal irritation and pain. The cause is unclear but may involve dietary intolerance and immune problems. The condition can be difficult to treat.

Anal glands – two glands located between the internal and external *sphincters* of the *anus*. They produce a thick brown secretion, with a distinctive odour, which contains *pheromones*. Its main function is that of scent marking on the animal's territory. In healthy dogs, the act of passing faeces results in the emptying of these sacs; however, the anal glands commonly become infected, requiring the vet to empty them manually. The surgical removal of the anal glands (*anal sacculectomy*) is sometimes of benefit to dogs with recurrent or non-responsive cases of anal gland problems. Also known as anal sacs.

Anal sac – see *Anal glands*.

Anal sacculectomy – surgical removal of the anal glands. Usually performed in dogs which suffer from persistent anal gland infections.

Anal sacculitis – inflammation of the anal sac, frequently caused by bacterial infection.

Analgesic drugs – drugs that provide short-term loss of pain without losing consciousness. Drugs within this category include non-steroidal anti-inflammatory drugs (NSAIDs) and opiates.

Anaphase – the third stage of cell division in both *mitosis* and *meiosis*. During this stage, the *centromeres* split and the *chromatids* move to opposite poles of the cell.

Anaphylactic shock – the body's immediate and extreme overreaction to coming into contact with an *antigen* to which the animal is sensitised (allergic). Large numbers of *antibodies* are produced causing wide-ranging and potentially life-threatening effects. *Hypovolaemia* can occur as the result of the loss of plasma into the tissues from leaking blood vessels. *Fluid therapy* is vital to restore circulating blood volume and improve tissue perfusion.

Anaphylaxis – an unusual or extreme allergic response. See also *Anaphylactic shock*.

Anastomosis – surgically joining two tubular parts together to continue unity.

Anatomical dead space – those parts of the respiratory tract that are filled with air during respiration, but that do not take part in *gaseous exchange*, eg nasal passages, *pharynx*, *trachea*, *bronchi* and *bronchioles*.

Anatomy – the scientific study of the structure of the body. See also *Physiology*.

Angiostrongylus – a parasitic *nematode* lungworm that is being recognised more often in dogs in the UK. Clinical signs of infection include coughing, dyspnoea, exercise intolerance and bleeding disorders.

Angiotensin I – a hormone produced in the kidney which is converted to angiotensin II by ACE when blood pressure is low. Angiotensin II causes constriction of blood vessels, release of *anti-diuretic hormone* (ADH) and *aldosterone*. This causes an increase in blood pressure.

Angiotribe – a surgical instrument used in *haemostasis*. Similar to, but much larger and more powerful than, a pair of *Spencer–Wells artery forceps*.

Anion – a negatively charged ion.

Annular cartilage – a layer of *cartilage* which surrounds and supports the vertical and horizontal canals of the *external auditory meatus*. See also *Auricular cartilage*.

Annulus fibrosus – a tough fibrous layer surrounding the semi-fluid centre, the *nucleus pulposus*, of an *intervertebral disc*.

Anode – a positively charged electrode that receives the beam of electrons from the cathode. They can be stationary (ie it does not move so the electrons hit the same area on the anode) or rotating (ie it continuously moves so the electrons hit different parts of the anode, increasing its life expectancy).

Anoestrus – the part of the reproductive cycle in female animals when there is no sexual activity. The reproductive hormones are at a basal level.

Anorexia – the loss of appetite, inappetance, or the lack of desire to eat. Can be caused by systemic illness and is often seen in nauseous animals. This lack of appetite may be one of the first signs an owner notices when their pet is unwell.

Anoxia – an absence of oxygen within the body tissues.

Anseriformes – order of birds that includes ducks, geese and swans.

Antagonist – a muscle which opposes the movement of an *agonist*.

Ante mortem – prior to or just before death.

Anterior chamber – one of the two chambers of the *eye*, containing the fluid-like substance, the *aqueous humour*, and divided from the larger *posterior chamber* by the *iris*. See also *Posterior chamber*.

Anthelmintic – medication given to kill *helminth parasites* (ie worms). Examples include ivermectin, selamectin, fenbendazole, milbemycin and praziquantel.

Antibiotic drugs – drugs which selectively kill bacteria (*bactericidal*) or prevent them from growing and dividing (*bacteriostatic*). Examples include penicillins, cephalosporins, potentiated sulphonamides, fluoroquinolones and tetracyclines.

Antibody – an antibody is an *immunoglobin* produced by *B lymphocytes* in response to a specific *antigen* as part of an *active immune response*. An antibody will then react with the antigen to neutralise it or the antibody will interact with killer *T lymphocytes* which destroy the invading *pathogen*. See also *Maternally derived antibodies*.

Anticholinergic drugs – drugs which inhibit the activity of the neurotransmitter *ACh* in the central and peripheral nervous system. Some are used as muscle relaxants (eg suxamethonium), others are used to block the activity of the parasympathetic nervous system (eg atropine) reducing bradycardia and causing dilation of the pupils.

Anticoagulant drugs – a drug used to reduce blood clotting. Examples are heparin and warfarin.

Anticonvulsant drugs – drugs used to prevent seizures, particularly in epileptic animals. The may be short-acting (eg diazepam) or longer acting (eg phenobarbitone, potassium bromide).

Antidiuretic hormone (ADH) – a *hormone* produced by the *pituitary gland* which acts on the kidney, increasing water reabsorption. Lack of ADH is called *diabetes insipidus.*

Antidote – a substance which reverses or neutralises a toxic substance in the body. Examples of suitable antidotes for use in poisoning cases include: *vitamin K* (used to treat *warfarin* toxicity), atropine (used to treat *organophosphate* toxicity), ethanol (used to treat *ethylene glycol* toxicity) and antivenins (treat bites from poisonous snakes etc). See also *Veterinary Poisons Information Service* (VPIS*)*.

Anti-dysrhythmic drugs – used to treat alterations in the rhythm of the heart. Examples are diltiazem, propranolol and lignocaine.

Anti-emetic drugs – used to reduce or prevent vomiting (*emesis*). An example is metoclopramide.

Anti-fungal drugs – kill (fungicidal) or retard the growth of (fungistatic) fungi. Examples include ketoconazole, griseofulvin, clotrimazole and miconazole.

Antigen – any substance which triggers an *active immune response*. Antigens are usually proteins on the surface of an invading *micro-organism*. If the animal does not already have *antibodies* to the invading antigen, an immune response is mounted and antibodies specific to the antigen are produced. The immune system has the ability to remember antigens, so if it encounters a pathogen it has met before, a swift response is mounted.

Antihistamine drugs – prevent the release of the inflammatory mediator histamine during hypersensitivity (allergic) reactions. They are used to treat allergies, and insect bites or stings. Examples are chlorpheniramine, hydroxyzine and cetirizine.

Antimicrobial drugs – the class of drugs that includes the drugs that kill or retard the growth and division of micro-organisms such as bacteria, fungi and viruses. Antibiotics, anti-fungals, anti-protozoals and anti-virals are all antimicrobial drugs.

Anti-neoplastic drugs – selectively target tumour cells. Examples are vincristine, doxirubicin, chlorambucil and cyclophosphamide. They kill cells (are *cytotoxic*) and therefore they may have a range of side-effects and must be handled very carefully.

Anti-protozoal drugs – used to treat protozoal infections such as *toxoplasmosis*. An example is clindamycin (although this drug is more commonly used for its antibiotic effects).

Antiseptic – a substance that provides *asepsis*, ie which inhibits the growth or spread of pathogenic *micro-organisms*, and is safe to use on animal skin and tissue. See also *Disinfectant, Disinfection.*

Antitoxin – an *antibody* which binds with and neutralises toxins. Eg tetanus antitoxin.

Antitussive drugs – suppress the cough reflex. Butorphanol is an example.

Anti-viral drugs – used to treat viral infections. Examples include aciclovir and idoxuridine.

Antrum – the distal part of the stomach which grinds and sieves the *ingesta* before it moves into the intestine for digestion.

Anuria – absence of urination.

Anus – the opening at the end of the alimentary canal, linking the *colon* to the exterior of the body at a mucocutaneous junction. Two muscles (the internal and external sphincter muscles) keep the anus closed and help prevent faecal *incontinence*. See also *Anal furunculosis, Anal glands, Rectum.*

Aorta – the largest artery in the body; it carries *blood* from the left *ventricle* of the *heart*. It then branches off into the brachycephalic trunk and the left subclavian artery before running through the *thorax* and *abdomen* and into the *pelvis*.

Aortic hiatus – one of three holes in the *diaphragm*, allowing the *aorta*, azygou vein and *thoracic duct* to pass through into the *abdomen*. The other two holes are known as the oesophageal hiatus and the foramen vena cava.

Aortic stenosis – a congenital heart problem where there is a narrowing in the valve area at the base of the aorta leading out of the heart. Some breeds such as boxers are more prone to this condition.

Aortic valve – a valve at the base of the aorta which closes after each contraction to prevent blood flowing back into the ventricles. (NB This valve is sometimes called a *semilunar* valve.)

Apneustic respiration – a prolonged pause between inspiration and expiration, particularly seen with the use of ketamine.

Apnoea – where breathing has stopped completely. Clinical signs of apnoea include an absence of chest movement and pale or *cyanotic mucous membranes*. If an anaesthetised patient shows signs of apnoea for more than 30 seconds, the anaesthetic agent should be turned off and *oxygen* administered by *intermittent positive pressure ventilation* (IPPV).

Apomorphine – a drug used to induce *emesis*, usually given to animals in cases of suspected poisoning to prevent further absorption of an ingested poison. The drug can be administered intravenously, normally causing the patient to vomit up the stomach contents shortly afterwards. As gastric contents remain in the stomach for up to 4 hours, inducing emesis after this period of time is ineffective.

Aponeurosis – a flat sheet of *tendon* which attaches *muscle* to another muscle or to *bone*. An example would be where the abdominal transverse and oblique muscles meet to form the midline. See also *Linea alba*.

Appendicular skeleton – one of three classified areas of the *skeleton* made up of the bones of the fore- and hindlimbs and the *scapula* and *pelvic* bones. Compare to *axial* and *splanchnic* skeleton.

Appraisal – a meeting with a manager or suitably qualified person to assess a person's work throughout the year. It is a forum whereby both parties can discuss disagreements, suggestions and goals. A written copy is given to each party.

Aquatic – an animal that lives in water.

Aqueous humour – the watery fluid contained in the *anterior chamber* of the *eye*, secreted by the *ciliary body*. See also *Vitreous humour*.

Arachidonic acid – one of the three essential fatty acids.

Arachnid – an invertebrate with two body regions (head and cephalothorax) and four pairs of legs, eg spider; some are ectoparasites such as mites.

Arachnoid layer – the middle layer of the *meninges*, the membranes which suspend and protect the *brain* and *spinal cord*. The arachnoid layer is a delicate, *avascular* membrane and its inner surface has fine filaments joining to the *pia mater*.

Arboreal – an animal that lives in the trees.

Arcuate arteries/veins – branches of the renal artery within the kidney.

Areolar tissue – *loose connective tissue* found between organs in the body and in the *subcutaneous* layer of the skin. Consists of a few fat cells (*adipocytes*), along with *collagen* fibres and elastic fibres. See also to *adipose tissue*.

Aromatherapy – the use of inhaled substances to treat a range of conditions.

Arrector pili muscle – each hair in the *dermis* has an arrector pili muscle adjacent to the follicle which acts to make the hair stand up. This may happen in cold weather as the raised hair will help to trap the air, thereby conserving body heat. The arrector pili muscle is also activated during stimulation of the *sympathetic nervous system*; if the animal is being threatened, the arrector pili muscles are stimulated and the fur stands up on end, thereby making the animal appear bigger to the potential aggressor.

Arrhythmia – an irregular heart rhythm.

Artefacts (radiography) – discrepancies seen on a radiograph, decreasing its quality, eg fingernail marks

Arteriole – a small branch of an *artery*, delivering blood to the *capillary* beds. Arterioles, unlike arteries, contain very little muscle in the vessel wall, but they play an important role in regulating resistance to blood flow and therefore *blood pressure*.

Artery – a blood vessel receiving *blood* from the *heart* and delivering it to the organs. Arterial blood is oxygenated and bright red (except for that in the *pulmonary artery* which carries deoxygenated blood). There are three layers in the artery wall: the inner *tunica interna*, the middle *tunica media* and the outer *tunica adventitia*. Arteries nearest the heart, which receive blood under the highest pressure, contain more elastic in the vessel walls to help absorb the pressure. See also *Aorta, Arteriole*.

Arthritis – an inflammation of the joints, causing pain and immobility. Arthritis is the result of any damage occurring to the joint. Traumatic arthritis (a sprain) usually only affects a single joint. The joint is painful and may be swollen and the animal may show signs of lameness on it. Treatment usually involves resting the animal and supporting the joint. See also *Osteoarthritis*.

Arthrodesis – surgically fusing a joint to improve stability or to reduce pain.

Arthrodesis wires – an implant used to fixate small bone fragments. Both points of the pin have trocar ends.

Arthrography – a contrast study of joints. Where radio-opaque liquid is injected into the joint, radiographs are taken.

Articular cartilage – found in *synovial joints* and made of *chondrocytes* and *collagen*, articular cartilage (usually *hyaline cartilage*) covers the articular surfaces of the joint bones to allow smooth movement, while also acting as a shock absorber to some of the forces to which the joint is subjected.

Arytenoid cartilage – the *cartilage* in the *larynx* which holds the attachment for the *vocal folds*.

Ascites – an abnormal accumulation of fluid in the *abdomen*. It is commonly seen in animals suffering from *chronic* right-sided heart failure, where the blood collects and builds up in the *veins* and organs, rather than being returned to the *heart*. This increased volume in the veins results in fluid being pushed out into the abdomen. *Diuretic* drugs can be administered to help clear the excess fluid.

Ascorbic acid (vitamin C) – a water-soluble vitamin; daily intake is required to prevent conditions such as scurvy. Any excess is excreted in the urine and not stored in the body.

Asepsis – describes freedom from *infection* by inhibiting the growth or spread of pathogenic *micro-organisms*.

ASIF/AO – ASIF (the Association for the Study of Internal Fixation) or AO (Arbeitsgemeinschaft Osteosynthesefragen). An organisation founded in Switzerland in 1958. A non-profit-making organisation that researches, promotes and provides education on their technique of internal fixation, using equipment such as the dynamic compression plate DCP.

Aspartate aminotransferase (AST) – an enzyme which is sometimes measured during a biochemistry blood profile. It is produced by liver cells and muscle cells and is increased when there is damage to liver or muscles cells.

Aspergillosis – a fungal infection of the nasal cavity caused by the mould *Aspergillus*. The disease is transmitted by the inhalation of the fungal *spores* and symptoms include a green *mucopurulent* nasal discharge.

Aspirate – a method of removing fluid or cells from the body, usually using a needle with or without a syringe.

Aspiration pneumonia – the inhalation of non-sterile fluid, foods or particles into the sterile lungs. Infection of the lungs follows.

Asternal rib – also called false ribs. The caudal four pairs of ribs which do not articulate directly with the sternum.

Asthma – respiratory disease which usually affects cats in which the airways become constricted and inflamed. Asthma attacks are usually caused by allergy although triggers such as excitement or cold may also be important. It is potentially life-threatening, and is treated with bronchodilators, mucolytics and anti-inflammatory agents. Recently the use of inhalers has enhanced medical management of this condition.

Asymptomatic – no signs or symptoms of a disease are presented or demonstrated.

Ataxia – describes unsteady walking, or a wobbly, unco-ordinated gait which may indicate a neurological disorder. Adjective: ataxic.

Atlas – the first of seven *cervical vertebrae*, the atlas articulates with the *skull* and has flattened *transverse processes* called the wings. Together with the *axis*, these two vertebrae form a pivot joint to allow the head to move.

Atom – a basic form of matter, a nucleus is present surrounded by electrons.

Atomic number – the number of protons in an atom's nucleus.

Atopy – an inherited tendency to develop allergic reactions to environmental allergens such as pollens and house dust mites. Some breeds, such as West Highland white terriers and shar peis, are more prone to developing atopy.

Atrial – relating to the atria. See also *Atrium*.

Atrioventricular node (AV node) – lying at the top of the *septum* in the heart, the AV node is involved in the conduction of the *nervous impulse* which controls the heart beat. The impulse is passed from the *sino-atrial node* on to the AV node, causing the *atria* to contract, then on to the *bundle of His* within the septum and then spreading out along the *Purkinje fibres*, causing the *ventricles* to contract.

Atrioventricular valves – two *valves* which lie between the left and right *atrium* and *ventricle*. The left atrioventricular valve is also known as the *mitral valve* or bicuspid valve and has two cusps, the right valve is known as the *tricuspid valve* because it has three cusps. Their main function is to control the flow of *blood* through the heart by preventing backflow back into the atria when the ventricles contract. The valves are anchored to the *papillary muscles* by fibrous strands called the *chordae tendinae*.

Atrium (pl. atria) – the two upper thin-walled chambers of the *heart*. The left and right atria are separated from each other by a *septum* and communicate with the *ventricles* via the *atrioventricular valves*. The right atrium receives deoxygenated blood from the body, the left receives oxygenated blood from the *lungs*.

Atropine – an antimuscarinic drug (one that blocks the action of muscarinic receptors of the *parasympathetic nervous sytem*) which, when administered, causes a similar response to the action of the *sympathetic nervous system*. It causes pupil dilation and reduces saliva production when given as a premedicant.

Auditory – relating to the hearing system in the ear (as opposed to the balance (vestibular) system).

Auditory canal – also known as the ear canal or *external acoustic meatus*. Consists of the horizontal and vertical canals which lead from the *pinna* to the *tympanic membrane*. *Ceruminous glands* in the walls of the canal secrete *cerumen* to help prevent particles and foreign bodies entering the ear. Some breeds have large numbers of hair follicles within the canal that can cause problems with the accumulation of ear wax and creating a dark, appealing environment in which ear mites (*Otodectes cynotis*) thrive. See also Lateral wall resection, Total ear canal ablation, Vertical canal ablation.

Auditory nerve – cranial nerve which transmits impulses associated with hearing and balance from the *inner ear* to the *brain*. See also *Vestibulocochlear nerve VIII*.

Auditory ossicles – three tiny bones in the middle ear called the *malleus* (hammer), *incus* (anvil) and *stapes* (stirrup) that amplify and transmit sound-wave vibrations across the *middle ear* onto the *oval window*, which then transmits the waves into the *cochlear*.

Auditory tubes – a tube which runs from the middle ear to the nasopharynx. They are also known as the Eustachian tubes. Their function is to allow the pressure in the middle ear to equalise with atmospheric pressure.

Aural – relating to the ear.

Aural haematoma – the development of a blood-filled pocket within the *pinna*. It is usually caused by excessive head shaking, often as a result of infection (*otitis externa*) or irritation (maybe because of the presence of a foreign body, eg a grass seed) in the ear itself. The repeated head shaking causes small blood vessels to rupture and the blood then collects in the space between the cartilage and the skin causing a swelling to form. Aural haematoma can occasionally be left to resolve naturally, but this often results in a deformed pinna. Surgical treatment involves making a small incision and draining the blood away. Sutures are then used to close the dead space created by the haematoma.

Auricular cartilage – the supporting *cartilages* of the *pinna* that determine its shape, which varies greatly from breed to breed. In some cases (eg cat/German shepherd dog) the pinna can be rotated to face the direction of the sound. In other breeds (eg cocker spaniel), the pinnae lie downwards, close to the head. See also *Annular cartilage*.

Auroscope – an instrument with speculum, magnifying glass and light enabling the external ear canal to be examined.

Auscultation – the art of listening via a stethoscope to the noises coming from the heart, lungs and abdomen. In this way, the heart rate can be counted, any heart murmurs can be detected and any unusual lung sounds can be assessed. See also *Borborygmi*.

Autoclave – a machine used to sterilise surgical instruments, equipment and materials by way of moist heat under pressure. Moist heat penetrates materials much more rapidly than dry heat because water conducts heat better than air. The autoclave is built to withstand great pressure because the temperature of steam increases as the pressure increases. Vacuum-assisted autoclaves are the most effective because high temperatures can be reached more quickly and also the moisture is removed at the end of the process to help dry the load. See also *Bowie Dick tape*, *Ethylene oxide*, *Hot-air oven*, *Vacuum-assisted autoclave*.

Autoimmune disease – a disease where the body's immune system attacks its own tissues. Examples include immune-mediated haemolytic anaemia, in which the body destroys its own erythrocytes, and keratoconjunctivitis sicca, in which the lacrimal gland is attacked by the immune system. Treatment usually involves suppressing the immune response.

Autolysis – breakdown and digestion (with cellular enzymes) of cells and tissues after death.

Automatic processor – a machine which automatically develops radiographs, usually within 3–5 minutes. Each machine will have its own protocol for maintenance.

Autonomic nervous system – part of the *peripheral nervous system*, it innervates all organs not under voluntary control. It can be divided into two parts – the *sympathetic* and *parasympathetic* nervous systems.

Autotomy – the ability of some animals to shed a body part (usually the tail) as a defence mechanism and then re-grow the body part. For example, lizards are able to shed their tails when being pursued or roughly handled. Starfish may also lose limbs in this way.

Avascular – without blood vessels, ie with no blood supply. The *cornea* is avascular.

Avian – relating to birds.

Avulsed – meaning torn or pulled away. An avulsed fracture is where the ends of the fractured bone have been pulled apart. An avulsed wound is where the tissue has become torn away and separated from its attachments. Animals that have been involved in a road traffic accident are often treated for such wounds.

Axial skeleton – one of three classified areas of the *skeleton* made up of the *skull*, the *vertebral column*, *ribs* and *sternum*. See also *Appendicular skeleton*, *Splanchnic skeleton*.

Axillary artery – arteries which branch off from the *aorta* and carry blood to the front legs. As they travel down the legs, they become known as the brachial arteries.

Axis – second of the seven *cervical vertebrae*, it has a process coming off it called the dens which projects cranially towards the *atlas*. The atlas and axis together form a pivot joint, allowing the head to move.

Axolemma – the outer membrane covering an *axon* (nerve).

Axolotl – an *amphibian*, an axolotl is the immature form of the salamander.

Axon – an elongated structure comprised of nervous tissue along which the nervous impulse travels away from the *cell body*. Many axons are wrapped in a *myelin sheath* made up of *Schwann cells* which increases the speed of impulse conduction. An axon may vary in length from less than a millimetre to many centimetres. See also *Action potential*.

Ayre's T-piece anaesthetic circuit (include Jackson-Rees modification) – a non-re-breathing anaesthetic circuit, used to deliver and maintain anaesthesia and also to remove waste gases. Comprises a length of corrugated tubing with no bags or valves. Patients up to 5 kg may use this circuit. The *Jackson-Rees modification* has an open ended re-breathing bag that is incorporated onto the original Ayres T-piece, this enables *intermittent positive pressure ventilation* to be performed. Patients up to 5 kg may use this circuit.

Azotaemia – the presence of abnormally high levels of urea and/or creatinine in the blood. It may be caused by pre-renal factors such as dehydration, renal factors such as renal failure, or post-renal factors such as bladder rupture or urethral obstruction.

B

B-lymphocyte – one of two types of *lymphocyte* (see also T-lymphocyte). They are made in the *bone marrow*, then travel to the *lymph nodes* and mature. When an *antigen* enters the lymph node, the B-lymphocytes multiply, swell and produce antibodies in response to this specific *antigen* as part of an *active immune response*.

Babcock tissue forceps – a surgical instrument used for handling soft tissue and viscera. The tips are triangular in shape. See also *Allis tissue forceps*.

Babesia – a tick-borne *protozoal parasite* which infects *erythrocytes* and causes anaemia. Not endemic to the UK but may be seen in animals which travel abroad.

Bacillus – may be used to describe any rod-shaped bacterium. There is also a genus of rod-shaped bacteria called *Bacillus* which includes *Bacillus anthracis*, the causative agent for anthrax.

Backhaus towel clip – surgical instruments used to anchor the *drapes* to the surgical field. They have a box joint and ratchet to hold them securely in place. Care should be taken when clipping these to the patient because the ends are pointed and sharp and can cause trauma to the tissue. See also *Cross-action towel clips*.

B

Bacteraemia – the presence of *bacteria* in the blood. Bacteraemia may occur when bacteria from a focus of infection enter the bloodstream and travel to other parts of the body. During bacteraemia the bacteria are not multiplying in the blood (compare with *septicaemia*).

Bactericidal – a substance which selectively kills bacteria. Examples of bactericidal antibiotics are fluoroquinolones, penicillins and cephalosporins. See also *Bacteriostatic*.

Bacteriostatic – a substance which prevents bacteria from growing and dividing (but does not kill them). Examples of bacteriostatic antibiotics are tetracyclines, sulphonamides and macrolides. See also *Bactericidal*.

Bacterium (pl. **bacteria)** – a group of *micro-organisms* with no distinct *nucleus*, surrounded either by a thick gelatinous capsule or a thinner slime layer. The function of this layer is to help protect the bacterium from the host's immune system. Bacteria have characteristic shapes, being spherical (*cocci*), rod-shaped (*bacilli*) or spiral (*spirochaetes*). Unstained bacteria are hard to see under the microscope, so stains (see also *Gram stain*) are used to help in identification. Some bacteria are able to produce *spores*, a dormant form of the bacterium, usually formed when conditions are unfavourable for survival. Not all bacteria cause *disease* – those that do are called *pathogens*. *Commensal* bacteria cause no damage to the host. See also *Antibiotic drugs*.

Bad debt – money owed by a client for services or goods supplied, which is unlikely to be repaid or cannot be collected.

B

Bain's circuit – a non re-breathing anaesthetic circuit, used to deliver and maintain anaesthesia and also to remove waste gases. Can be parallel (two pieces of tubing alongside each other) or co-axial (two pieces of tubing inside each other). In co-axial circuits fresh gas enters the patient via the inner tube and waste gas is breathed out into and removed by the outer tube. Uses higher flow rates than the Lack circuit but can be used for intermittent positive pressure ventilation. Used in patients over 7 kg.

Ball and socket joint – a type of *synovial joint* found in the shoulder and hip. In the shoulder, the head of the *humerus* articulates with the *glenoid cavity* of the *scapula*. In the hip, the head of the *femur* articulates with the *acetabulum* in the pelvis. See also *Hip dysplasia*.

Band neutrophil – an immature *neutrophil* with a band-shaped nucleus, often released into the blood during overwhelming bacterial *infection* or *inflammation* when there is a huge increase in demand for neutrophil cells.

Barbiturates – drugs used to induce general anaesthesia and in some cases to controls fits. Three categories of barbiturates are used for general anaesthesia:

❖ oxybarbiturates (short-acting barbiturates); these are not often used, eg pentobarbital
❖ thiobarbiturates (ultrashort-acting barbiturates), eg thiopentone sodium
❖ methylated barbiturates, eg methohexital.

Long-acting barbiturates, eg phenobarbital, would be used to control fits.

Bargaining (communication) – where two people engage in a heated discussion or even argue over a situation or what has being said.

B

Barium hydroxide lime – a chemical used for absorbing carbon dioxide, usually housed in a canister within a re-breathing anaesthetic circuit.

Barium meal (barium sulphate) – the patient is fed a meal containing barium sulphate before *contrast radiographic studies* of the alimentary canal are carried out. The barium is *radio-opaque* and shows up any obstructions or abnormalities of the *oesophagus, stomach* and *intestines*. It should not be used if perforation of the intestines is suspected.

Barnsley receiver – a canister used within an active scavenging system.

Baroreceptor – a sensory receptor located in the artery walls that detects the degree of stretch in the vessel wall. This gives information about the *blood pressure* level which then initiates responses from the *sympathetic* and *parasympathetic nervous systems* to adjust *cardiac output* and blood vessel resistance. If the blood pressure falls, cardiac output and *vasoconstriction* are increased. If the blood pressure is too high, the opposite occurs.

Barrier nursing – also called isolation nursing, this is a strict protocol on how to nurse an *infectious* patient to prevent the *infection* from spreading to other susceptible patients in the hospital. It involves isolating the patient from others and using separate bedding, bowls and equipment solely for that one patient. Ideally one member of staff only should be dealing with the infectious patient, but as this is likely to be impractical, protective clothing should be worn and scrupulous hygiene procedures should be followed after handling any infectious animal. See also *Zoonosis*.

Basal cell tumour – *benign skin tumour* of the basal cell. Now known as Trichoepithelioma.

Basal energy requirement (BER) calculation – the calculation is:

❧ Under 5 kg: BER = 60 × bodyweight
❧ Over 5 kg: BER = 30 × bodyweight + 70

The calculation allows you to work out the total number of calories the animal requires a day.

Basal metabolic rate (BMR) – the rate at which energy must be used to maintain vital functions such as respiration, heartbeat, peristalsis and biosynthesis (construction of protein and other molecules). The BMR is controlled by thyroid hormones and is higher in younger animals to allow for growth.

Basement membrane – more correctly called the basal lamina. This is a non-cellular layer which supports cells and separates tissues.

Basophil – rarest of the *granular leukocytes*, produced in the *bone marrow*. The nucleus is bi-lobed or shaped like a kidney bean. The *cytoplasm* contains many granules of *histamine* and *heparin*, which stain blue and which are released at the site of inflammation.

B

Benign – opposite of *malignant*, ie not harmful.

Benzodiazepine drugs – a group of drugs that induce tranquillity and relaxation but not sedation. Can be used alone or in combination with other drugs for use as a premed. Can also be used to treat fits. Examples of this group are diazepam, midazolam.

Bereavement – feeling the loss of a loved one, feeling sad or lonely following the death of a pet. Bereavement counselling is available for those who would benefit from this (where feelings can be discussed with a professional); there is usually a charge for this service.

Beta (β) cells – cells found in the *islets of Langerhans* in the *pancreas*. Beta cells secrete insulin when blood glucose levels increase (eg after a meal).

Bicarbonate – an anion found in the body containing hydrogen, carbon and oxygen (HCO_3^-), which plays an important role as an extracellular buffer in maintaining correct hydration levels and therefore the *pH* of *blood*.

Biceps brachii – a two-headed *muscle* of the proximal forelimb. It flexes the elbow and extends the shoulder.

Biceps femoris – a two-headed *muscle* of the hindlimb. It makes up part of the group of muscles known as the hamstring. It extends the hip, *stifle* and *hock*. See also *Semimembranosus muscle*, *Semitendinosus muscle*.

Bicuspid valve – the left *atrioventricular valve*, also known as the *mitral* valve. Made up of two cusps, it is found between the left *atrium* and *ventricle* in the heart. The cusps are anchored to the *papillary muscles* by the *chordae tendinae* and their function is to close after the atrium contracts to prevent the back-flow of blood from the ventricle into the atrium. See also *Atrioventricular valves, Tricuspid valve.*

BID – means twice daily (from latin *bis in die*).

Bifurcation – a fork into two branches, eg in the area of the *mediastinum*, the *trachea* divides into the left and right *bronchi*, which supply the left and right *lungs*. This point is known as the bifurcation of the trachea.

Bilateral – affecting both sides (left and right) of the body.

Bile – a liquid which is produced in the liver and stored in the gall bladder. It contains bile acids which emulsify fats during digestion.

Bile acid stimulation test – a diagnostic test used to assess liver function by measuring *bile acids* pre- and post-feeding. In dogs with liver dysfunction the post-feeding bile acids are much higher than in normal dogs.

Bile acids – a group of acids which are produced in the liver and make up part of *bile*. Bile acids are secreted into the gut in bile, are almost completely reabsorbed, and pass back into the liver.

Bile duct – the tube which carries *bile* from the *gall bladder* to the duodenum.

Bilious vomiting – vomit containing bile.

Bilirubin – a yellow pigment derived from the breakdown of *erythrocytes*. It is usually recycled through the gut and liver, or passes out of the body in the faeces. An increase in plasma bilirubin results in *icterus* (jaundice).

B

Binary fission – the type of asexual reproduction which occurs in bacteria and other *prokaryotes* during which the bacterium divides in two to produce two daughter cells.

Binocular – an optical instrument where both eyes are used, eg microscope with two eyepieces.

Biochemistry – the chemistry of living organisms. Biochemistry profiles from blood and urine samples are used to assess the health of animals, and the progress of diseases. They are also used to monitor the effects of drugs and procedures on the body.

Biohazard – any biological waste, pathogenic material or contaminated biological material.

Biopsy – a tissue sample taken from a live animal. Can be *incisional*, where a sample of the lesion or organ is taken, or *excisional*, where the whole lesion is removed. The sample can then be submitted for *histopathology*. See also *Punch biopsy*.

Bipolar – rare type of *neurone* that has two processes arising from the *cell body*. This type of neurone can be found in the eye, ear and nose. See also *Multipolar*, *Unipolar*.

Bird of prey – a bird, such as a hawk or an owl, which hunts other animals for food.

Bitter spray – a spray that is bitter to taste; can be used on unbroken skin or fur to prevent licking or patient interference.

B

Bladder – a distensible storage organ of the urinary system found in the pelvic cavity. The *ureters* carry the *urine* from the *kidneys* and enter the bladder (at the *trigone*) at an oblique angle. This helps to prevent the back-flow of urine into the ureters as the bladder fills. The bladder consists of a double layer of *smooth muscle* lined with *transitional epithelium* cells. These are able to stretch as the bladder fills. The *urethra* leaves the bladder and carries urine to be passed out of the body. See also *Cystocentesis, Urination*.

Blepharospasm – excessive blinking or holding the eyelid closed. A sign of ocular discomfort, often caused by the presence of a foreign body or injury to the *cornea*.

Blood – a red fluid which circulates round the body in a system of tubes (blood vessels). Consists of a fluid part ($\simeq$60%) and a solid part ($\simeq$40%). The solid part consists of cells (corpuscles) and fragments of cells; the fluid is straw-coloured and called *plasma*. There are two groups of cells found in mammalian blood – *erythrocytes* (red blood cells), (*thrombocytes* (platelets)) and *leukocytes* (white blood cells). There are five types of white blood cell – *lymphocyte, neutrophil, monocyte, eosinophil* and *basophil*. Blood is the major transport medium of the body and allows substances, eg glucose, oxygen or hormones, to be transported to tissues and cells throughout the body. It also transports waste products, eg urea and carbon dioxide, away from the cells to the organs responsible for their elimination and excretion. See also *Cardiovascular system, Haemostasis*.

Blood–brain barrier – barrier between the blood vessels of the *central nervous system* (CNS) and the CNS itself. Brought about by reduced permeability of the *capillaries* in nervous tissues; prevents many molecules, including antibiotics, from diffusing from the blood to the *brain* and *spinal cord*, making treatment of CNS infections difficult.

B

Blood gas analyser – a piece of equipment that can measure arterial carbon dioxide levels and arterial oxygen levels. Blood must be obtained from an artery, stored on ice and used for analysis within 2 hours of its being taken.

Blood pressure (BP) – the pressure of the *blood* within the main arteries. Sensed by *baroreceptors*, which then relay the information to the *medulla*. If it is high, the medulla will reduce *sympathetic activity*, so lowering the heart rate, increase *parasympathetic activity*, causing the heart to slow down, and produce *vasodilation*, lowering peripheral blood pressure. If it is low, this mechanism works in the opposite direction. It is important to maintain adequate blood pressure to ensure that sufficient tissue perfusion is achieved, allowing enough oxygen to be delivered to the tissues and enough carbon dioxide to be removed. If blood pressure is too low, there is a danger of *hypoxia*. See also *Blood pressure monitor*, *Vasoconstriction*.

Blood pressure monitor – a device which allows the monitoring of a patient's *blood pressure*. Usually a Doppler detector is used along with an occlusive cuff. A distal *pulse* is located in the patient's limb and the Doppler receiver is used to detect the pulse. Then the cuff is wrapped around the *proximal* part of the limb and inflated so that the arterial flow to the limb is gradually occluded and the pulse can no longer be detected. The cuff is then slowly deflated. The pressure at which the Doppler receiver detects the pulse returning is the *systolic* pressure.

B

Blood transfusion (including **blood storage)** – the transfer of blood from one patient to another which must be of the same species. Blood should be collected from healthy, vaccinated patients – dogs over 30 kg and cats over 4 kg. Cats must also be screened for feline leukaemia virus, feline immunodeficiency virus and feline coronavirus before collection. Storage should be as follows:

❖ if collected into a heparinised tube/syringe then it must be used within 48 hours

❖ if collected into a citrate phosphate dextrose (CPD) collection bag then it may be stored at 1–6 °C for 28 days

❖ if collected into an acid citrate dextrose (ACD) collection bag then it may be stored at 1–6 °C for 21 days.

Blood type – a category used to describe the patient's individual blood group. These are classed according to the type of antigens found on the surface of the red blood cells. There are three feline blood groups, and eight canine blood groups.

Blue sensitive film – radiography film that is sensitive to ultraviolet, violet and blue light. It is important that the correct intensifying screen is used, ie a screen that emits green light, eg calcium tungstate screens, which only emit blue light.

B-mode (brightness mode) – a type of image display used in ultrasound. It produces a two-dimensional, cross-sectional image; movement of structures can also be seen. The most commonly used mode.

Bobbins – used in flow meters to indicate the gas level. They are read off the top not the centre.

Bodock washer – a rubber washer fitted between the gas cylinder and its connector to prevent leakage. They perish so need regular replacement.

B

Body bandage – a bandage used around the thorax or abdomen to aid compression of air, fluid or blood. Elastoplast should be used for the tertiary layer because a self-conforming bandage can tighten and may obstruct.

Body language – communication through facial expression, postures and gestures.

Bolus (food or medication) – an amount given in a single dose.

Bone – hard, white connective tissue consisting of a matrix of *calcium*-containing minerals and *collagen* fibres. Bones make up the internal *skeleton* of mammals (*axial*, *appendicular* and *splanchnic*) and can be classified as one of five types – *long bones*, *short bones*, *flat bones*, *irregular bones* and *sesamoid bones*. Bone structure is described as being either spongy (*cancellous*) or compact (*cortical*). Bones develop by one of two ways – *endochondral* or *intramembranous ossification*. Lengthening of bones during growth occurs at the growth plates (*epiphyseal plates*). When growth has finished, the growth plates are replaced with bone and are said to have closed. The age at which this happens varies greatly between species and breeds. See also *Pneumatised bone*.

Bone-cutting forceps – surgical instrument used for cutting through bone or through pieces of bone; has flat, sloping blades to cut through the bone cleanly.

Bone-holding forceps – surgical instrument used for holding bone, facilitating manipulation and reduction of fragments or fractures, eg Kern bone-holding forceps.

B

Bone marrow – the soft, vascular tissue found in the *medullary cavity* of *long bones* that produces *red* and *white blood cells*. See also *Haematopoieisis*.

Bonus – an additional amount of money paid on top of normal earnings or wages.

Booster vaccination – a vaccination usually administered annually after the initial course of the primary *vaccination* to maintain *immunity*. If the immune system is not exposed to the diseases it has been vaccinated against, the number of memory cells decreases and the animal's immunity gradually wears off. For this reason boosters are given to remind the immune system of which *pathogens* to be prepared for.

Borborygmi – rumbling sounds from the gut; may be increased in animals with gastrointestinal disease.

Bordetella bronchiseptica – a *Gram-negative bacterium*, one of the several *pathogens* causing *kennel cough* and other respiratory tract infections of the dog and cat.

Boric acid – a white crystalline powder that, in veterinary use, is used to preserve urine samples for culture and sensitivity tests. Plastic pots with a red label and lid contain boric acid and are usually ready prepared. The standard pot containing boric acid should be filled with 30 ml urine to ensure that the ratio of boric acid : urine is correct.

B

Bowie–Dick tape – indicator tape used to seal *autoclave* packs. Its function is to monitor sterilisation methods. Heat-sensitive stripes on the tape turn from beige to dark brown at 121 °C but it gives no indication as to the exposure time, or for how long this temperature was maintained. Can also be used in conjunction with *ethylene oxide*, when the stripes turn from beige to green. See also *Sterilisation*.

Bowman's capsule – also called the glomerular capsule; it is a cup-shaped structure in the *renal cortex*, at one end of the *nephron*, that encloses the *glomerulus*. It is here that fluid from the plasma is filtered through the wall of the arteriole in the glomerulus and collects into the Bowman's capsule. Fluid produced by this process is called glomerular filtrate.

Brachial plexus – a group of nerves (plexus) from the caudal cervical/cranial thoracic spinal cord that is located deep in the axilla (armpit). The nerves of the brachial plexus control sensation and movement in the forelimb.

Brachial pulse – a pulse on the medial aspect of the humerus.

Brachialis – *muscle* of the upper forelimb that flexes the elbow.

Brachiocephalicus muscle – *muscle* of the neck and shoulder that advances the forelimb, extends the shoulder and moves the head and neck laterally.

Brachycephalic – description of short-faced, wide-headed skull shape, as seen in breeds such as bulldogs, pugs, boxers and Persian cats. See also *Dolichocephalic*, *Mesocephalic*.

Bradycardia – an abnormally slow heart rate.

Bradypnoea – a decreased respiration rate.

Brain – the brain is a large organ housed in the *cranium*. It can be divided into three main areas, the *fore-*, *mid-* and *hindbrain*. The forebrain is made up of the *cerebrum*, *thalamus* and *hypothalamus*. The brain is connected to the *spinal cord* by the brainstem and, together, the brain and spinal cord make up the *central nervous system*. The *ventricles* are four connected cavities within the brain containing *cerebrospinal fluid*. See also *Blood–brain barrier, Cranial nerve*.

British Small Animal Veterinary Association (BSAVA) – founded in 1957, an organisation to aid veterinary surgeons who treat small animals (companion animals). It promotes education, teaching and research of small animal medicine and surgery.

British Veterinary Association (BVA) – the BVA represents the veterinary profession nationwide and has 51 divisions. Membership is voluntary.

Broad ligament – a sheet of connective tissue which suspends the *uterus* and *ovaries* from the dorsal surface of the abdominal cavity. The part which supports the uterus is called the *mesometrium*, and the part which supports the ovaries is called the *mesovarium*.

Bronchial tree – the structure of air passages in the *lungs* formed by the subdivision of *bronchi* and *bronchioles*.

Bronchiole – a small division of the *bronchi* in the *lungs*. Each bronchiole subdivides, becoming smaller with each division. The terminal bronchioles give rise to *alveolar ducts*, which allow the air to reach the *alveoli*.

B

Bronchoconstriction – narrowing of the *bronchi*, which may occur in allergic airway disease or following inhalation of irritants.

Bronchodilator – a drug which is used to dilate the lower airways that allows respiration to occur more easily and aids in removal of accumulated mucus, eg theophylline, terbutaline and clenbuterol.

Bronchus (bronchi) – the *trachea* divides into two large airways called the bronchi. These supply air to the left and right *lungs*. The bronchi at this point have strengthening C-shaped rings of *cartilage* to maintain their shape. The bronchi then start to subdivide to become small *bronchioles* and the cartilage rings disappear.

Browne's tube – a sterilisation-monitoring method. Sealed glass tubes change from red to green when a specified temperature has been reached but there is no indication as to how long this temperature was maintained. Browne's tubes can be used in *hot-air ovens* and *autoclaves*. See also *Bowie–Dick tape*, *TST indicator strips*.

Brunner's glands – glands in the duodenum that secrete alkaline material, which assists in the digestive process.

Bruxism – tooth grinding, often a sign of pain in small mammals.

Buccal – relating to the buccal cavity, or mouth.

Bucky – see *Potter–Bucky grid*.

Buffer (radiography) – maintains the pH of fixer.

Buffy coat – the layer which sits on top of the erythrocytes in a centrifuged blood sample. The buffy coat contains white blood cells and platelets.

B

Bulbo-urethral glands – a pair of glands that lie at the caudal end of the penis in the cat and contribute to *seminal fluid.*

Bulbus glandis – an expansion of erectile tissue near the base of the *penis* in the dog; sometimes called the bulb of the penis.

Bulla(e) – see Tympanic bulla.

Bulla osteotomy – the surgical removal of the lining of the *tympanic bulla*, often performed during a *total ear canal ablation*. Hearing is severely impaired following this procedure, which is occasionally used for the treatment of *chronic otitis externa* and *media.*

BUN – blood urea nitrogen. See *Urea.*

Bundle of His – specialised cells within the *heart* septum that conduct the electrical impulse from the *atrioventricular node* to the *Purkinje fibres.*

Buprenorphine – a Schedule 3 opiate and partial agonist. It has a slow onset of action and a duration of action of 4–6 hours. It can be administered either *subcutaneously* or *intramuscularly.*

Burn – a tissue injury usually caused by the application of heat. Can be caused by dry heat (fire, hot household appliances, heat pads, hairdryers, etc), chemicals (caustic substances or acids), electricity (electric shock or lightning strike) or radiation. Burns can also result from prolonged contact with ice or liquid nitrogen. They are characterised by tissue necrosis, skin peeling and fluid loss.

B

Bursa (pl. **bursae)** – a small fluid-filled sac found in tissue and around tendons whose function is to reduce friction and aid smooth movement.

Buttress support – used in internal fixation when a fracture cannot be completely reduced. The entire potential load is borne by the implant (either a plate or an external fixator).

C

Cachexia – weight loss, muscle loss, weakness and general ill-health, usually associated with an underlying condition.

Cadaver – a corpse.

Caecotroph – partially digested faecal matter passed out of a rabbit which the rabbit then re-ingests to allow it to be fully digested. This usually takes place during the night, so the owner may not be aware that it occurs at all. If the rabbit is obese or has dental disease, it may not be physically able to re-ingest the caecotroph – this can then lead to digestive disorders and fur soiling.

Caecum – a blind-ending section of gut at the junction between the ileum and the colon. It has little function in the dog and cat but is an important feature of the digestive system in herbivorous animals such as rabbits and horses. The caecum acts as a large fermentation vat where cellulose is broken down.

Caesarean section (*C* section) – a surgical incision into the womb to deliver a *fetus* whilst the mother is anaesthetised. It is performed due to *dystocia* for several reasons, including *uterine inertia*, oversized or malformed fetus or an unusually narrow birth canal. A *ventral midline* incision is made with the patient in *dorsal* recumbency. Once the fetuses have been removed from the *uterus*, they are passed to an assistant for resuscitation. Once the uterus has been checked for any remaining fetuses, it is repaired and the abdominal wound is closed.

Calciferol – see *Vitamin D*.

Calcinosis cutis – deposition of calcium in the skin which occurs in animals with *hyperadrenocorticism*.

Calcitonin – a hormone that is secreted by the C cells in the *thyroid gland* and that lowers blood *calcium* levels by reducing calcium resorption from bone.

Calcium – a mineral found in *bones*, teeth and *blood*, it is also required for normal *nerve* and *muscle* function. The body's calcium requirements increase during growth, pregnancy and lactation. Calcium deficiency in young animals results in skeletal deformities. Hypocalcaemia in lactating bitches causes *eclampsia*.

Calcium alginate dressings – also known as interactive dressings, they exchange sodium ions for calcium ions to aid wound healing and also help to stop haemorrhage, although they are not intended for intraoperative use.

Calcium-channel blocker – a group of dugs used to lower blood pressure, through actions on the blood vessels and heart, eg amlodipine.

Calculus (calculi) – **1.** also known as dental calculus or tartar, a gritty, brown deposit which builds up on teeth and is formed from *plaque* and inorganic substances in *saliva*. If it is not removed (by means of a tooth scale and polish while the animal is anaesthetised), calculus builds up and causes *gingivitis* and *periodontitis*. To prevent it building up in the first place, owners should be advised to regularly brush their pet's teeth and to feed dried food rather than wet. **2.** urinary calculi (or uroliths) are formed when urinary crystals clump together. The presence of calculi in the *bladder* is always abnormal and should be investigated. Calculi are formed from a variety of crystals which include *struvite*, *oxalate*, *urate* and *cystein*. See also *Urinalysis*.

Calibration – a process of checking a piece of equipment's results against a standard to ensure the equipment is working correctly, eg laboratory equipment will need calibrating.

Calicivirus – one of the agents associated with feline *upper respiratory tract disease* ('cat flu'). The virus multiplies in the local *lymph nodes* before affecting the epithelial cells of the respiratory tract and *conjunctiva*.

Calling (cats) – vocal exercises performed by female cats in season, letting other male cats know they are ready to mate. The cats often roll around and can look and sound as if they are in pain but they are not.

Callipers – an instrument used to measure the thickness of tissue, commonly used in radiography.

Callus – formed in the early stages of fracture healing and consisting of fibrous tissue, immature bone and cartilage. As healing continues the callus changes to contain mainly bone, providing strength to the fracture site. Eventually the two bone ends of the fracture meet and this is *clinical union*.

Campylobacter jejuni – a bacterium which affects the gastrointestinal tract and can cause vomiting and diarrhoea. *Campylobacter* can be zoonotic (passed from animals to humans).

Canaliculus – a very small channel which leads from the eyelid to the lacrimal sac, allowing tears to pass into the nose. Also a narrow channel in bone or the liver.

Cancellous bone – also known as spongy bone. The *Haversian systems* are spread more widely apart than in *cortical bone* and the spaces between are filled with red *bone marrow*. Found in the *vertebrae*, *flat bones* and at the *epiphyses* of *long bones*.

Cancellous screw – a surgical implant used during orthopaedic procedures. A screw used for securing a plate to *cancellous bone*. It has a coarser thread than a *cortical screw* for a better bite into the spongier bone.

Cancer – abnormal growth of tissue; refers to both *malignant tumours* and *leukaemia*. A term usually reserved for malignant neoplasia (tumours). See also *Neoplasia*.

Candida albicans – a yeast which may cause infection of the *mucous membranes* (mouth and genital tract in particular). *Candida* infection is known as thrush or candidiasis.

Canine – adjective relating to dogs.

Canine tooth – one of four well-developed teeth between the *incisors* and *premolars* in the dog and cat. They have a large, single root, a pointed crown and are used for piercing flesh and holding prey.

Capillary – a very small blood vessel which runs between an *arteriole* and a *venule* within the body tissues. It has a thin, easily permeable wall which allows the exchange of oxygen, nutrients and waste products between the tissues and the *blood*.

Capillary refill time (CRT) – a quick and easy way to assess shock or circulatory failure in a patient. Pressing with a finger on the pink gums in the patient's mouth causes a whitening of the tissue. The refill time (time it takes for normal tissue colour to return) is then measured in seconds. Normal CRT is less than 2 seconds; a CRT longer than 2 seconds indicates poor peripheral perfusion. See *Dehydration*.

Capnograph – a piece of monitoring equipment which is useful during anaesthesia to calculate the concentration of exhaled *carbon dioxide*. Consists of a sensor placed in the breathing circuit or in a tube that carries the exhaled gases back to the analysing device within the capnograph so that carbon dioxide levels can be monitored.

Capsid – the protein coat that surrounds a *virus* and gives it its shape.

Capsomere – *polypeptide* molecules that make up the *capsid*.

Carapace – the *dorsal* part of a *chelonian* shell. See also *Plastron*.

Carbohydrate – an organic compound that can be classified as a monosaccharide, disaccharide or polysaccharide. Carbohydrates are usually stored in the body as *glycogen* or they can be laid down as fat in times of excess.

Carbon dioxide – a colourless, odourless gas which is present in the air and which is formed by the tissues as a waste product during *respiration*. It diffuses into the *blood* from the tissues, is carried to the *alveoli* and is breathed out of the body. See also *Capnograph*.

Carbon monoxide – a poisonous, colourless and odourless gas that is produced by incomplete combustion of some fuels, eg gasoline. Prevents oxygen from being carried around the body by binding irreversibly to haemoglobin.

Carcinogen – a substance that causes *neoplasia* or *cancer*.

Carcinoma – a suffix (see suffix appendix) denoting a malignant growth of the *epithelial tissues*. An example would be a *squamous cell carcinoma* – a *malignant* tumour of the squamous epithelium, commonly seen on the tips of the *pinnae* in white/pale cats. See also *Sarcoma*.

Cardia (stomach) – the cranial portion of the *stomach* which is attached to the *oesophagus*.

Cardiac – adjective relating to the heart.

Cardiac arrest – a life-threatening situation in which the *heart* stops beating. Clinical signs include *cyanotic mucous membranes*, increased *capillary refill time*, no *pulse*, no heart beat, dilated *pupils*. The patient will need to be *intubated* and *IPPV* will need to be performed, along with *cardiac compression*. Cardiac arrest may occur as the result of an overdose of anaesthetic agents or cardiac disease.

Cardiac compression – a technique also known as *cardiopulmonary resuscitation* (CPR) performed when *cardiac arrest* has occurred. It is carried out in conjunction with *intermittent positive pressure ventilation*. The aim is to push *blood* through the *heart* and therefore provide *cardiac output*. In cats and small dogs the chest wall can be compressed from side to side. In larger dogs the patient is placed in right lateral recumbency and compressions are carried out on one side of the chest wall at a force appropriate to the size of the animal. Aim for 80–120 compressions per minute. The patient must be ventilated every third to fifth compression.

Cardiac muscle – *muscle* found only in the *heart*; a muscle under involuntary control. Contractions are generated from within the heart but are modified by the *parasympathetic nervous system*. Cardiac muscle is unique in that it is the only muscle not to tire following repeated contractions, unlike *skeletal muscle*. See also Atrioventricular node, Bundle of His, Purkinje fibres, Sino-atrial node.

Cardiac output – the volume of *blood* ejected by the *heart* every minute. Cardiac output = stroke volume × heart rate.

Cardiogenic shock – condition caused by a failure of the *heart* to pump, leading to reduced tissue perfusion. Can be caused by dilated *cardiomyopathy*, where the heart muscle is no longer strong enough to force the *blood* out of the *ventricles* and round the circulatory system.

Cardiomyopathy – disease of the heart muscle (*myocardium*). The two main types are:

❧ *dilated cardiomyopathy* where the myocardium becomes thinner and loses its ability to contract efficiently (this is more common in large-breed dogs)
❧ *hypertrophic cardiomyopathy* where the myocardium becomes thickened and the diameter of the chambers is reduced (this is more common in cats and small-breed dogs).

Cardiopulmonary resuscitation (CPR) – *first-aid* treatment for a patient whose heart has stopped beating and who is not breathing. *Cardiac compressions* are carried out whilst air is blown into the patient's lungs by *intermittent positive pressure ventilation.*

Cardiovascular drugs – drugs which act on the heart and/or circulatory system, eg drugs which act on the heart such as *anti-dysrhythmics* and *inotropes* and drugs which act on the blood vessels such as the *ACE inhibitors* and *venodilators.*

Cardiovascular system – describes the system of the *heart* and *blood vessels* around the body. See also *Artery, Vein.*

Carnassial – found in carnivores, the carnassial teeth are upper premolar 4 and lower molar 1; designed to crush and cut food.

Carnivore – a meat-eating animal. A cat is an obligate carnivore, meaning it must have meat in its diet to obtain the necessary nutrients (see also Taurine) required to keep it healthy. See also *Herbivore, Omnivore.*

Carotid artery – a pair of arteries in the neck which branch off the *aorta* and supply oxygenated *blood* to the *brain.*

Carotid pulse – a pulse found on both the right and left sides of the neck.

Carotid sinus – an area in the carotid artery wall containing *baroreceptors*, which measure *blood pressure*.

Carpal – describes the area around the *carpus*, equivalent to the human wrist.

Carpal arthrodesis plate – a specially designed plate that tapers at one end to enable arthrodesis of the carpal joint.

Carpal pulse – a pulse found on the palmar aspect of the carpus.

Carpus – the joint in the forelimb made up of a number of bones, including the *carpal* and *metacarpal* bones. Equivalent to the human wrist.

Carrier animal – an animal that has come into contact with an *infectious* agent and may be harbouring the *disease* without showing any clinical signs (*healthy carrier*) or who has recovered from the disease (*convalescent carrier*).

Cartilage – *avascular* type of supporting *connective tissue* which is found mainly at joints and between *bones*. Produced by *chondrocytes*, there are three types: hyaline cartilage, fibrocartilage and elastic cartilage. *Hyaline cartilage* is mainly found covering bone ends at *synovial joints*, providing a smooth surface which eases movement, whilst also acting as a shock absorber to some of the forces applied to the joint. *Elastic cartilage* is found in the *pinna* of the ear, while *fibrocartilage*, the strongest of all the cartilage tissues, is found within the *intervertebral discs* and at the *pubic symphysis*.

Cartilaginous joint – also called a synchondrosis, this is a type of joint between two bones which allows a small amount of movement, eg the *mandibular* and *pubic symphyses*.

Case records – records that are kept and maintained regarding a patient's health and treatment. These records are confidential.

Cassette – a rigid or flexible case that houses radiography film. May also be loaded with intensifying screens.

Casting material – materials used to provide a hard and rigid dressing to aid fracture healing or to provide support. Materials include thermoplastics (plastic polymers), plaster of Paris and resin-impregnated material (fibreglass).

Castration – an operation performed under general anaesthesia to surgically remove both testicles.

Castroviejo scissors – a delicate ophthalmic surgical instrument used to cut away the lens capsule of the *eye* during *cataract* surgery. They have a spring action, pear-shaped handle and tiny blades.

Casts (urine) – tubular structures sometimes found in urine that originate from the *renal tubules*. The presence of casts indicates disease in the renal tubules. Casts may be hyaline (made of mucoprotein), cellular (made of cells such as erythrocytes, leukocytes or epithelial cells), granular (degenerate cellular casts) or waxy (very degenerate cellular casts).

Cat 'flu' – an upper respiratory viral disease of cats caused by feline herpes virus and/or feline calicivirus. There is often also a secondary bacterial infection. Clinical signs include sneezing and ocular and nasal discharge. Cats which have been infected remain carriers throughout their lives. There are many vaccines available to protect cats against these viruses.

Catabolism – breakdown of complex molecules into simpler ones with the production of energy (usually in the form of ATP). Catabolism is the opposite of *anabolism*.

Catagen – stage two of the hair cycle. During catagen, the hair follicle atrophies and the hair shaft weakens. See also *Anagen*, *Telogen*.

Cataract – a condition causing opacity (or cloudiness) of the *lens* in the eye. Vision can be severely affected or lost completely. Causes include age-related changes in the lenses of older animals, *congenital* cataracts, diabetes mellitus and trauma to the eye. In many older animals with cataracts, they are able to cope using a combination of the remaining vision and their other senses (eg smell, hearing). In more complete cataracts, vision can be lost altogether. In these cases, the problem can sometimes be corrected surgically by an *ophthalmologist*. This may include extraction of the whole lens or removal of the cataract material through a small incision in the *cornea*.

Catecholamines – hormones such as *adrenaline* and *noradrenaline* which are produced in the *adrenal gland* and promote activity of the *sympathetic nervous system*.

Catgut – a natural, multi-filament suture material made from sheep intestine that is gradually absorbed by the body by enzymatic degradation and phagocytosis. Catgut is mainly used for placing sutures in *subcutaneous* tissue, *muscle*, hollow *viscera* and for *ligatures*. It is available as plain or *chromic catgut*.

Cathartic – an agent used to purge the bowels, used in severe constipation.

Catheter – **1.** a *urinary* catheter is a very long, thin tube which is passed into the *bladder* via the *urethra*. Available in a variety of shapes, sizes and materials, commonly used catheters include the *Jackson cat catheter, Tiemann's, Foley,* Portex and metal catheters. May be used to obtain a *sterile urine* sample for *bacteria* and *culture* sensitivity tests, to empty the bladder before surgery, to introduce *contrast media*, to maintain constant and controlled bladder drainage and to provide a *patent urethra*, for hydropropulsion methods to dislodge particles/crystals stuck in the urethra and to monitor urine output. Complications with catheterisation can occur from urinary tract infection, trauma, patient interference or blockage. **2.** an *intravenous* catheter is a small tube with attached connection port inserted into a vein to allow *fluid therapy* to be administered to a patient. Common types of catheter include over-the-needle and butterfly catheters. The *vein* should be *aseptically* prepared using *antiseptic* solution and spirit before inserting the catheter. A dressing is required on the limb to protect the 'catheter and giving set' from patient interference. See also *Venepuncture*.

Cathode – a coil of wire (filament) similar in appearance to that found in a light bulb; it is usually made of tungsten and is negatively charged. By applying heat to the filament via milliamperage a cloud of electrons is produced and can be measured in milliamps (mA).

Cation – a positively charged ion eg H^+, Na^+.

Cauda equina – meaning 'tail of a horse', this is the *caudal* portion of the *spinal cord* where it splits into a large number of *nerve* fibres, the structure of which resembles a horse's tail.

Caudal – towards or near the tail. See also *Cranial*.

Caudo-cranial (CdCr) – a term used in radiography for views of both the fore- and hindlimbs above the carpus joint or tarsal joint.

Cavy (cavies) – a group of various tailless South American rodents of the family Caviidae, which includes the guinea-pig, capybara, coypu and agouti.

Cell – the basic structural and functional unit of all living organisms. Cells have specialised characteristics dependent on their function within the body, but most consist of a *cell wall*, *cell membrane*, *nucleus*, *cytoplasm* and various cell *organelles*.

Cell body – part of a *nerve cell* containing the *nucleus* and *cytoplasm*.

Cell membrane – also called the plasma membrane, it separates the *cell* contents from the outside environment. Comprises a double layer of *phospholipids*, *proteins* and *carbohydrates*. It is selectively *permeable,* allowing the transport of some substances in and out of the cell. *Cholesterol* also forms an important part of the cell membrane. See *Osmosis*.

Cell replication – the process by which cells divide to form new cells. Cell replication can occur either by *mitosis* or *meiosis*.

Cell wall – the layer surrounding the cell in bacteria, plants and fungi; cells of eukaryotic animals such as mammals do not possess a cell wall.

Cellulitis – inflammation of the connective tissues, usually caused by bacterial infection. The subcutaneous tissues are most commonly affected. Clinical signs include oedema, inflammation, pain and swelling.

Cement – covers the roots of teeth; has a similar structure to bone but is very resistant to wear.

Central nervous system (CNS) – a division of the nervous system that includes the *brain* and *spinal cord*. See also Cranial nerves, Peripheral nervous system.

Central venous pressure (CVP) – measurement of blood pressure within large central veins, eg anterior vena cava. Used to monitor patients with right-sided heart failure and those receiving fluid therapy.

Centrifuge – a piece of laboratory equipment used to spin liquids at high speed. **1.** an electric centrifuge spins samples of liquids (eg *blood, urine*) at high speeds so the more dense particles sink to the bottom and the lighter particles float on the top. The deposit at the bottom of the sample after centrifugation is called the *sediment*; the liquid on top is the *supernatant*. **2.** a *microhaematocrit* centrifuge is used to separate blood samples in microhaematocrit capillary tubes to allow an accurate measurement of the *packed cell volume*.

C

Centriole – a structure found in the *cytoplasm* that migrates to opposite poles of the cell during *cell replication*, laying down microtubules to form the spindle as they go. See *Meiosis, Mitosis*.

Centromere – a structure holding the two *chromatids* together during *cell replication*.

Cephalic vein – the *vein* in the forelimb of an animal which carries the *blood* returning to the *heart* from the legs. Often used as a site for *intravenous* injections and to insert indwelling *intravenous catheters*.

Cerclage wire (orthopaedic wire) – wire that looks similar to fuse wire. Used in fragment fixation to improve stability of internal fixation (cerclage/hemicerclage wiring), inter-fragmentary wiring (eg wiring a fractured jaw), and tension band wiring (a figure of eight to counteract the pull of muscles, tendons and ligaments).

Cere – the soft fleshy tissue at the base of the beak in a bird which contains the nostrils. In some species, such as budgerigars, the sex of the bird can be determined from the colour of the cere.

Cerebellum – part of the *hindbrain* which is divided into two cerebral hemispheres. Controls balance and co-ordination of posture and locomotion. See also *Medulla oblongata, Pons.*

Cerebrospinal fluid (CSF) – a fluid similar to *plasma* but containing far less *protein* and very few cells. It is secreted by the *choroid plexuses* located in each of the *brain ventricles.* It circulates around the brain and *spinal cord,* acting as a cushion and protecting the area from disturbances in *blood pressure.* Sampling of CSF can be very useful when investigating *neurological* disease – whilst the animal is anaesthetised, a needle is carefully inserted into the *cisterna magna* and a sample of CSF is collected for analysis.

Cerebrovascular accident (CVA) – a stroke, or rupture of a *blood vessel* in the *brain.* Very rarely seen in veterinary practice. May be confused with vestibular syndrome by owners.

Cerebrum – the largest part of the *forebrain* composed of two cerebral hemispheres separated into lobes: the frontal lobe, parietal lobe, occipital lobe and temporal lobe. The centre for functions such as sensation, olfaction, vision and hearing. See also *Hypothalamus, Thalamus.*

Cerumen – earwax. Produced by *ceruminous glands,* it helps prevent debris and dust passing into the inner parts of the *ear.*

Ceruminous gland – produces *cerumen;* found in the outer parts of the *ear* canal.

Cervical vertebra – the seven vertebrae that make up the neck. The first vertebra which articulates with the skull is called the *atlas*; the second is the *axis*. These two vertebrae form a pivot joint which allows the head to move. See also *Coccygeal vertebra, Lumbar vertebra*.

C

Cervix – the thick-walled caudal segment of the uterus which functions as a *sphincter* to prevent passage of material in and out of the *uterus*. The cervix is opened during parts of the reproductive cycle, and during *parturition*. The word cervix comes from the Latin meaning 'neck'.

Cestode – a tapeworm. See also Dipylidium caninum, Echinococcus granulosus, *Taenia*.

Channel hangers – used in wet development of radiographs. The channel hanger has slots down both sides enabling the film to be 'slotted in' and held while the film is processed.

Cheatle sterilising forceps – instrument used in theatre to allow unscrubbed personnel to open sterile theatre packs. They have angled beak-shaped tips to allow items to be grasped and manipulated.

Chelonian – order of reptiles which includes tortoises, terrapins and turtles.

Chemoreceptor – a receptor found in the aortic and carotid bodies which monitors the *oxygen* levels of the *blood*. Stimulated by a change in the *pH* of blood; if this is detected, information is sent to the respiratory centre in the *medulla oblongata* of the *brain*, which then initiates an appropriate response. For example, if the chemoreceptors detect a rise in *carbon dioxide* levels, the respiratory centre will stimulate an increase in *respiratory rate* to remove the excess carbon dioxide.

Chemoreceptor trigger zone (CTZ) – the area of the brain which causes *vomiting* as a response to some drugs, hormones or toxins.

Chemosis – oedema of the *conjunctiva* in the eye; commonly associated with *conjunctivitis*.

Chemotherapy – the use of medication to selectively destroy neoplastic cells. Chemotherapy drugs include *cytotoxic drugs*, which must be handled with extreme caution and adequate precautions must be taken to avoid coming into contact with them by accident. The choice of chemotherapy agents is determined by the type of *tumour* and its susceptibility to different drugs.

Cherry eye – a prolapse of the *nictitans gland* so that it appears as a smooth, red swelling at the *medial canthus* of the eye. Treatment involves suturing the gland back into place. This condition is more often seen in bulldogs, mastiffs and rottweilers.

Cheyletiella – a non-burrowing mite which is found on dogs, cats and rabbits and may cause hypersensitivity reactions in people. Infestation with *Cheyletiella* may be called 'walking dandruff' because on a dark background the mites may be seen moving with the naked eye.

Cheyne–Stokes respiration – a distinctive pattern of breathing, usually seen just before death, demonstrated by an alternating pattern of deep, convulsive gasps for breath and shallow breaths at infrequent intervals.

Chiasmata – cross-links which form between pairs of *homologous chromosomes* during *meiosis* that allow exchange of genetic material to take place and give rise to genetic variation.

Chinchilla – 1. small South American rodent, bred in captivity for its soft, silvery-grey fur. Often kept as pets but can be very sensitive and easily frightened. Rough handling can cause the coat to be shed (*fur slip*). **2.** the Chinchilla cat is a popular long-haired breed and is in fact a type of Persian. It has a long, thick, silky coat, round face and large eyes. The coat is usually white with black tipping.

Chinese finger suture – a type of suture used to secure tubing and certain drains to the skin.

Chisel – a surgical instrument used during orthopaedic procedures to shave away bone. Bevelled on one side only to allow it to sit flush with the bone. Not to be confused with an *osteotome*.

Chitin – the tough material which forms the exoskeleton (outside layer) of many insects, and is a component of the cell wall in many fungi.

Chlamydia psittaci – recently renamed as *Chlamydophila*, the name of the intracellular bacterium which causes chlamydiosis. This is a zoonotic disease which causes chronic *conjunctivitis* in cats. It can also cause abortion of fetuses and infertility in breeding cats. There is a *vaccine* against it, most commonly given to animals kept for breeding purposes. See also *Psittacosis*.

Chlorhexidine – a *bactericidal* skin cleanser or surgical scrub.

Chloride (Cl⁻) – a negatively charged form (ion) of the element chlorine. Chloride is measured in the electrolyte panel in a biochemistry profile and is used to assess acid–base status. For example, low chloride (hypochloraemia) may be caused by vomiting (loss of hydrochloric acid from the stomach), which is an example of *metabolic alkalosis*.

Cholangiohepatitis – inflammation of the gall bladder, bile duct and liver. The commonest causes are toxic and infectious (usually bacterial or viral).

Cholecystokinin – a hormone which is secreted in the presence of fats in the duodenum. Causes gall bladder contraction and is important for the digestive process.

Cholestasis – obstruction to the flow of *bile* from the liver. May be within the liver (intra-hepatic) or in the bile ducts (post-hepatic). Associated with increased bilirubin and alkaline phosphatase on a basic biochemistry panel. *Icterus* (jaundice) may occur secondary to cholestasis.

Cholesterol – a *steroid* produced by the liver and ingested in the diet that has many useful functions in all tissues and is the precursor for steroid *hormones* such as *cortisol* and *testosterone*. Measured in a blood biochemistry panel: increased levels may reflect recent feeding, hepatopathy, endocrinopathy or *pancreatitis*; decreased levels are associated with liver disease, such as *portosystemic shunt*, and protein-losing enteropathies.

Chondroblast – a *cartilage*-forming cell that deposits *calcium* salts during *bone* formation by *endochondral ossification*.

Chondrocyte – a mature *cartilage* cell found in the small cavities called *lacunae* and surrounded by *collagen* fibres. See also *Chondroblast*.

Chordae tendinae – fibrous strands in the *heart* which anchor the *atrioventricular valves* to the *papillary muscles*.

Chorion – the outermost fetal membrane which protects the fetus and forms part of the placenta.

Choroid – part of the *uvea*, the choroid makes up the middle layer of the eyeball. It is a pigmented layer which lines the internal surface of the *sclera*. The reflective surface of the *tapetum lucidum* can also be found in this layer. See also *Ciliary body, Iris.*

C

Choroid plexus – a vascular region situated in each of the *ventricles* in the *brain*, it secretes cerebrospinal fluid (CSF).

Chromatid – found in the *nucleus* during *cell replication*. Each *chromosome* can be seen as two identical chromatids attached by a *centromere*. See also *Meiosis, Mitosis.*

Chromic catgut – a natural multi-filament suture material made from sheep intestine, absorbed by the body by enzymatic degradation and phagocytosis. Coated in chromic salts that slow down its absorption, increase its strength and decrease the tissue reaction to it. See also *Catgut.*

Chromosome – a thread-like structure found in the *nucleus* of a *cell* and comprising two coiled strands of *deoxyribonucleic acid* (DNA). Each coiled strand is made up of sequences of bases (adenine, guanine, cytosine and thiamine) which act as the code for the synthesis of all *proteins* made by the cell. Each species has a fixed number of chromosomes; cats have 38, dogs have 78.

Chronic – symptoms or conditions that are prolonged or long-term.

Chronic renal failure – loss of renal function characterised by gradual and irreversible loss of functional renal tissue. Causes include inherited disease, infectious diseases (bacterial infections in particular) and tumours. Affected animals are usually *azotaemic* and may be suffering from *uraemia*. Long-term prognosis is poor but with treatment the quality of life may be good and progression of the disease may be slowed.

Chyle – a milky fluid absorbed by the lymphatic vessels (*lacteals*) of the intestine. Carried in the lymphatic vessels, known as the *cisterna chyli*, and formed by the absorption of fats by the lacteals during the digestive process.

Chylomicron – lipid particles formed during fat digestion and absorbed through the *lacteals* of the intestinal *villi*; make up part of *chyle*.

Chylothorax – the presence of chyle in the pleural cavity, usually caused by damage to the thoracic duct. Clinical signs include dyspnoea and a pleural effusion can be seen on thoracic radiography.

Chylous effusion – the presence of *chyle* in the pleural cavity or abdomen. May be caused by damage to the lymphatic system or thoracic duct.

Chyme – a liquid mixture of partially digested ingesta and gastric juice found in the stomach. NB Do not confuse with *chyle*.

Chymotrypsin – a proteolytic enzyme in *pancreatic juice* involved in protein digestion in the small intestine.

Ciliary body – part of the *uvea* that supports the *lens* and contains the ciliary muscles which help the *lens* to focus. It also produces the *aqueous humour* for the *anterior chamber* of the eye.

Ciliated – an adjective used to describe the presence of *cilia*.

Cilium (pl. **cilia) – 1.** hair-like projection on the cell surface used to waft fluid or *mucus* over the cell. Particularly important in the movement of mucus in the upper respiratory tract. **2.** can also be used to describe eye lashes.

Circle anaesthetic circuit – a re-breathing anaesthetic circuit used to deliver and maintain anaesthesia and also to remove waste gases. It can be parallel (two pieces of tubing alongside each other) or co-axial (two pieces of tubing inside each other). Uses soda lime to absorb carbon dioxide. Nitrous oxide should not be used with his circuit. Use in patients over 15 kg.

Circulation – description of the flow of *blood* from the *heart* around the body in a network of *arteries*, *veins* and *capillaries* and then back to the heart. See also *Hepatic portal vein*.

Cirrhosis – replacement of functional hepatic tissue with fibrous scar tissue. A consequence of severe or chronic liver damage and may eventually result in liver failure.

Cisterna chyli – a small pouch in the *lymphatic system*, located in the *dorsal abdomen*. Formed by the convergence of lymphatic vessels from the gut and caudal abdomen. See *Chyle*.

Cisterna magna – an enlarged subarachnoid space between the *medulla oblongata* and the *cerebellum*. Can be used as a point to collect *cerebrospinal fluid* or to inject *contrast media* for *radiography*.

Cisternal puncture – the more commonly used approached in myelography, using the cisterna magna for inserting the contrast into the subarachnoid space.

Citrate – an anti-coagulant used when coagulation profiles are required.

Citrate phosphate dextrose collection bags – a prepared blood collection bag used to collect blood from the donor patient during blood transfusions. May be stored at 1–6 °C for 28 days.

Clavicle – the collar bone; absent in the dog. It may be seen on radiographs as a slender piece of bone in cats and is reduced to a tiny piece of bone in dogs, which may not be visible on a radiograph.

Clean contaminated surgery – second in the order of priority for theatre surgical procedure lists, an example would be gastrointestinal surgery where no break into the gastrointestinal tract occurs. See also *Clean/sterile surgery, Contaminated surgery, Dirty surgery*.

Clean/sterile surgery – first in the order of priority for theatre surgical procedure lists, an example of clean surgery would be an orthopaedic procedure. See also *Clean/contaminated surgery, Contaminated surgery, Dirty surgery*.

Clearing (fixing) agent (radiography) – used to dissolve and remove unexposed silver halide crystals from the film; contains either sodium thiosulphate or ammonium thiosulphate.

Cleft palate – a *congenital* defect seen in the *neonate* – the *midline* of the *hard palate* has not fused correctly, leaving a gap. This causes serious feeding and suckling problems and the animal is unlikely to survive.

Clinical signs – symptoms (that are variable) produced or demonstrated by the patient.

Clinical union (surgical nursing) – where the bone ends of the fracture have met and are held securely by the callus.

Clinical waste – waste material comprising animal tissue, body fluids, excretions, drugs or any product that may be hazardous to health. Governed by the *Collection and Disposal Waste Regulations 1992* and *Control of Pollution Act 1974*. Placed in yellow clinical waste bags and collected by official companies who then incinerate the waste.

Clipper rash – a red skin rash caused when electric clippers have been used incorrectly, eg the blade not at the same angle as the skin.

Clitoris – the female version of the penis; consists of erectile and nervous tissue. May be difficult to see because it is concealed in a fold called the clitoral fossa.

Cloaca – the cavity into which both the intestinal and genito-urinary tracts empty in reptiles, birds, amphibians and many fish.

Closed anaesthetic circuit – a classification of circuits that has now been largely superseded by the term re-breathing circuits, eg circle circuit.

Closed carrier – a patient harbouring an infectious agent but not shedding the agent into the environment. Can also be a healthy carrier (showing no symptoms of the infection) or a convalescent carrier (recovering from the infectious agent).

Closed question – a style of question which is formulated to collect facts from the person being questioned. An example of a closed question is 'so his drinking is normal'? See also Open and Leading Questions.

Clostridia – a group of bacteria that includes *Clostridium tetani* (which causes tetanus), *Clostridium botulinum* (which causes botulism) and *Clostridium perfringens* (which causes gangrene and food poisoning).

Clotting – see *Coagulation*.

Clotting cascade – a complex process involving a series of reactions in the *blood* with the aim of forming a *fibrin* clot to prevent large volumes of blood being lost. When the injury occurs, thromboplastin is released from the damaged tissue and from the *platelets*. This reacts with the circulating prothrombin and *calcium* to form thrombin, which in turn reacts with circulating fibrinogen to produce a fibrin clot. See also *Haemorrhage*, *Haemostasis*.

Cluster (seizures) – a group of seizures occurring close together (within a few hours), usually in an epileptic animal. May lead to *status epilepticus* and should therefore be treated promptly.

Cnemidocoptes pilae – a burrowing mite which affects birds. Causes scaly face in caged birds, eg budgerigars.

Coagulant – an agent which causes *coagulation*, used to control *haemorrhage*, eg ferric chloride is commonly used to stop a claw bleeding after an over-enthusiastic claw clip. See also *Anticoagulant drugs*.

Coagulation – meaning the formation of *blood* clots at the site of an injury to prevent large volumes of blood being lost. Lack of *thrombocytes*, *vitamin K deficiency* and presence of anticoagulants, eg warfarin, all cause increased coagulation times. See also *Clotting cascade*.

Coagulopathy – a disease which affects the ability of the blood to clot normally, eg haemophilia, *Von Willebrand's disease* and poisoning with warfarin-based *rodenticides*.

Cobalamin – see Vitamin B-complex.

Cocci – bacteria that are spherical in shape, eg Staphylococci (bunches of cocci) and Streptococci (strings of cocci).

Coccidia – *protozoal parasites* that usually live in the gut and cause diarrhoea, eg *Eimeria*. An important cause of disease in poultry.

Coccygeal pulse – a pulse found under the base of the tail.

Coccygeal vein – a *vein* carrying blood back from the tail; can be used as a site for blood sampling in reptiles.

Coccygeal vertebra – also called the caudal vertebrae. On average there are 20 (dependent on species) and they form the tail. See also *Cervical vertebra*, *Lumbar vertebra*.

Cochlea – a system of coiled tubes in the *inner ear* that resembles a snail's shell. Contains the *organ of Corti*, the organ of hearing.

Cochlear window – see *Round window*.

Codman's triangle – a radiographic feature associated with the malignant bone tumour *osteosarcoma* in which the *periosteum* becomes elevated from the surface of the bone.

Coelomic cavity (coelom) – a hollow body cavity; in animals without a diaphragm (such as fish) the coelomic cavity contains the cardiac, respiratory, reproductive, urinary and digestive tracts all in the one cavity.

Coenurus – a type of *metacestode* (part of the life cycle of tapeworms) which consists of a fluid-filled bladder with many inverted *scolices*. An example of a tapeworm which forms a coenurus is *Taenia multiceps*, which affects dogs and sheep.

Cold abscess – similar to an abscess; there is pus present but no inflammation. Treatment requires surgical excision.

Cold application (wound care) – can be used in wound care to reduce heat and blood loss by causing vasoconstriction; examples of cold applications include swabs soaked in cold water and latex gloves filled with cold water.

Cold chemical sterilisation – a way to *disinfect* items that are too delicate or fragile to be *autoclaved* or put in a *hot air oven*. Involves submerging the item in a liquid *disinfectant* for a specified length of time. The concentration of the liquid should be calculated with care, according to the manufacturer's guidelines.

Collagen – a structural *protein* found in *cartilage*.

Collapse – an inability to rise to a sitting or standing position. May occur with or without loss of consciousness. Causes may include weakness as a result of pain or neurological conditions; reduced cardiac output; seizures; or metabolic conditions such as uncontrolled diabetes mellitus or hypoadrenocorticism.

Collecting duct – the tube which takes *urine* from the *nephron* to the *renal pelvis* and into the *ureter*. The collecting duct has important roles in electrolyte and water balance, and is the site of action of *antidiuretic hormone*.

Collie eye anomaly – a hereditary condition during which there is incomplete development of the retina. The condition can result in retinal detachment and intra-ocular haemorrhage. Any collie breed may be affected; there are a number of schemes that aim to identify affected animals and avoid their use in breeding.

Collimation – limiting the field of the primary beam by use of a light-beam diaphragm or cones.

Colloid – a plasma replacement fluid, used if whole blood or plasma is unavailable. It expands the plasma volume by retaining the large molecules within the circulation; required in cases of hypovolaemic shock, hypotension and extensive burns.

Colon – the portion of the gastrointestinal tract leading from the *ileocaecocolic junction* to the *rectum*. The main functions are reabsorption of water and *electrolytes* from the digested material. *Vitamin K* is produced in the colon. The distal colon stores and periodically expels *faeces*.

Colostrum – the first milk produced by the mother following *parturition*. Different from the milk produced throughout the rest of *lactation* and has a number of important functions: a concentrated source of nutrients for the *neonate*, containing high levels of *protein*, *glucose* and *iron*; also rich in *maternally derived antibodies* which pass *immunity* to the neonate and provide some *passive immunity* against disease. These antibodies can only be absorbed by the neonate for the first 24 hours of life so it is vitally important that the neonate starts to suckle as soon as possible.

Columbiforme – order of birds that includes pigeons and doves.

Columnar epithelium – epithelial tissue composed of tall column-shaped epithelial cells which may or may not possess cilia. Found lining the small intestine, various glands (unciliated) and the oviducts (ciliated).

Coma – the patient is unconscious and does not react to external stimuli. May occur following trauma.

Commensal – a micro-organism (usually bacterial) that lives in close contact with an animal but does not cause any harm, eg the normal gut and skin bacteria.

Comminuted fracture – a bone fracture with multiple fracture lines and bone fragments at the fracture site. See also *Avulsed, Compound (open) fracture, Depressed fracture*.

Communication (types and methods)

❖ verbal communication – in person, over the telephone, internet link

❖ written communication – letter, memorandum, email, fax

❖ non-verbal communication – body language, sign language, images.

Complementary medicine – Medicine or therapy used alongside conventional therapy. Eg magnetic therapy, acupuncture or hydrotherapy used alongside conventional pain therapy.

Complete fracture – a bone fracture across both cortices.

Compliance – owner compliance is needed to ensure the patient receives the correct treatment and medication. The following factors are needed to ensure owner compliance:

❖ understanding

❖ skill

❖ good communication over any conflicting beliefs

❖ perception

❖ financial

❖ general good communication.

Complicated fracture – a bone fracture where there is another serious injury involved, such as when important organs or structures near the fracture site are damaged, eg fractured *rib* penetrating the *lung* tissue. See also *Avulsed, Comminuted fracture, Compound (open) fracture, Depressed fracture.*

Compound (open) fracture – a bone fracture where part of the bone has penetrated the skin, causing an open *wound*. With this type of fracture there is a high risk of infection. See also *Avulsed fracture*, *Comminuted fracture*, *Compound fracture*, *Depressed fracture*.

Compression – pressure applied to an area, either purposely, as in a compression bandage or due to trauma as in a compression fracture.

Compression plate – see *Dynamic compression plate*.

Computerised axial tomography (CAT) – uses ionising radiation. Patient lies on a table and enters a 'polo'-shaped CAT scanner. The part being examined is seen as a cross-section. Tissue will be seen as varying shades of grey, while bone and air appear as they would on standard X-ray film.

Conceptus – a term used to describe a fertilised ovum from the moment of fertilisation until birth. Other terms are also used to describe specific parts of the process such as *zygote*, *embryo* and *fetus*.

Condenser – the part of the *microscope* that focuses light onto the slide.

Condyle – a rounded prominence at the end of a bone.

Cone (eye and radiography) – **1.** a photoreceptor cell found in the retina that receives light and converts it to electrical impulses. **2.** a metal, shaped cone used for collimation in radiography; these have largely been superseded by light beam diaphragms.

Confidentiality – a person's right that data regarding them or their pet are not disclosed or discussed with unauthorised people.

Conflict – situation where two or more people disagree.

C

Conforming bandage – a material used for the secondary layer in a bandage, can be of the net variety or crepe.

Congenital – an adjective describing an abnormal condition present at birth, eg *cleft palate*. Congenital conditions may or may not be hereditary.

Congestive heart failure (CHF) – a medical condition in which the heart is unable to pump blood forwards (from the left ventricle) effectively. The result is build-up of blood in the pulmonary circulation, which may cause *pulmonary oedema*. Blood may also build up in the veins and organs (particularly the liver) and can result in *ascites*. Causes of congestive heart failure include valvular disease and cardiomyopathy.

Conjugation – transfer of genetic material from one bacterium to another during bacterial reproduction.

Conjunctiva – the *mucous membrane* lining the inner surface of the eyelid. See also *Conjunctivitis*.

Conjunctivitis – inflammation of the *conjunctiva*, may be caused by chemical or physical irritation to the conjunctiva, tear film abnormalities and bacterial/viral infections among other things. Clinical signs include *blepharospasm*, *chemosis* and *epiphora*.

Connective tissue – a type of tissue which provides support and structure for different parts of the body. Examples are fat, bone, cartilage and blood.

Consent form – a form legally required to be signed by the owners or agent giving permission for any procedure including anaesthesia. The person signing the form has to be over 18 years old.

Constipation – a condition whereby the *faeces* become impacted (wedged) in the *colon* and *rectum*. It can be caused by *dehydration* or a sedentary lifestyle, or by an enlarged *prostate gland* or rectal *tumours*. See also *Dyschezia*, *Tenesmus*.

Constrict – to widen or enlarge an opening or hollow structure beyond its usual size, such as the pupil of the eye or a blood vessel. See also *Dilate* and *Vasoconstriction*.

Constructive criticism – offering a person advice or opinions regarding their work. Both positive and negative suggestions are usually made but expressed in a positive manner, usually leading to a higher standard of work.

Contagious – a *disease* that is able to spread by contact from one animal to another. See also *Infectious*.

Contaminated surgery – third in the order of priority for theatre surgical procedure lists, examples would include *pyometra* or bowel resection surgery, both of which involve a break into infected organs. See also *Clean/contaminated fracture*, *Dirty surgery*.

Continuous suture pattern – a type of suture pattern that is a running stitch and is rapidly placed. Because the suture relies on a single knot at either end if one end of the suture comes undone, the whole length of suture material will pull away. See also *Interrupted sutures*.

Contract (communication) – a legally binding document between two parties (usually an employer and employee) stating working conditions and pay. Company policies are sometimes stated within the contract or it may refer you to the company handout (which states all company regulations and policies). Contracts must be signed by both parties and each party should have a copy as well as any company handout booklet.

Contraction (wound care) – reduction in wound size by movement of normal tissue migrating towards the centre of the wound.

Contraindication – a specific circumstance during which the use of a particular drug or treatment is not advisable, eg the use of steroids is contraindicated in pregnant animals because it may cause termination of the pregnancy.

Contrast medium – substance used in radiographic studies to highlight a hollow organ. *Positive contrast* media are more *radio-opaque* than the surrounding tissue, eg *barium sulphate*, *iodine* compounds. *Negative contrast* media are more *radiolucent* than the surrounding tissue, eg *oxygen*, air. *Double contrast* involves using a small amount of positive contrast followed by negative.

Contrast study – a radiographic technique using a contrast medium to enhance or outline structures that are not usually visible on a radiograph. This technique is most often used in cystography, to outline the alimentary tract or to examine one kidney, ureters and bladder.

Control of Substances Hazardous to Health (COSHH) 1999 – act of legislation requiring all practices to make a thorough assessment of all the potential hazards that are in the workplace.

Controlled area – the area around the primary beam where radiation levels are in excess of the safe level, usually within a 2-metre radius of the primary beam.

Controlled drug – specific category of Prescription Only Medicine (POM) drugs consisting of five classes or schedules. Special legislation exists regarding the use of controlled drugs and strict regulations cover their purchase, storage and disposal (See also The *Misuse of Drugs Act 1971*). Schedule 1 drugs are not used in veterinary practice but include cannabis and LSD. Schedule 2 drugs include morphine, fentanyl, pethidine. Schedule 3 drugs include buprenorphine, pentobarbitone, phenobarbitone. Schedule 4 drugs include diazepam. Schedule 5 drugs include certain preparations of codeine or morphine, e.g. kaolin and morphine antidiarrhoeal suspension.

Convalescent – a patient that is recovering from illness, injury or surgery.

Convalescent carrier (latent carrier) – a patient who has recovered from the infectious agent. See also *Closed carrier*.

Convulsion – a *seizure* or fit; violent, uncontrolled, unconscious contractions of the body muscles. Convulsions result from disruption of the electrical activity in the *brain*. See also *Epilepsy*, *Seizure*, *Status epilepticus*.

C

Coprophagia – the normal practice by rabbits of eating partially digested faecal matter (*caecotrophs*) to allow it to pass through the digestive process for a second time. Rabbits that are unable to do this because of obesity or dental disease may suffer from weight loss and digestive disorders.

Copulation – see *Mating*.

Core temperature – the operating temperature of an organism, specifically in the deep structures of the body such as the *Liver*, as opposed to the temperature of the peripheral tissues. The temperature taken with a thermometer inserted into the *rectum* is closest to core temperature. Maintaining a stable core temperature is one of the body's *homeostatic* mechanisms designed to create an optimum environment to allow *enzymes* to work in chemical reactions.

Cornea – the highly sensitive outer layer of the *eye*. Transparent to allow light rays to enter the eye; also plays a role in bending the light rays to help focus them onto the *retina*. Corneal injury is seen frequently, ranging from superficial scratches through to corneal perforations. See also *Corneal reflex*, *Corneal ulcer*.

Corneal reflex – gently touching the *cornea* normally elicits a blink reflex. This is a reflex action designed to protect the cornea from damage. If the blink reflex is absent, it is a sign that death has occurred.

Corneal ulcer – a defect in the surface of the *cornea* that can be seen when stained with the dye *fluorescein*. A corneal ulcer can occur following trauma to the eye (eg scratch from a cat claw), as the result of the presence of a *foreign body* in the eye or an eyelash abnormality (see also Distichiasis, Entropion). Superficial injuries can be treated topically, deeper injuries need to be examined under general anaesthetic, usually by an ophthalmologist.

Coronavirus – the causal agent of *feline infectious peritonitis*.

Corpus luteum – the area left by the ruptured *follicle* on the surface of the *ovary* following *ovulation*; produces the hormone *progesterone*.

Corpuscle – a term used to describe the initial filtering portion (the *glomerulus* and *Bowman's capsule*) of the nephron. Also an old-fashioned term for a red or white blood cell.

Cortex (pl. **cortices)** – **1.** the outer, darker layer of the *kidney.* **2.** the outer layer of the *adrenal gland* where *corticosteroid* hormones, eg *mineralocorticoids* (eg *aldosterone*) and *glucocorticoids* (eg *cortisol*) are produced. **3.** the hard, outer layer of bone. See also *cortical bone.* **4.** the extensive outer layer of grey matter of the cerebral hemispheres, largely responsible for higher brain functions. See also *cerebrum.*

Cortical bone – also known as *compact bone.* Found on the outer surfaces of bones, giving the bone overall strength. *Haversian systems* within cortical bone are located close together, forming a hard white tissue. See also *Cancellous bone.*

Cortical screw – a surgical implant used during orthopaedic procedures; a screw used for securing a plate to *cortical bone*. Has a finer thread than the *cancellous screw*, a blunt head and hexagonal hole in the head.

Corticosteroids – steroid *hormones* secreted by the *adrenal cortex* which include *glucocorticoids*, *mineralocorticoids* and *sex hormones*. The most important glucocorticoid is cortisol; the most important mineralocorticoid is *aldosterone*.

Cortisol – a steroid hormone produced by the cortex of the adrenal gland. Production of cortisol is stimulated by ACTH. Important for enabling an animal to cope with physical and mental stress; involved with production of glucose through protein and carbohydrate metabolism, also causes immune suppression and has anti-inflammatory effects. Cortisol levels are high in stressed animals.

Costal – adjective referring to the ribs.

Costal arch – the costal cartilages of ribs 9 to 12 overlap to form the costal arch.

Costochondral junction – the point where the dorsal bony part of the rib meets the ventral costal cartilage part of the rib.

Cough reflex – a reflex action that prevents the unwanted inhalation of food pieces or solid particles into the *trachea*. Any contact of solid particles with the mucosa of the *larynx* causes the cough reflex. A sharp blast of air is expelled, thus blowing the particles out of the way.

Countersink – contouring the top of the screw hole (before drilling the screw into the bone) to fit the screw head; prevents fractures of the bone fragment.

Counterstain – usually carbol fuschin, used to stain Gram-negative organisms so they can be viewed under the microscope. The counterstain does not affect the colour of Gram-positive organisms.

Coupage (or percussion) – a type of physiotherapy that helps to clear fluid and secretions within the lungs involving very gentle percussion (or hitting) of the *thorax* using cupped hands; helps prevent *hypostatic pneumonia*. Must be carried out from the *caudal* end of the chest to the *cranial* end and aims to encourage coughing, which helps with the gradual removal of secretions.

Cradle – a plastic trough, useful for patient positioning particularly in surgery and radiography. Most troughs are radiolucent so can be radiographed without them altering the quality of the radiograph.

Cranial – adjective used to describe an area or anatomical position towards or near the head. See also *Caudal*.

Cranial nerve – there are 12 pairs of cranial nerves which arise directly from the *brain*, numbered cranially to caudally.

Cranial tibial muscle – a hindlimb muscle which causes flexion of the hock.

Cranio-caudal (CrCd) – a term used in radiography for views of both the fore- and hindlimbs above the carpus joint or tarsal joint.

Cranium – the *skull*; the bones enclosing the *brain*.

Crash box – a box that contains sufficient equipment and drugs to cope with emergencies such as a cardiac arrest. It should be regularly maintained and re-stocked immediately after use.

Creatine kinase (CK) – a muscle enzyme which is often measured in blood biochemistry profiles; elevated in animals with acute or ongoing muscle damage.

Creatinine – a molecule produced by the breakdown of creatine from muscles which is commonly measured in a biochemistry profile. Produced at a constant rate and filtered freely by the kidneys. Increase in plasma creatinine can therefore result from a reduced glomerular filtration rate (GFR), which may be pre-renal, renal or post-renal.

Cremaster muscle – a muscle which surrounds the testis and is used to draw it closer to the body in cold conditions. Relaxation of the muscle allows the testis to move away from the body to prevent over-heating in warm conditions.

Crenation – a term used to describe the shrunken and spiky appearance of dehydrated cells on a smear; usually an artefact caused by slow drying of the smear.

Crepitus – a grating or crunching sensation that may be felt or heard when the broken ends of bone move against each other. One of the clinical signs that a *fracture* has occurred.

Crepuscular – an animal that is active at dusk and at dawn.

Crescent or crimp marks – artefact found on radiographs, usually caused during handling of the radiograph by fingernail imprints.

Cricoid cartilage – a cartilage structure found in the *hyoid apparatus* in the *larynx*.

Crocodile forceps – a distinctive-looking surgical instrument, often used to extract a foreign body from within the ear canal or nose. Easily identifiable by the long, thin shaft with crocodile-type jaws at the tip.

Crop – a distensible sac found in birds, associated with the distal oesophagus, which stores food before digestion.

Crop feeding tube – used in birds that are unable or unwilling to eat. A special feeding tube is inserted into the oesophagus as far as the crop. A Spreull's needle may also be used for this purpose.

Cross-action towel clip – surgical instruments used to anchor the surgical drapes to the surgical field. They are identifiable by their spring-type cross action. See also *Backhaus towel clip*.

Cross-infection – the risk of a *disease* or *infection* passing from one patient to another, either by direct or indirect contact, by *fomites*, *vectors* or *aerosols*.

Crossed grid – a type of stationary grid; two grids, either parallel or focused, are superimposed on one another.

Crown – the part of the tooth above the gum line.

Cruciate ligaments – *ligaments* found within the *stifle joint* that normally provide stability for the joint. They are commonly damaged during exercise and the patient often requires surgery to correct the problem.

Cryotherapy – the use of extreme cold applied directly to neoplastic cells to destroy them. Usually used to remove small skin neoplasms such as *papillomas*.

Cryptorchid – having one or both testicles not fully descended into the scrotum. The testicle may be located within the abdomen, in the inguinal canal, or under the skin close to the scrotum. If only one testicle is retained the animal is described as a *unilateral* cryptorchid; if both are retained the animal is a *bilateral* cryptorchid.

Crypts of Lieberkühn – deep folds in the small intestinal mucosa lined with glands that secrete alkaline fluid into the small intestine.

Crystalloid – a type of fluid used to maintain hydration, and correct dehydration or electrolyte abnormalities. Not retained within the circulation and will be excreted in urine.

Ctenocephalides felis – known as the cat *flea*, the commonest flea found on both cats and dogs, it will also bite humans. It is a wingless insect with a laterally compressed body which feeds exclusively on *blood*. Severe flea infestation can result in *anaemia,* particularly in puppies and kittens. Hypersensitivity reactions can occur to flea saliva (feline allergic dermatitis). They act as an *intermediate host* for the *tapeworm Dipylidium caninum*, and can act as a *vector* for other diseases.

Cuboidal epithelium – epithelial tissue composed of non-ciliated cube-shaped epithelial cells, these cells line the thyroid gland and renal tubules.

Culture – a laboratory technique where a microbiological organism (usually bacterial but also fungal or viral) is encouraged to grow on special media. The technique is used to produce a larger quantity of the organism so that it can be identified more easily; and to assess the sensitivity of the organism to treatment.

Cushing's disease (hyperadrenocorticism) – also called *hyperadrenocorticism*, this is caused by excessive production of *corticosteroids* by the *adrenal cortex*. This can occur because of a *tumour* on the adrenal or pituitary gland, or because of excessive growth of the adrenal gland. Clinical signs include lethargy, hair loss, pot belly, thirst. Diagnosis can be confirmed by an *ACTH stimulation test*.

Cutaneous – relating to the skin.

Cutting needle – a type of surgical needle with a sharp point and sides. Triangular in cross-section, it is used for suturing skin and other dense tissues. See also *Round-bodied needle*.

Cyanosis – describes a blueish tinge to *mucous membranes*, tongue or skin that indicates insufficient oxygen is reaching the tissues. See also *Perfusion*.

Cyclic vomiting – repeated acts of vomiting, seen in conditions such as inflammatory intestinal disease.

Cyclosporin(e) (now spelt ciclosporin) – an immunosuppressive drug which is used in the management of immune-mediated conditions such as keratoconjunctivitis sicca and canine atopy.

Cyst – an abnormal, walled sac lined with epithelium and containing fluid, or occasionally semi-solid material. Often benign but can cause damage to local structures, particularly if they burst or become inflamed/infected.

Cystic calculius – a stone formed from mineralised material which is found in the bladder (urolith). May be asymptomatic if small but can cause recurrent cystitis, bacterial infections and even urinary tract obstructions in some cases.

Cysticercoid – a type of *metacestode* (part of the life cycle of tapeworms), only found in invertebrates such as fleas and lice. An example is the tapeworm *Dipylidium caninum* which produces cysticercoids inside the intermediate host (the flea).

Cysticercus - a type of *metacestode* (part of the life cycle of tapeworms), consists of a fluid-filled bladder with a single inverted *scolex*. An example of a tapeworm which produced a cysticercus is *Taenia hydatigena* which affects dogs and sheep.

Cystine crystals – a type of crystal which occurs uncommonly in the urine. Cystine crystalluria occurs most commonly in concentrated acidic urine and in animals with the hereditary disease cystinuria.

Cystitis – inflammation of the *bladder*, can be caused by *bacterial infection*, trauma, *urine crystals* or *calculi* or *neoplasia*. Symptoms include discomfort on urination, *dysuria*, *haematuria* and the animal may spend a lot of time licking the *perineum*. Treatment involves determining the underlying cause and treating accordingly.

Cystocentesis – the use of a sterile needle and syringe to withdraw uncontaminated urine directly from the bladder. A useful technique if urine culture is required because it reduces contamination with bacteria from the urethra and skin.

Cystotomy – surgical incision into the bladder. May be performed to remove bladder stones or tumours from inside the bladder.

Cytology – the study of cells using a *microscope*. The cells are collected using techniques such as *fine-needle aspiration*, tracheal washing and impression smears. The cells are then stained with stains such as Wright–Giemsa or Papanicolaou and examined for evidence of disease. Note that *histology* is the study of tissues using a microscope.

Cytoplasm – the semi-fluid content of a cell which contains the *nucleus* and *cell organelles*; also where products are stored, eg *lipid, carbohydrate* and *glycogen* granules.

Cytosol – the cystol as (opposed to *cytoplasm*, which also includes the *organelles*) is the internal fluid of the cell, and a large part of cell *metabolism* occurs here.

Cytotoxic drugs – drugs that are toxic (poisonous) to *cells*. May be used as part of a *chemotherapy* regimen. Extreme care must be used when dealing with cytotoxic drugs and manufacturer's guidelines regarding personal safety must be strictly followed.

D

Dacryocystitis – *infection* and *inflammation* of the *naso-lacrimal duct*; can cause the duct to become occluded. Often seen in *brachycephalic* animals and in rabbits with dental disease or *Pasteurella* infection.

Dam – describes the female parent of an animal.

Dangerous Wild Animal Act – a law passed to ensure that all potentially dangerous animals, eg wild cats, primates or poisonous reptiles, insects and spiders, can only be kept by people with the appropriate licences. Licences can only be issued by a veterinary surgeon and an environmental health officer once housing, welfare and safety criteria have been met by the owner.

Dark room – a specific room allocated for the development of radiographs.

Dartos muscle – muscular subcutaneous tissue of the scrotum covering the testes. The dartos muscle works with the *cremaster* muscle to keep the testes at the correct temperature. In the cold the dartos muscle contracts, causing wrinkling of the skin of the scrotum, which helps to retain heat. In warmer temperatures the dartos muscle relaxes.

Data Protection Acts 1984 and 1998 – These Acts give a person the right to be informed about any personal data relating to themselves on payment of a fee.

Dead space – **1.** the parts of the upper respiratory tract that are filled with air during respiration but that do not play a role in oxygen exchange are termed anatomical dead space. Structures making up this dead space include the nasal passages, *pharynx*, *trachea*, *bronchi* and *bronchioles*. **2.** the volume of the anaesthetic circuit from the patient's end to the point up to which to-and-fro movement of expired gas takes place. Often known as apparatus dead space.

Deamination – the process of removal of an amino group from a protein that occurs when proteins are metabolised.

Debilitation – severe loss of energy, fatigue and weakening, possibly affecting movement.

Debit – collection of payment from an account.

Debridement – a procedure to clean up an old or devitalised *wound* by surgically cutting away dead and contaminated tissue to allow healthy tissue to granulate.

Debris – very small object of solid material, eg dirt.

Debtor – a person who owes a debt.

Debulking – a surgical technique used to remove the bulk of a large *tumour* without removing it completely or taking clear margins around the tumour. Often used when the mass is *benign* and when the size of the mass is causing the animal difficulty in moving, eg a large *lipoma* situated in the axilla area.

Deciduous teeth – the first set of teeth that erupt, replaced by the permanent teeth, usually around the age of 7 months.

Decolouriser – an agent that removes the purple stain from Gram-negative bacteria only. The agent used is often acetone.

Decubitus ulcer – a red sore on the *skin* caused by prolonged lying down in one position. Usually found over bony prominences, eg elbow, hock. The patient may seem restless or uncomfortable and there may be some bleeding or ulceration of the skin. Nursing care includes carefully cleaning and drying the area, applying extra padding and turning the recumbent patient regularly to avoid lying for long periods in the same position.

Defamation – damaging the reputation or character of someone. Can be libel and/or slander.

Defecation – the act of passing *faeces* from the body through the *anus*.

Deferent duct – often called the *vas deferens*. A tube which arises from the tail of the *epididymis* in the testicle, and extends to join the *urethra* at the level of the *prostate gland*. Its function is to carry *sperm* from the epididymis to the urethra.

Definitive host – see *Final host*.

DEFRA (Department for the Environment, Farming and Rural Affairs) – a Government-controlled regulatory body whose main role in small animal veterinary terms is to control and update the laws and requirements of the *Pet Travel Scheme (PETS)*.

Degenerative disease – diseases caused by failure of the body to renew or repair damaged or worn out tissues, eg degenerative joint disease.

Degloving injury – a wound where the skin has been torn or peeled away.

Deglutition – the act of swallowing.

Degu – a small, gerbil-like rodent native to Chile. Sometimes referred to as the trumpet-tailed rat (although not related to the rat family) and is occasionally seen in the veterinary practice. Degus should not be picked up by the tail, as, like the gerbil, they can shed their tail as a way to escape from predators.

Dehiscence (of wounds) – wounds that have broken down and failed to heal. Can happen for a number of reasons, including poor suturing technique, poor aseptic technique, infection already present, poor surgical technique, poor post-operative care, decreased blood supply to the wound or use of steroids.

Dehydration – a reduction in the total amount of water in the body. Can be caused by many conditions, including excessive and/or prolonged *vomiting* or *diarrhoea*, severe *burns*, *hyperthermia*, excessive panting, *unconsciousness*, prolonged inappetance, eg because of a fractured jaw or the animal having no access to water. Will lead to a decrease in circulating *blood* volume and the animal will become *hypovolaemic*. Signs associated with dehydration include skin tenting, sluggish *capillary refill time*, tacky *mucous membranes*, sunken eyes, collapse, *shock* and death. Tests for dehydration include measuring the *packed cell volume* and checking the *specific gravity* of the *urine*. To reverse dehydration, immediate *intravenous fluid therapy* is required.

Delayed healing – wounds that are taking longer than expected to heal. Can happen as a result of poor health, old age, diabetes mellitus, poor suturing technique, wrong suture material used, use of steroids, radiation therapy or location of the wound, eg over a joint.

Delayed union – fractures that are taking longer than expected to reach clinical union.

Deltoideus – one of the muscles of the shoulder, making the joint flex.

Demeanour – the way in which a patient behaves towards other people and animals.

Demodex canis – a cigar-shaped, burrowing mite which may be a *commensal* organism in the hair follicles and sebaceous glands. In animals that are predisposed or immune-suppressed, *Demodex* mites may multiply and cause skin disease (demodectic mange or *demodicosis*).

Demodicosis – condition describing the presence of *Demodex* mites on a patient. The mites cause various symptoms, including *non-pruritic alopecia* and scaly, thickened skin. The skin lesions are often localised on the head or forelimbs but they can spread to the rest of the body and feet, where it becomes more difficult to treat. Demodicosis can be treated with weekly baths in Amitraz, an *organophosphate*, so the product must be handled and used with great care.

Dendrite – a short process that extends out of the *cell body* of a *nerve* cell, through which *nervous impulses* are received from other *neurones*.

Dental – **1.** pertaining to the teeth. **2.** a procedure performed under general anaesthetic that involves scaling and polishing the teeth with extractions if required.

Dental elevator – a dental instrument used to rupture the periodontal ligament and to elevate the tooth from the socket.

Dental formula – a list stating the numbers of each kind of tooth for each species.

Dentine – a layer found below the enamel in each tooth.

Deoxyribonucleic acid (DNA) – a double-stranded molecule found in the *nucleus* of every *cell*; carries coded information for reproducing new cells. A strand of DNA is made up of individual *genes*. Each gene issues the instructions for the assembly of a specific *protein*. A *chromosome* is composed of a larger molecule of DNA.

Depolarising neuromuscular blocking drugs (NMBDs) – used in anaesthesia to achieve a high level of muscle relaxation, eg suxamethonium.

Depressed fracture – a fragment of bone is pushed below its normal level, usually seen in the *cranium* after a forceful blow to the *skull*. See also *Avulsed, Comminuted fracture, Complicated fracture, Compound (open) fracture.*

Depression (medical nursing) – a state of low mood; the animal is often withdrawn and may also refuse to eat and drink.

Depth gauge – an instrument used to provide measurement of hole depth, to enable selection of the correct size screw.

Dermal – relating to the skin.

***Dermatophagoides* sp.** – house dust mites; common in many homes and may be a cause of allergic reactions in dogs with *atopy*.

Dermatophyte – a fungus that causes *ringworm*, affecting the skin, hair and claws. Penetrates the hair shaft and causes an inflammatory response. Can sometimes be detected using a *Wood's lamp*. See *Dermatophytosis.*

Dermatophytosis – also known as *ringworm*; a *zoonotic*, fungal infection affecting skin, hair and claws. Clinical signs include circular areas of *alopecia*, scaling, inflammation and also *pruritis*. Care must be taken when handling affected patients as this is a *zoonotic pathogen*. Common species of the fungus include *Microsporum canis* and *Trichophyton mentagrophytes*. Many cases resolve spontaneously. See *Dermatophyte.*

Dermis – the layer of connective tissue below the *epidermis* of the *skin*. It is here that nerve endings, *blood vessels*, *glands*, hair follicles and the *arrector pili muscles* are located.

Designated area – a room specifically designed for radiography.

Designated people – any person whose name is stated on the local rules can work within the designated area.

Developer – a solution used to develop the image on a radiograph by converting silver halide crystals to metallic silver. The developing or reducing agent is either hydroquinone or phenidone.

Developer splashes – an artefact seen on a radiograph as black patches.

Dexamethasone suppression test – See *High-dose dexamethasone suppression test*, *Low-dose dexamethasone suppression test*.

Dextrose – a type of fluid used to correct conditions such as hypoglycaemia or to maintain blood glucose levels. Should be administered along with a crystalloid.

Diabetes insipidus – deficiency in *antidiuretic hormone* (ADH) synthesis/release (central diabetes insipidus), or failure of the kidneys to respond to ADH (nephrogenic diabetes insipidus). Results in the inability of the kidneys to concentrate urine. The primary clinical signs are severe *polyuria* and *polydipsia* (PU/PD). Diagnosis involves ruling out other causes of PU/PD and then performing a *water deprivation test*.

Diabetes mellitus – an *endocrine* disorder in which there is
persistent *hyperglycaemia* as the result of a lack of *insulin*
production in the *pancreas* (insulin-dependent/type 1
diabetes mellitus); or tissue resistance to the actions of insulin
(non-insulin-dependent/type 2 diabetes mellitus). Clinical
signs include PU/PD, *polyphagia*, and weight loss.
Cataracts may develop and *diabetic ketoacidosis* is a
serious complication.

D

Diabetic ketoacidosis (DKA) – a serious complication
associated with poorly controlled *diabetes mellitus*. Occurs
when the body breaks down fats for energy, producing
large quantities of ketones. These cause *metabolic acidosis*
and exacerbate the existing condition. Clinical signs include
anorexia, vomiting, lethargy and a strong-smelling ketotic
breath (ketones smell like pear-drops). Ketones can be
detected in the urine (*ketonuria*). The condition is life-
threatening and requires aggressive therapy.

Diagnosis – identifying a condition from signs and symptoms.

Diaphragm – **1.** a domed sheet of *muscle* and *tendons* which separates the *thoracic cavity* from the *abdominal cavity*. During *respiration*, the diaphragm contracts, lowering the pressure within the *thorax*. At the same time, the *intercostal muscles* contract, pushing the ribcage up and out. Air flows into the thorax from the atmosphere until the pressure is equal inside the thorax and out. This is called *inspiration*. At this point, the muscles of the diaphragm relax, reducing the thorax volume and pushing air out. This is called *expiration*. There are three holes in the diaphragm (the aortic hiatus, the oesophageal hiatus and the *foramen vena cava*) which allow important structures to pass through it from one cavity to the other. See also Diaphragmatic rupture/tear, Diaphragmatic hernia. **2.** the iris diaphragm is an adjustable opening beneath the stage on a light *microscope* which is used to vary the amount of light directed onto the stage.

Diaphragmatic hernia – a defect in the *diaphragm*, usually caused by trauma. See *Diaphragmatic rupture/tear*.

Diaphragmatic rupture/tear – a rupture/tear in the *diaphragm*; usually occurs as the result of a road traffic accident (RTA) and should be repaired as soon as possible because *abdominal* contents can move into the *thorax* through the tear. The patient will often be *dyspnoeic*, so careful *anaesthetic* monitoring is essential. Surgery causes a *pneumothorax* because air from the atmosphere travels through the diaphragmatic tear into the thorax, so a chest drain is usually placed to help remove the excess air.

Diaphysis – the shaft of a *long bone* formed from a primary centre of ossification during *endochondral ossification*, contains the *bone marrow*.

Diarrhoea – faeces that are unformed and more liquid than normal. Degree of severity can range from slightly softer stools than normal to brown watery liquid. Can be caused by disease of the *small* or *large intestine* and can be *acute* (usually an *infectious* or inflammatory response) or *chronic* (often linked to *malabsorption*). Prolonged episodes of diarrhoea can cause *dehydration* and *electrolyte* imbalance as a result of excess fluid loss.

Diarthrosis – a freely movable synovial joint between two bones.

Diastema – the toothless gap between the incisor teeth and the molar teeth in animals such as rabbits and horses.

Diastole – the relaxation period of the *cardiac muscle* between heart beats. See also *Systole*.

Diastolic pressure – the pressure of the *blood* in the *veins* when the *heart* is relaxed, or in diastole. This is normally relatively low.

Diathermy – a method of controlling *haemorrhage* during surgery. An electric current is used to create heat, which is then applied to the tissues so the blood *coagulates* at the site of application. This technique can also be used to cut through tissue.

Dichroic fog – a film fault caused by incorrect washing, seen as yellow-brown stains on the radiograph.

Diffusion – the movement of molecules from an area of high concentration to low concentration until their concentration is equal in all areas. Can apply to molecules in a gas or in solution.

Diffusion hypoxia – a condition in which nitrous oxide molecules can remove and replace oxygen molecules within the lungs.

Digastricus – one of the masticatory muscles of the dog and cat, innervated by the *trigeminal nerve* (cranial nerve V). It runs from the base of the *skull* to the *mandible* and it makes the jaw open.

Digestion – the process of breaking down complex food molecules to simpler molecules so that they can be used for growth and repair, and to provide energy within the body; eg the breaking down of proteins to polypeptides and amino acids with enzymes in the stomach and small intestine. Waste products are then excreted. See also Digestive system.

Digestive system – system of organs through the body concerned with digestion; includes the mouth, tongue, teeth, salivary glands, *pharynx, oesophagus, liver, stomach, duodenum, pancreas, gall bladder, jejunum, ileum, caecum, colon, rectum, anus*.

Digital radiography – development of the image is performed digitally and the image is viewed on a computer screen.

Digital thermometer – a thermometer that provides digital readings.

Dilate – the enlargement or expansion of a structure.

Dimorphism – having two forms. It usually means that an organism has two distinct forms, for example, males and females of some species look different, and are said to be sexually dimorphic.

Dioestrus – a short period of sexual inactivity which occurs after a season in the cat, before the next pro-oestrus begins.

Diplococci – bacterial *cocci* which are arranged in pairs.

Diploid – describes a cell that contains two sets of *chromosomes*, a paternal set and a maternal set. When a cell has divided by *mitosis*, two *diploid* cells are produced. See also Haploid, Meiosis.

Diptera – flies such as bluebottles and greenbottles (blowflies). Some diptera lay eggs on damaged skin (or even intact skin in some cases) and the larvae (maggots) hatch out and feed on the skin and tissues. Infestation with dipteran larvae is called *myiasis* or fly strike.

Dipylidium caninum – a common tapeworm parasite of the small intestine of dogs and cats. Flea larvae are usually the intermediate hosts.

Direct trauma – damage caused by high impact, such as road traffic accident.

Dirty screens (intensifying) – intensifying screens with debris, such as dirt or hair, contaminating them; there will be artefacts on all radiographs.

Dirty surgery – last in the order of priority for theatre surgical procedure risks, an example of dirty surgery would be a dental. See also *clean/contaminated surgery*, *contaminated surgery*, *clean/sterile surgery*.

Dirty wound – a classification of a wound which is over 6 hours old or a surgical wound with infection present.

Disaccharide – a pair of joined monosaccharides.

Discharging patients – returning the patient to the owner (usually with after-care instructions) following treatment within the practice/hospital.

Disease – a condition affecting the health of a patient.

Disease factor – used when calculating energy requirements in patients who are being tube fed. Basal energy requirement (BER) × disease factor where disease factors are as follows:

- ❧ Cage rest – 1.2
- ❧ Surgery trauma – 1.3
- ❧ Multiple surgeries – 1.5
- ❧ Sepsis/cancer – 1.7
- ❧ Burns – 2.0.

Disinfectant – a chemical product used to achieve *disinfection* by destroying *pathogenic micro-organisms*. See also *Disinfection*.

Disinfection – a physical or chemical means of removing *micro-organisms* (but not usually *spores*) from contaminated surfaces, eg surfaces, floors, kennels, equipment. See also *Sterilisation*.

Disorientation – loss of awareness.

Displacement activity – where a physical device is used for transferring anxiety during confrontation/discussion, eg biting nails, playing with hair.

Disseminated intravascular coagulation (DIC) – a severe and usually fatal condition where widespread blood clotting occurs, eventually all the coagulant factors have been used up and the animal starts to haemorrhage. Can be caused by many other conditions such as haemolytic anaemia, neoplasia, shock , sepsis and transfusion reactions.

Distal – furthest away; see also *Proximal*.

Distal convoluted tubule – the part of the *nephron* leading from the *loop of Henlé* to the *collecting duct*.

Distemper – a common *infectious disease* of the dog and ferret caused by a *morbillivirus*. Colloquially known as 'hard pad', its symptoms include depression, *anorexia*, *pyrexia*, dysphasic temperature, *hyperkeratosis* of the skin. Spread of the disease is largely controlled by the use of regular *vaccines*.

Distichiasis – a painful *congenital* condition caused by having an extra row of eyelashes that are turned inwards towards the eyeball. Symptoms include *epiphora*, *corneal ulceration* and *blepharospasm*. Treatment may involve plucking, electrolysis or surgical excision of the affected area.

Diuretics – drugs that increase the amount of fluid excreted from the body by the kidneys. Used in the treatment of heart failure and oedema. Examples include frusemide, spironolactone and hydrochlorothiazide. Side-effects can include dehydration and electrolyte imbalances.

Diurnal – describing an animal which is active during the day; see also Nocturnal.

Dolichocephalic – a description of a long-nosed, slender skull shape, as seen in greyhounds, whippets, salukis and Afghan hounds. See also *Brachycephalic*, *Mesocephalic*.

Dominant gene – when an animal carries two different copies of a gene (ie is *heterozygous*) one copy usually masks the effects of the other (is *dominant* over it). The less dominant gene is called the *recessive gene*, eg in dalmatians the black form of the spotting gene (**B**) is dominant over the liver-coloured spot form (**b**); a dalmation carrying **BB** or **Bb** genes will have black spots, but one carrying **bb** will have liver spots because there is no dominant gene to mask its effects.

Donor – a patient who gives organs, tissue, blood, etc to another patient.

Doppler – uses sound waves and produces an audible noise; used in equipment such as blood pressure monitoring.

Dorsal – a directional term meaning towards the animal's back. See also Ventral.

Dorsal root ganglion – area containing the *cell bodies* of the *sensory neurones* entering the *spinal cord*.

Dorsoventral (DV) – a term used in radiography to describe the view; the beam enters the dorsal surface and leaves through the ventral surface.

Double contrast study – a contrast study where two contrast agents are used to provide better contrast and detail, eg air and ionic contrast medium.

Double exposure – two exposures on the same piece of radiographic film, superimposed one on the other.

Dowe's catheter – an indwelling urinary catheter, not commonly used.

Doxapram – a respiratory stimulant which works on the *central nervous system*. Most commonly administered in drop form under the tongue of *neonates* to stimulate *respiration* during resuscitation after a *Caesarean section*.

Doyen bowel clamp – a surgical instrument used for occluding or clamping the intestines or stomach during abdominal surgery. There is a gap between the grasping surfaces so they are as atraumatic as possible when holding the delicate tissue.

Drape – a pre-sterilised sheet, can be made from paper, cotton or plastic and is used to cover the patient before and during surgery. Acts as a barrier against contamination of the surgical site. A drape can be fenestrated (with a window cut into the drape to operate through) or plain (no window).

Dressings – coverings, using various materials with/without other agents impregnated, used to place over wounds to aid healing.

Drill – a device used to apply implants such as screws into bone.

Drill bit – an orthopaedic instrument used to drill a hole into a bone before fixing a plate. See *Dynamic compression plate, Sherman compression plate, Venables compression plate*.

Drill cover/shroud – a material cover that encases the whole drill. Can be sterilised, enabling surgeons and theatre staff to use it in a sterile manner.

Drill guide – allows accurate control of the drill bit, preventing damage to surrounding tissue.

Drip rate – the rate and amount required to maintain hydration. Calculation of the fluid requirements should take into account the size of the animal and the giving set used (ie standard giving set drop rate = 20 drops/ml; paediatric giving set drop rate = 60 drops/ml). Fluids should be maintained at 50–60 ml/kg per day to replace daily losses. An example is given here of the maintenance rates for a 5-kg cat using a standard giving set:

* maintenance fluid requirement = 50 ml/kg per day = (50 ml × 5 kg)/day = 250 ml/day
* requirement per hour = 250 ml ÷ 24 = 10 ml
* requirement per minute = 10 ml ÷ 60 = 0.16 ml
* giving set drop rate = 20 × 0.16 ml = 3.2 drops/min
* drip rate = 60 seconds/3.2 drops = 1 drop every 18 seconds.

Drug-induced – a condition caused by the administration of a drug, eg vomiting caused by the administration of apomorphine is drug-induced.

Dry-dry dressing – used in infected wounds that are secreting large amounts of exudates, eg dry swabs are placed in or over the wound and bandaged in place. The dressing would be removed after 24 hours, removing infected and necrotic tissue.

Dry eye – see *Keratoconjunctivitis sicca*.

Drying (radiography) – in wet development the radiograph needs to be hung in a dust-free area to allow complete drying.

Duct – a channel or tube used for secretion or excretion of liquids, eg bile flows down the *bile duct* from the *gall bladder* into the *duodenum*. See also *Nasolacrimal duct*, *Thoracic duct*.

Ductus deferens – See *Deferent duct*.

Duodenum – the most *proximal* portion of the small intestine; it is fairly short, extending from the *pylorus* of the stomach to the point where the small intestine enters the *mesentery* (where the *jejunum* begins). The bile duct and pancreatic duct both enter the duodenum providing bile and pancreatic juice for digestion.

Dura mater – the tough, protective outer membrane of the *meninges*, made out of dense connective tissue.

Duty of care – nurses are personally responsible for their own professional standards and negligence; they should act at all times in the best interest of the animal.

Dynamic compression plate – an orthopaedic implant used for fracture fixation and compression, rectangular in shape with oval holes. See also *Sherman compression plate*, *Venables compression plate*.

Dyschezia – difficulty or pain when passing *faeces*. Owners usually notice the animal straining excessively. Can be associated with *constipation*, rectal *tumours* or an enlarged *prostate gland*. See also *Tenesmus*.

Dysecdysis – describes abnormal shedding of skin in snakes. The skin is shed in lots of small pieces, rather than as one or two large pieces. Can be caused by low humidity in the snake's environment or inadequate/lack of bathing facilities in the *vivarium*.

Dysphagia – difficulty eating, although the animal can often be very hungry; can be caused by dental disease, neurological disorders or a foreign body in the throat or *oesophagus*.

Dysphonia – a change or loss of voice; may occur with damage/disease to the larynx.

Dysplasia – abnormal size, shape or arrangement of cells that is not *neoplastic*. Dysplasia may be caused by irritation to a tissue and may sometimes precede neoplastic changes.

Dyspnoea – difficulty in breathing or laboured breathing. See also *Mouth breathing*.

Dysrhythmia – an abnormal alteration to the *heart* rhythm. See also *Sinus arrhythmia*.

Dystocia – difficulty with *parturition*, or giving birth. The two main causes of dystocia are maternal factors (*uterine inertia* and obstruction of the birth canal) and fetal factors (fetal oversize or abnormality of fetal alignment). See also *Caesarean section*.

Dysuria – difficulty or pain when passing *urine*. See also *Cystitis, Pollakiuria*.

E

E. coli – see *Escherichia coli*.

Ecchymoses – a leakage of *blood* from vessels into tissues, forming a bruise or *haematoma*. See also *Petechia*.

Echinococcus granulosus – an uncommon tapeworm parasite; an important *zoonotic* agent because its *metacestode* is a *hydatid cyst* that can develop in a number of *intermediate hosts* including humans. The final host is the dog or fox.

Echocardiogram – a piece of equipment that allows the vet to assess the structure and function of the *heart* using *ultrasound* to assess the thickness and contractibility of the *ventricular* walls and also the functionality of the heart valves. Useful in detecting *cardiomyopathy*, pericardial effusions and *endocardiosis*. Abnormal soft tissue masses, such as *tumours* or lesions on the heart valves, can be detected and *blood flow* through the heart can also be assessed. See also *Electrocardiograph (ECG)*.

Eclampsia – a life-threatening condition caused by hypocalcaemia, usually in the first few weeks of lactation (or rarely towards the end of pregnancy). Clinical signs include weakness, tremors and occasionally seizures. Small-breed dogs with large litters may be at increased risk of developing eclampsia.

Ectoderm – a layer of tissue formed in an *embryo* which goes on to develop into the *integument* and nervous system.

Ectoparasite – a *parasite* living on the surface of the *host*, eg *fleas, ticks, lice, mites*. See also *Endoparasites*.

E

Ectoparasiticides – drugs used to kill external parasites such as fleas, lice, ticks and mites. May be injectable (eg ivermectin), spot-on (eg selamectin, fipronil, moxidectin, imidacloprid), oral preparations (eg lufenuron) or baths (eg amitraz).

Ectopic – a structure occurring in the wrong place, eg ectopic *cilia* are hairs growing out of the *conjunctiva*, causing irritation to the *cornea*; ectopic *ureters* may enter the *bladder* at a place other than the *trigone* and may cause *incontinence*; an ectopic *pregnancy* is where the *embryo* attaches and starts developing outside the *uterus*.

Ectropion – an outward drooping of the eyelid, often related to the breed conformation. Can result in chronic *conjunctivitis* or *keratitis* if the animal is not able to close its eyelids properly. In extreme cases, surgical correction is required. Commonly affected breeds include St Bernards, Bassett Hounds and Mastiffs. See also *Entropion*.

Effector – usually a *muscle* or *gland* that responds to a nervous stimulus.

Efferent – conducting away from, eg an efferent *nerve* carries a *nervous impulse* away from the *spinal cord.* See also *Afferent.*

Effusion – accumulation of fluid in a body cavity. See also *Ascites, Pleural effusion.*

Ehmer sling – a bandage used to support the hindlimb, eg following hip dislocation.

E

Ejaculation – the passage of semen through the urethra and out of the urethral orifice. Occurs during mating so that semen is transferred to the female reproductive tract to fertilise the ova.

Elastin – a *protein* that is found in elastic *connective tissue.* Found in places where flexibility is needed such as in the lining of *blood vessels* and in the *lungs.*

Elbow dysplasia – a genetic disease causing abnormalities of the elbow joints that can lead to osteoarthritis changes and lameness.

Elbow dysplasia scheme (elbow score) – scheme run by the BVA and kennel club; involves examining radiographs of elbows from dogs and bitches and grading their elbows on a scale from 0 to 3 depending on the severity of elbow dysplasia. Used for breeding purposes, to reduce/control elbow dysplasia.

Elective surgery – non-urgent surgery, a procedure that can be scheduled ahead of time to suit the owner and vet, eg routine *dental* procedures, routine *neutering.*

Electrocardiograph (ECG) – a machine used to measure the electrical activity of the heart; a normal ECG trace consists of a *P-wave* which represents depolarisation of the atria, a *QRS-complex*, which represents depolarisation of the ventricles, and a *T-wave*, which represents re-polarisation of the ventricles.

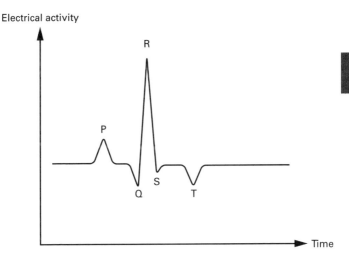

Electrolytes – elements dissolved in the body's tissues in the form of positively or negatively charged ions. Have many functions in the body and are often measured as part of a biochemistry profile. Examples are sodium (Na^+), chloride (Cl^-), potassium (K^+), calcium (Ca^{2+}), magnesium (Mg^{2+}) and bicarbonate (HCO_3^-).

Electromagnetic radiation – a method of transporting energy, identified by energy, wavelength and frequency.

Electron – a negatively charged particle that surrounds the nucleus of an atom in shells.

Elimination – anaesthetic drugs can be excreted via the liver, kidneys and lungs depending on the drug used; their level of function should be assessed before administering these drugs.

ELISA (enzyme-linked immunosorbent assay) – a biochemical technique used to detect the presence of an antibody or antigen in a sample; a colour change is produced in the test kit when the antigen or antibody is present. Examples of ELISA tests used commonly in practice are the feline leukaemia virus, feline immunodeficiency virus and parvovirus test kits.

E

Elizabethan collar – a clear plastic collar (similar in shape to a lampshade) to prevent patient interference. A range of sizes is available to accommodate patients from birds through to large dogs.

Emaciation – severe or excessive weight loss.

Embryo – the stage of development from when the *zygote* starts to divide until all the organs are developed (when the embryo becomes a *fetus*).

Emesis – meaning *vomiting*. See also *Emetic*.

Emetic – a substance used to induce *emesis* or to make the patient *vomit*; would be given in suspected *poisoning* to prevent further absorption of the poison by removing it from the animal's stomach. Emesis must only be induced, however, if the ingested poison is non-corrosive. Examples of emetics include *apomorphine*, washing soda crystals or salt water. See also *Activated charcoal, Adsorbent*.

Emulsion – a layer between the protective coat and the base of radiographic film, containing gelatin and silver halide micro-crystals.

Enamel – a hard calcified material coating the crowns of teeth.

Encephalitis – inflammation of the brain.

Encephalitozoon cuniculi – a fairly common *protozoal* parasite which affects rabbits. May cause neurological problems, renal failure and cataracts; can be transmitted across the *placenta* during development, or in the urine.

E

End tidal carbon dioxide – the amount of carbon dioxide present at the end of expiration.

Endemic disease – (sometimes called *enzootic* disease) a disease which is present in the population and causes intermittent disease. For example feline leukaemia virus and feline immunedeficiency virus are endemic in the cat population in the UK.

Endocardiosis – a progressive thickening of the heart *valves*, gradually rendering them unable to function effectively and causing them to leak severely when they should be closed. Congestive heart failure often follows.

Endocarditis – inflammation of the inner lining of the *heart* (*endocardium*), in particular the heart *valves*. Associated with *bacterial infection* that has spread to the heart. Symptoms include heart murmur, coughing, *dyspnoea* and *pyrexia*.

Endocardium – the endothelial layer lining the inner walls and *valves* of the *heart*.

Endochondral ossification – the formation of *bone* based on a *cartilage* model formed within the *embryo*. Centres of *ossification* appear within the cartilage where *osteoclast* cells erode the cartilage and *osteoblasts* replace it with new bone matrix. During this time, blood vessels grow and start to penetrate into the bone matrix, eventually forming the *bone marrow* cavity. See also *Diaphysis*, *Epiphysis*, *Intramembranous ossification*.

Endocrine gland – a *duct*less gland that synthesises and secretes *hormones* directly into the bloodstream, eg the *pituitary gland*, *adrenal glands*, *thyroid gland* and *pancreas*. See also *Endocrine system*, *Exocrine gland*.

Endocrine system – a system of glands that controls and co-ordinates many functions of the body. Various *endocrine glands* synthesise and secrete hormones directly into the bloodstream (see also *Exocrine gland*) – these travel to their target organ, bind with receptors and elicit a response.

Endoderm – a layer of tissue formed in an *embryo* that goes on to develop into the digestive system and associated glands, and the respiratory system.

Endolymph – the fluid contained within the membranous labyrinth in the *inner ear*.

Endometrium – the inner surface of the uterus, it is lined with many glands.

Endoneurium – the *connective tissue* surrounding each *nerve* fibre.

Endoparasites – a parasite living inside its host, eg *roundworms* and *tapeworms*. See also *Cestode*, *Ectoparasite*, *Nematode*.

Endoparasiticides – drugs used to kill internal parasites such as roundworms, tapeworms, flukes and protozoa. May be injectable (eg ivermectin, levamisole), spot-on (eg selamectin, moxidectin), or oral preparations (eg fenbendazole, praziquantel).

Endoplasmic reticulum (ER) – cell *organelle* concerned with the synthesis and storage of proteins. In places the ER is coated with *ribosomes* (where protein synthesis takes place). Where the ER is coated with ribosomes, it is called rough ER, the rest is called smooth ER.

Endoscope – medical instrument used to visualise internal structures and organs and to allow biopsy samples to be taken. Made from fibre optics, mirrors, lenses and a light source, they carry an image of the tissue in question back to the operator. They can be flexible (generally used to examine structures such as the stomach) or rigid (generally used to examine structures such as the nose or joints). Need careful cleaning and handling because they are very fragile.

Endoscopy – an examination using an endoscope.

Endospore – see *Spore*.

Endotoxic shock – an inadequate perfusion of the body tissues caused by an inflammatory response to severe bacterial infection. See also *Anaphylactic shock, Cardiogenic shock, Hypovolaemic shock*.

Endotoxin – a component of the *cell wall* of *Gram-negative* bacteria that is released when the bacteria die and degrade. Has many effects, ranging from *pyrexia* and *hypotension* through to *endotoxic shock* and death. The effects are the result of the immune system's reaction to the toxin rather than the toxin itself.

Endotracheal tube (ET tube) – a rubber or plastic tube inserted into the *trachea* of an anaesthetised animal to maintain a patent airway and allow the administration of oxygen and anaesthetic gas. Available in a wide range of sizes and either with or without an inflatable cuff. The cuff should be inflated not only to reduce the risk of the patient inhaling saliva, blood or vomit, but also to limit the escape of anaesthetic gases into the environment. The cuff can cause damage to the trachea if over inflated.

Enema – introduction of fluid into the rectum to empty the bowel or aid bowel movement (will require anaesthesia).

Enterectomy – surgical removal of a section of intestine.

Enteritis – inflammation of the small intestine. Causes include bacterial or viral infection, or parasites.

Enteroplication – surgically securing the intestines in folds to prevent intussusception re-occurring.

Enterotomy – surgical incision and opening into the intestine.

Entropion – the inversion of the eyelid so that the eyelashes roll inwards and cause irritation to the *cornea*. Symptoms include *epiphora, blepharospasm* and *corneal ulceration*. Can be corrected surgically by excising a small strip of the eyelid to allow the lid to sit in a more natural position. Commonly affected breeds include those with lots of facial folds, eg Shar Pei, Labrador, Chow and many others. See also *Ectropion*.

Enucleation – the surgical removal of the whole eyeball. Generally carried out because of severe trauma to the eye, *infection*, *neoplasia* or as a means of providing pain relief for the animal when the vision has already been lost, eg as a result of *glaucoma*.

Envelope – the outer layer of many viruses, made of lipoprotein.

Environmental Protection Act 1992 – act of law covering the disposal of all domestic and industrial (including *clinical*) *waste*.

E

Enzootic disease – see Endemic disease.

Enzyme – a protein in cells that acts as a catalyst during chemical reactions in the body. Speeds up the reaction, without itself becoming involved in the reaction.

Eosinopaenia – a decrease in the number of circulating eosinophils in the blood. Causes may include steroid therapy and hyperadrenocorticism.

Eosinophil – a *granulocyte* produced in the *bone marrow*, numbers increase in the bloodstream during allergic reactions and *parasite* infestations. Can be identified by the fact that the granules in the *cytoplasm* stain orange/red. They make up around 5% of total white blood cell count. See also Leucocyte.

Eosinophilia – an increase in the number of eosinophils in the blood. Causes may include parasitic infestation, allergic conditions, tissue damage and some types of tumour (such as mast cell tumour).

Eosinophilic granuloma complex – a common inflammatory skin disease of cats characterised by a group of lesions affecting the skin, oral cavity and mucocutaneous junctions. Thought to be caused by hypersensitivity reactions to food or parasites.

Eosinophilic ulcer – (also called rodent ulcer or indolent ulcer) a cutaneous or oral lesion that is part of the *eosinophilic granuloma complex*. Usually painless.

Epaxial muscle – muscle lying *dorsal* to the vertebral column. Attaches to the vertebrae and ribs and acts to extend the spine. See also *Hypaxial muscle*.

Epicardium – the outer surface of the heart. See also *Endocardium, Myocardium*.

Epidemic disease – (sometimes called *epizootic* disease) an epidemic describes a sudden steep rise in the incidence of infection with a particular disease, eg the recent foot and mouth disease outbreak in the UK, or an outbreak of *parvovirus* in a kennel block.

Epidermis – the outer layer of the skin, formed from stratified squamous epithelial tissue. Made up of four layers (from lowest to highest), namely the stratum germinativum, stratum granulosum, stratum lucidum and stratum corneum. See also *Dermis*.

Epididymis – part of the testicle in male animals that stores spermatozoa. A coiled tube connecting the efferent tubules from the testis to the *deferent duct*.

Epidural space – a space within the spinal column, where the dura mater is not closely attached. Analgesia may be administered into this area, as can local anaesthetics, creating an epidural or spinal anaesthesia (an aseptic technique is required for both these procedures).

Epiglottis – a flap of tissue and *cartilage* at the base of the tongue which covers the entrance to the *larynx* during swallowing to prevent the accidental inhalation into the lungs of food or drink particles. See also *Cough reflex*.

Epilepsy – a condition in which the patient suffers from unpredictable *convulsions* or *seizures* occurring as a result of abnormal electrical activity or chemical imbalance in the *brain*. Seizures are often triggered by stress. An epileptic seizure can be divided into three phases:

- pre-ictal stage, a few minutes before the seizure starts, where the animal is restless and excitable
- ictal stage, the seizure itself, when the animal will show jerky, uncontrolled movement and will often lose consciousness
- post-ictal stage, the animal is often disorientated and restless.

First-aid involves ensuring the animal does not damage itself or the owner during the fit. Treatment can include administering anti-convulsants. See also *Status epilepticus*.

Epineurium – *connective tissue* surrounding the whole *nerve*.

Epiphora – excessive tear production; can lead to discoloration of the fur in the area around the eye. Often caused by blocked *nasolacrimal ducts*.

Epiphyseal plate – also known as a growth plate, this is a strip of cartilage between the developing *diaphysis* and the *epiphysis* of a growing *bone*; becomes calcified once bone growth is complete and is visible on radiographs as the epiphyseal line. See also *Endochondral ossification*.

Epiphysis (pl. **epiphyses)** – the area of bone development towards the ends of the *bone*. See also *Epiphyseal plate*.

Epistaxis – haemorrhage (bleeding) from one or both nostrils.

Epithelial tissue (epithelium) – tissue which covers all surfaces of the body, inside and out. There are several types of epithelial tissue – simple squamous, cuboidal or columnar, stratified squamous and transitional epithelium.

Epithelialisation – the movement of epithelial cells across a wound bed during wound healing.

Epithelium – a type of tissue made up of layers of cells. A lining tissue that coats the surface of body cavities, glands and the gastrointestinal, reproductive, urinary and respiratory tracts; it also covers the outer surface of the body. There are different types of epithelium, all specialised for their function, eg *squamous, stratified squamous, cuboidal, columnar* and *transitional*. Some is ciliated (covered with *cilia*).

Epizootic disease – see *Epidemic disease*.

Erosion – focal loss of some or all of the epidermis, eg under a blister. Erosions heal without scarring because the dermis is unaffected.

Erythema – reddening of the skin as a result of dilation of the skin capillaries. Often associated with inflammation.

Erythrocyte – a mature *red blood cell*; the most numerous blood cell in the body. Carries oxygen to the tissues in the form of oxyhaemoglobin. Has no *nucleus* and therefore has a short life span of around 4 months. The cells are bi-concave to increase the surface area for oxygen–carbon dioxide exchange to occur during *gaseous exchange* and *respiration* and to make them flexible to squeeze through capillaries. See also *Erythropoeisis*, *Haemoglobin*, *Reticulocyte*.

Erythropoeisis – production of *erythrocytes* which takes place in the *bone marrow*.

E

Erythropoeitin (EPO) – a hormone produced in the *kidney* in response to a drop in blood oxygen levels. Stimulates the production of more *erythrocytes*.

Escherichia coli – a species of bacteria living in the intestinal tract of animals and humans. Many of the different strains of E. coli are harmless but some can cause severe enteritis and are potentially zoonotic.

Essential amino acids – amino acids make up protein and are joined together by peptide bonds. There are 11 essential amino acids that cannot be made by the body and therefore are required in the daily diet.

Essential fatty acids (EFA) – polyunsaturated fats that cannot be made by the body and therefore are required in the daily diet.

Estimate – an approximation of how much a treatment or procedure is likely to cost.

Ethmoid bones – located in the nasal cavity, these bones are covered with olfactory mucosa. They detect chemicals in the inspired air and send the information via the *olfactory nerve* (cranial nerve I) to the olfactory centre in the *brain*. This information is then converted into a sense of smell. This sense is highly developed in both the dog and cat.

Ethylene glycol (antifreeze) – toxic to dogs and cats but unfortunately has an attractive sweet taste. Symptoms of ingestion include vomiting, weakness, convulsions and collapse. The antidote is ethanol.

Ethylene oxide – a gas used for *sterilisation*; it destroys *micro-organisms* by inactivating their *DNA*. Can be used to sterilise *endoscopes*, plastic equipment, delicate equipment and other items not suitable for *autoclave* or *hot-air oven* sterilisation. *COSHH* (Control of Substances Hazardous to Health) regulations must be strictly followed because the gas is toxic, highly flammable and irritant to tissues.

Eukaryote – an organism of which the cells have a *nucleus* and membrane-bound cell *organelles*. All plants and animals are eukaryotes, as well as *fungi* and *protozoa*. See also *Prokaryote*.

Euphoria – a feeling of great elation and happiness, can be drug-induced.

Eustachian tube (auditory tube) – a tube in the *middle ear* communicating with the *nasopharynx*. Allows the air pressure to be equalised (kept the same as the outside air pressure) on either side of the *tympanic membrane*.

Euthanasia – meaning 'good death', it is the humane killing or 'putting to sleep' of an animal to relieve suffering.

Euthyroid – having normal thyroid function.

Evisceration – exposure of the abdominal contents.

Excisional biopsy – when a whole mass is surgically removed with wide margins and submitted for *histopathology*. See also *Incisional biopsy, Punch biopsy*.

Excitatory – increased excitement or stimulation.

Excitatory synapse – if a *neurotransmitter* creates an *action potential* in a second *neurone* across the *synapse*, then it is known as an excitatory synapse.

Excoriation – scratches or abrasions of the skin, seen in some skin conditions, eg dermatitis.

Excretion – eliminating waste products from the body such as urine and faeces.

Exhalation (or expiration) – breathing out.

Exocrine gland – a *gland* that secretes via a *duct* onto a surface of a cavity or the *skin*, eg *salivary glands*, *sebaceous glands* and *sweat glands*.

Exocrine pancreatic insufficiency – deficiency in pancreatic digestive enzymes such as amylase, lipase and proteolytic enzymes. This leads to maldigestion. Most commonly seen in young dogs, the clinical signs include production of voluminous pasty diarrhoea which contains undigested material. Affected animals are usually extremely thin and very hungry.

Exotic – a term used in veterinary practice to describe an animal that is not a dog or cat! Usually describes *rodents*, rabbits, birds, *reptiles*, *amphibians* and fish.

Exotoxin – toxins released by bacteria that can have a local or systemic action, eg the *Clostridium botulinum* toxin, which causes flaccid paralysis of the muscles, and the *Clostridium tetani* toxin, which causes muscle spasms.

Expectorant – a drug that is used to encourage removal of mucous secretions in the respiratory tract by stimulating the cough reflex, eg ipecacuanha.

Expiration – process by which air flows out of the *thorax*, caused by relaxation of the *diaphragm* and the *intercostal muscles* reducing the volume of the thorax and so forcing the air out; a passive process. See also *Diaphragm, Inspiration*.

Expiratory dyspnoea – difficulty breathing on inspiration.

Expiratory valve – found on anaesthetic circuits; allows waste gas to escape in semi-closed systems.

Exploratory laparotomy (Ex lap) – a surgical procedure involving opening the abdominal cavity to identify the cause of a disease, eg may be performed to detect and retrieve an intestinal foreign body in a vomiting dog.

Extension – describes the movement of a joint when the joint is opened, eg straightening the knee.

External abdominal oblique muscles – one of four groups of *abdominal* muscles running caudoventrally and inserting onto the *linea alba* through an *aponeurosis*. See also *Internal abdominal oblique, Rectus abdominis*.

External auditory meatus – see *Auditory canal*.

External cardiac massage – an emergency procedure to maintain circulation when the heart ceases to beat. Chest compressions are performed on the outside of the chest along with artificial respiration (either by mouth to nose, via an endotracheal tube or by ambu bag).

External ear – consists of the *pinna, external auditory meatus* and *tympanic membrane*. See also *Inner ear, Middle ear*.

External fixation – a method for repairing fractures, using connecting bars, clamps and small pins such as Ellis pins. Pins are placed through the skin and through either one or both cortices of the bone. Part of this framework is visible on the outside of the body.

Extracellular fluid – body fluid which is not within the cells; made up of *interstitial fluid, plasma, transcellular fluid* and *lymph*.

Extraction forceps – a surgical instrument used during dental procedures to extract teeth. Having cup-like tips, it is especially useful for extracting multi-rooted teeth. See also *Dental, Periosteal elevator*.

Extravascular – outside the blood vessel.

Extubate – remove the endotracheal tube.

Exudate – a build-up of fluid that is high in protein and cellular content, eg pus.

Eye contact – non-verbal communication; involves directly looking at another person's eyes.

E

Eye position – Normal eye position – looking forwards, the eyeball is not rotated in anyway. During anaesthesia the eyeball rotates ventrally and the third eyelid moves across slightly – this is the ideal eye position during anaesthesia.

F

F₁ generation, F₂ generation, etc – terms used in genetics to describe the offspring from a cross between two individuals. F_1 describes the first generation of offspring, F_2 describes the second-generation offspring (ie F_1 individual crossed with another F_1 individual), and so on.

Fabella (pl. **fabellae)** – a pair of *sesamoid bones* associated with the *stifle* joint, located on the *caudal* aspect of the distal *femur*, within the origins of the *gastrocnemius* muscle.

Face mask – non-static rubber or clear plastic cone-shaped mask, placed over the nose and mouth to administer oxygen only or oxygen with anaesthetic gases. Should not be used to administer nitrous oxide nor should it be used by pregnant women to administer anaesthetic gases.

Facial nerve – seventh (VII) *cranial nerve* concerned with the sensation of taste and with the function of the *muscles* of the face, scalp and neck.

Facultative anaerobe – a bacterium that grows well in the presence of air (aerobically) but can metabolise anaerobically if necessary.

Fading puppy/kitten syndrome – occurs within hours of birth, signs include general weakness, dehydration and failure to suckle. Possible causes include parvovirus, low birthweight, congenital abnormalities and trauma during parturition. Mortality rates are very high.

Faeces – waste material excreted via the *anus* at the end of the digestive tract, mainly comprises unabsorbed food (fibrous matter) and water. Act of passing faeces is called *defecation*. To assess a patient's faecal output, the following characteristics should be noted – appearance (should be sausage-shaped), amount (two or three 'sausages' should be passed once or twice a day), consistency (formed, not runny), odour and colour. See also *Constipation*, *Diarrhoea*.

Falconiformes – order of birds that includes the *birds of prey*, eg falcon, hawk.

Fallopian tubes – see *Uterine tubes*.

False (asternal) rib – the *caudal* four pairs of *ribs* that do not articulate directly with the *sternum*. Their costal cartilages overlap to form the *costal arch*. See also *Floating rib*.

Fanconi syndrome – an inherited disorder of the *renal tubule* that results in loss of glucose and many other substances into the urine. Typically there is *glucosuria* with normal blood glucose. Basenjis are more commonly affected than other breeds.

Fascia – a sheet of fibrous *connective tissue* that surrounds *muscles* and muscle groups and other internal organs.

Fast (high speed) intensifying screens – intensifying screens containing large phosphor crystals that emit more light, they compromise detail but allow for lower exposure factors.

Fast (ultra speed) film – radiograph film containing large silver halide crystals, allows for lower exposure factors but compromises detail. Useful with low output machines.

Fat – formed from fatty acids and glycerol; provides energy, is a carrier for fat-soluble vitamins, increases palatability and provides the essential fatty acids. See also *Lipid*.

Fat-soluble vitamins – vitamins A, D, E and K; any excess is stored within the body.

Fatty acid – a component of fat; when fats are broken down by enzymes (lipases), fatty acids and glycerol are produced.

Fe – chemical symbol for iron.

Feather cyst – a condition occasionally seen in birds. A swelling is seen at the base of a feather, especially on the wings, that can be mistaken for a *tumour*. It can usually be removed surgically.

Feather plucking – a condition seen in birds where they obsessively preen and pull out their own feathers. It can be a sign of *infection* or *parasites*, but it can also point to psychological disorders caused by poor husbandry. Treatment includes preventing the plucking by use of a suitably small *Elizabethan collar*, improving the bird's diet, providing the bird with more attention or enriching the environment with toys, distractions and increased exercise.

Fee – the amount a service, procedure or product costs.

Felicola subrostratus – a biting louse which occurs in the
cat.

Feline immunodeficiency virus (FIV) – caused by a
lentivirus, the *disease* is spread by direct contact with *saliva*
(bite wounds). The virus can remain dormant for many years
in the body until signs of *immunosuppression* start to
develop. Clinical signs include *pyrexia*, weight loss,
anaemia, *chronic gingivitis*, respiratory infections.

Feline infectious anaemia (FIA) – caused by the parasite
mycoplasma haemofelis and *Rickettsia elmeria*, can be
spread through bites, *fleas*, blood transfusions, in utero and
by mating. The bacteria multiply in the *red blood cells*,
causing them to rupture. Clinical signs include *anaemia*,
anorexia, weakness, *tachycardia*, *tachypnoea* and
splenomegaly.

Feline infectious enteritis (FIE) – also known as feline
panleukopenia, it is a highly infectious disease caused by a
parvovirus. The *virus* attacks the gut and *bone marrow* and
causes abnormally low numbers of all circulating *white
blood cells*. Depression, *vomiting*, *diarrhoea* and a high
temperature are all symptoms of the disease and it can
sometimes be fatal.

Feline infectious peritonitis (FIP) – caused by a *coronavirus*, spread by direct and indirect contact (*urine* and *faeces*) and can also be passed transplacentally to unborn fetuses. The *virus* multiplies in the intestines. Two forms are seen:

❧ dry FIP – the cat is *pyrexic, anorexic*, has *diarrhoea* and is losing weight
❧ wet FIP – causes an enlarged *abdomen* because of an accumulation of ascitic fluid.

Most animals infected with *coronavirus* do not develop FIP.

Feline leukaemia virus (FeLV) – caused by a *retrovirus*, spread by direct or indirect contact between cats. The virus multiplies in the lymph nodes of the throat and tonsils. Clinical signs include *anorexia*, depression, *lethargy*, non-regenerative *anaemia*. Diagnosis can be rapidly confirmed using an in-house *ELISA* test. There is a *vaccine* available for this disease.

Feline lower urinary tract disease (FLUTD) – a group of conditions affecting the bladder and urethra in cats that includes *cystitis*, bladder stones and bacterial infections. Clinical signs include *dysuria, haematuria, pollakiuria* and *stranguria*. It is not uncommon for plugs to form that can block the urethra completely making the cat unable to urinate. Treatment depends on the cause and may be life-long.

Feline Odontoclastic resorptive lesions (FORL) – also known as *neck lesions*. A lesion on the teeth of cats which erodes into the sensitive *dentine*. Their cause is unknown, however they could arise as the result of an *autoimmune response*, the *calicivirus* or metabolic imbalances relating to *calcium* regulation. Cats with FORLs may show hypersalivation, oral bleeding, or have difficulty eating, but many cats do not show any obvious clinical signs. Intra-oral *radiography* is helpful in making a definitive diagnosis.

Feline upper respiratory tract disease (FURTD) – also known as 'cat flu', this disease is caused by a *calicivirus* and *herpes virus* and is spread by inhalation (see also *Aerosol*). The *virus* affects the epithelial cells of the respiratory tract and *conjunctiva*. Clinical signs include sneezing, *conjunctivitis*, ocular and nasal discharge, coughing, *anorexia*, *pyrexia* and depression. There is a vaccine available.

Femoral – relating to the femur.

Femoral pore – found on the medial thigh of some lizards, more developed in the male and can be used to distinguish the sexes.

Femoral pulse – a pulse found on the medial aspect of the femur.

Femur – *long bone* of the hind limb, it is the thigh bone, running from a *ball and socket joint*, which it forms with the *pelvis*, down to the *stifle joint*.

Ferric chloride – agent which causes *coagulation* of the *blood*, eg can be applied to treat a claw that is bleeding after an overenthusiastic claw clip.

Fertilisation – the fusion of the male *gamete* (*spermatozoon*) with the female gamete (*ovum*).

Fertility – the ability to produce healthy offspring; depends on many things including age, health status, sexual behaviour, conformation and nutrition.

Fetal – relating to the *fetus*.

Fetal oversize – a cause of dystocia resulting from excessive size of fetus. This is particularly common when a small-breed bitch is mated with a larger breed dog, or when there is a single fetus.

Fetus – the stage of development following the embryonic stage. The *embryo* becomes a fetus when all the organs have developed. The developing animal is then described as a fetus until birth.

Fibre (roughage) – formed from indigestible polysaccharides, eg cellulose, that are usually plant material. Aids bowel function, provides faeces with bulk and prevents constipation.

Fibreglass cast – light-weight, quick-drying material used for casting.

Fibrin – an insoluble *protein* in the *blood*, formed when thrombin reacts with circulating *fibrinogen* and involved in the *clotting* process. A mesh of insoluble fibrin fibres, known as a clot, forms at the site of injury to prevent blood loss. See also *Clotting cascade*, *Coagulation*.

F

Fibrinogen – a soluble precursor of *fibrin*; a *plasma protein* produced in the liver. Involved in the *clotting* cascade, forms fibrin when exposed to the *enzyme* thrombin, and is also produced during inflammation.

Fibroblast – a cell of *fibrous connective tissue* that produces *collagen* fibres.

Fibrosarcoma – a *malignant tumour* of the *fibrous connective tissue*.

Fibrous (dense) connective tissue – comprises *collagen* and elastic fibres, it provides strength and support in *ligaments*, *tendons* and *fascia*.

Fibrous joint – a *dense connective tissue joint* between two adjacent *bones*. This type of joint allows very little movement and occurs mainly between the bones of the *skull*. In a young animal, they allow the skull to expand as the animal grows. Also known as sutures.

Fibula – a thin bone that lies on the *lateral* aspect of the *tibia* in the hind limb. Runs from the *stifle* to the *hock*.

Filiaroides osleri – a lungworm parasite affecting dogs.

Filing – placing record cards or information in a particular order, usually alphabetical.

Film – see *Radiographic film*.

Film badges – a type of dosemeter, usually blue, comprising pieces of radiographic film worn by personnel, which are then developed and measured by the degree of blackening.

Film focal distance – the distance between the focal spot and the radiographic film, as this is increased the intensity of the beam is reduced.

Film speed – the speed of radiographic film is denoted by the size of the silver halide crystals present within it. Generally the smaller the crystal the finer the detail; however, higher exposure factors will be required the 'slower' the film is. Films are available as:

❀ Fast (ultra speed)
❀ Medium (standard)
❀ Slow (fine detail).

Filter (for safelight) – a filter used in front of light bulbs in the darkroom. This is to alter the colour of light so radiographic film is not exposed to white light. The filter needs to correspond with the colour of radiographic film used.

Filtrate – the part of a solution left after passing through a filter mechanism. An example of a filtrate is the fluid which passes into the *renal tubule* at the *glomerulus*, leaving behind cells and proteins that are too large to pass through.

Fimbra (pl. **fimbriae)** – a finger-like or fringed projection, eg the fringed edge of the uterine tube where the ovum is collected at ovulation and the finger-like projections on the surface of some bacteria that allow them to adhere to surfaces.

Final host – also called the definitive host, a term used in parasitology to describe the host in/on which sexual reproduction takes place.

Fine-needle aspirate (FNA) – a sample of cells or material obtained by placing a needle into a lesion and applying gentle suction, or simply redirecting the needle. The material collected is placed on a slide, stained and examined under a microscope. This technique is used to identify lesions such as tumours and cysts.

Finger badges – a type of dosemeter worn by equine radiography staff. Placed inside the protective gloves that are worn.

First-aid treatment – immediate medical assistance that can be administered by anyone in an emergency without the need for drugs or specialist equipment. See also *Cardiopulmonary resuscitation*, *Recovery position*.

First intention healing – occurs in clean surgical wounds that are sutured; the wound heals over a period of 14 days.

Fistula – an abnormal tract connecting the *skin* and a mucosal surface. Can be acquired, eg *anal furunculosis*, or *congenital*, eg rectovaginal fistula, linking the *vagina* to the *rectum*.

Fit – see *Seizure*.

Fixer – an agent used to fix the image on a radiograph by dissolving and removing unexposed silver halide crystals from the radiographic film. The clearing or fixing agent is either sodium thiosulphate or ammonium thiosulphate.

Flaccid – a very relaxed state, there is a decrease in muscle tone and muscles appear limp.

Flagellate – a protozoan possessing a *flagellum* (whip-like projection) that is used for locomotion, eg *Giardia*.

Flank gland – a pigmented scent gland in the skin of both flanks of hamsters, better developed in males.

Flat bone – bones formed by *intramembranous ossification*; flat and broad, offering a large surface area for muscle attachment and protection for soft tissue, eg *scapula*, *wing of ilium* and bones of the *skull*.

Flat head screwdriver – instrument used to remove screws with only one groove on the head from internal implants.

Flatulence – excessive gas in the intestines.

Flea – wingless insect parasites that feed exclusively on blood as adults, eg *Ctenocephalides felis, Ctenocephalides canis*.

Flexion – describes the movement of a *joint*, flexion is when the angle of a joint is reduced, eg bending the *stifle joint*. See also *Extension, Flexor*.

Flexor – *muscle* whose action brings about the *flexion* of a joint.

Floating rib – the 13th pair of *ribs* which are very short and whose end lies free within the muscle wall. See also *False (asternal) rib*.

Flow meter – a device with a marked scale controlling gas flow to the patient; they are gas specific.

Flow rate (include calculations) – The level of carrier gas required by the patient.

a) Respiratory rate × tidal volume = minute volume
b) Minute volume × circuit factor = flow rate carrier

The answer gives the total amount of gas, if using nitrous oxide, at least 30%, or this total must be oxygen.

Fluid deficit requirements – amount of fluid required to correct any fluid imbalances.

 ❧ Vomiting or diarrhea – 3–4 ml/kg per episode
 ❧ Pyrexia – 3 ml/kg per % increase in body temperature
 ❧ Surgery – 5–10 ml/kg per hour
 ❧ Packed cell volume (PCV) – 10 ml/kg per 1% increase in PCV
 ❧ Dehydration deficit – 10 ml/kg per % dehydrated.

Fluid therapy – administering prepared fluids to maintain hydration and correct any imbalances. Can be administered orally, subcutaneously, intraperitoneally or intravenously.

Fluorescein – a fluorescent dye placed in the *eye* to help detect any injury to the *cornea* or the presence of *corneal ulcers*. If there is an injury or ulcer on the cornea, this area will take up the fluorescein dye and become visible. The dye can also be used to check the patency of the *nasolacrimal duct* if a blockage is suspected.

Fluoride oxalate – an anticoagulant used for measuring glucose in blood samples. Fluoride oxalate tubes usually have yellow lids.

Fly strike – a distressing condition more commonly seen in the summer months. It is caused by an adult fly (bluebottle, greenbottle) laying eggs on a host. The larvae (maggots) then hatch out and feed on the host, causing great tissue damage, pain and distress. The fly is initially attracted to the host by smell, either of faecal matter or an injury. It is often seen in rabbits which are too fat, ill or old to groom the perineal region, but is also seen in debilitated, incontinent dogs and cats. Treatment involves picking the maggots off the animal, clipping away the soiled fur and carefully cleaning the exposed wounds. Sometimes it may also be necessary to suture deep wounds back together. If the tissue damage is extensive, the animal will quickly go into shock and may die. Also known as myiasis.

F

Foam dressings – non-adhesive wound dressings with good absorptive properties but maintaining moisture in the environment.

Focal spot – a specific area on the anode where the electrons collide after acceleration from the cathode.

Focused grid – a type of stationary grid where the lead strips are angled towards the centre.

Focusing cup – made of a metal called molybdenum, it shapes the beam and directs the electrons in one direction only, towards the anode.

Folate – one of the B complex vitamins, a daily intake is required.

Foley catheter – a type of indwelling urinary catheter used in bitches. Held in place by a balloon that is filled with air once fitted.

Follicle – a sac-like structure. **1.** the ovary contains follicles within which the ova develop. **2.** each hair grows from a follicle within the skin. **3.** the thyroid gland contains follicles that secrete thyroid hormones.

Follicle stimulating hormone (FSH) – hormone produced in the anterior pituitary gland that controls the growth and maturation of ovarian follicles.

Folliculitis – inflammation of the hair follicles caused by infection or irritation. Folliculitis caused by *Staphylococcal* infections is quite common in puppies.

Fomite – an inanimate object, eg feeding bowl, toy or bedding, that can be involved in the spread of infection from one patient to others. See also *Barrier nursing*.

Foramen (pl. **foramina)** – a hole, or passageway, usually through a bone. See *Foramen magnum*, *Foramen vena cava*.

Foramen magnum – a large opening at the base of the *skull* that allows the *spinal cord* to pass out of the *cranium*.

Foramen vena cava – one of three holes in the *diaphragm*, allowing the *vena cava* to pass through it from the *thorax* into the *abdomen*.

Forebrain – one area of the *brain* made up of the *cerebrum* (*cerebral hemispheres*), the *thalamus* and *hypothalamus*. See also *Hindbrain*, *Midbrain*.

Foreign body – an object within the body that should not be there, eg a grass seed lodged in the ear, or a thorn embedded in a paw. *Gastric* or small intestinal foreign bodies are sometimes seen in dogs and cats, treatment usually involves surgery (*gastrotomy* or *enterotomy*) to remove them.

Foreshortening – the image on the radiograph appears shorter than the part actually is because the part in question is not parallel to the radiographic film.

Formal saline (formalin) – a 40% solution of dissolved formaldehyde gas. It fixes or hardens tissue samples.

Fossa – a small depression in a bone, eg the trochanteric fossa at the proximal end of the femur where bone marrow samples are often taken.

Fostering – caring for a patient (young or old) on a temporary basis.

Fovea – an area on the *retina* of the *eye* that provides the sharpest vision because of the high density of *cone cells* located there. Also known as the macula lutea (yellow spot).

Fracture – a forcible break in the continuity of the bone, often caused by direct trauma (eg road traffic accident) or by disease (eg *tumours* or *calcium/vitamin D* deficiency). Clinical signs of a fracture include pain, swelling, *crepitus* and loss of normal function. Fracture types include complete, incomplete, *complicated*, *comminuted*, *compound*, *avulsed* or *depressed*. See also *Metabolic bone disease*.

F

Free-catch urine sample – simplest method of obtaining a urine sample. Performed when the patient is passing urine normally or when the bladder is manually expressed, use a suitable dish or container to catch the urine.

Frenulum – the thin fold of tissue on the underside of the tongue that is attached to the floor of the mouth. Its function is to prevent excessive movement of the tongue.

Frontal sinus – an air-filled cavity within the frontal bone of the *skull*. Its function is not completely understood, but it may help with insulation and protection of the *brain*.

Fructosamine – a protein with a glucose molecule attached, can be measured in a biochemistry profile to assess whether an animal has been hyperglycaemic over the previous 2–3 weeks. Used to diagnose and monitor diabetes mellitus.

Fructose – a monosaccharide sugar.

Fundus – **1.** the back of the eye, which can be examined with an ophthalmoscope. Includes the retina, optic disc and blood vessels. **2.** part of the stomach distal to the cardia which acts as a storage vat for ingesta.

Fungi – *eukaryotic* organisms that are *saprophytic*, *parasitic* or form *symbiotic* relationships with other organisms; divided into three groups: the yeasts (eg *Malassezia pachydermatis*), the moulds or filamentous fungi (eg *Microsporum canis*, *Trichophyton mentagrophytes* and *Aspergillus* sp.) and the dimorphic fungi, which have both yeast and filamentous forms (eg *Histoplasma*).

Fungicide – an agent that kills fungi. May be given orally (eg griseofulvin, ketoconazole), or topically (eg clotrimazole, miconazole, itraconazole).

Fur slip – a *chinchilla* will shed its fur if it is stressed, frightened or roughly handled, this is known as fur slip.

Furunculosis – a deep-seated skin infection affecting the hair follicles and sweat glands, usually bacterial and may be difficult to treat, eg *anal furunculosis*, interdigital furunculosis (between the toes).

Fuzzies – young mice with a fine coat, used as food for carnivorous animals such as snakes.

G

Gag reflex – a swallowing/retching reflex, used to judge when a recovering but still anaesthetised animal should have the *endotracheal tube* removed. In dogs, the tube should be removed once the gag reflex has returned; in cats, the tube should be removed just before the gag reflex returns.

Gall bladder – a structure attached to the *liver* for the storage of *bile*. Connected to the *duodenum* by the *bile duct*. After a meal, stimulated by the hormone *cholecystokinin*, the gall bladder contracts, expelling the bile into the duodenum.

Gamete – a male or female reproductive cell (*spermatozoon* or *ovum*) containing a *haploid* number of *chromosomes*. Cell division in gametes occurs by *meiosis*. See also *Diploid, Mitosis*.

Ganglion – a group of *cell bodies* of *neurones* on a peripheral *nerve*.

Gaseous exchange – the diffusion of oxygen molecules from the air into the blood and of carbon dioxide molecules from the blood into the air that occurs in the *alveoli* in the lungs. See also *Respiration*.

Gastric – relating to the stomach, eg gastric torsion.

Gastric dilatation/volvulus (GDV) – a life-threatening condition of deep-chested dogs where the *stomach* becomes distended with food and gas. It may then twist on itself so that outflow is occluded, resulting in more gas build-up. Blood flow is affected as the distended stomach presses on the *vena cava*. The animal quickly goes into *shock* and will die unless the condition is corrected surgically. Symptoms include unproductive retching, a bloated abdomen, restlessness, discomfort, respiratory distress, shock, death. Deep-chested dogs are more susceptible because the stomach has more room to move, commonly affected breeds include Greyhounds, Wolfhounds, Dobermans, Weimeraners. GDV can however occur in any breed and even in cats. Overfeeding followed by exercise soon after the meal is a common cause of GDV.

Gastric lavage – *first-aid* treatment in the case of poisoning. Involves anaesthetising the animal and flushing out the *stomach* contents using warm water; only effective if carried out within 4 hours of ingestion of the poison because *gastric* contents move out of the stomach after this time. See also *Activated charcoal*, *Adsorbents*, *Emesis*.

Gastric torsion – see *Gastric dilatation/volvulus*.

Gastric ulcer – an erosion of the mucosa of the stomach resulting in pain, vomiting and sometimes haematemesis and melaena. Gastric ulcers may be caused by or exacerbated by the use of non-steroidal anti-inflammatory drugs. It is unclear whether *Helicobacter* sp. bacteria (which cause gastric ulcers in humans) are linked with gastric ulceration in dogs and cats.

Gastrin – a hormone secreted by cells in the stomach that stimulates increased release of gastric juice when there is food in the mouth or stomach.

Gastrocentesis – emergency *first-aid treatment* of a *gastric dilatation/volvulus*, this involves passing a wide-bore needle through the abdominal wall into the distended *stomach* to release the build-up of gas and relieve the pressure.

Gastrocnemius – the *muscle* of the lower hindlimb that runs from the distal *femur* to the *os calcis* of the *tibia*. It *extends* the *hock* and *flexes* the *stifle*.

Gastropexy – the surgical correction of a *gastric dilatation/volvulus*, involves untwisting the *stomach* and anchoring it to the abdominal wall to prevent it twisting again.

Gastrostomy tube – a feeding tube surgically placed into the stomach to enable artificial feeding.

Gastrotomy – a surgical incision into the stomach.

Gauge (bore) – the diameter of tubes and needles.

Gavage – feeding a patient through the nose or mouth via a tube.

Gelpi retractors – a surgical instrument with single pronged, outward-turning tips used for muscle and joint retraction. Gelpis are self-retaining retractors. See also *Langenbeck retractor*.

Gene – part of the DNA molecule that carries instructions for the synthesis of a polypeptide or protein.

General anaesthesia (GA) – a reversible state of total unconsciousness; unable to feel, respond to or remember noxious stimuli.

Generalised – a condition affecting the whole body, or whole system, eg *demodicosis* may be localised (affecting just a small area) or generalised (affecting the whole skin).

Genetics – the science of inheritance, ie the study of how characteristics are passed on from parent to offspring. See *Chromosome, Gene.*

Genome – the complete set of genetic information contained in each cell of an organism, includes all the DNA and RNA.

Genotype – the genetic make-up of an animal contained in its DNA; determines the *phenotype*, but also includes genes that are not expressed (the recessive genes).

Giardia – a flagellate protozoan parasite that causes chronic diarrhoea in dogs and cats and may be zoonotic. Infection with *Giardia* is called giardiasis.

Giemsa stain – a type of stain used for blood smears and cytology specimens; more commonly used in combination with Wright's stain.

Gillies needle holders – a surgical instrument used for holding needles and cutting *sutures*. Their distinguishing feature is that one handle is shorter than the other with a large thumb/finger grip. See also *Olsen–Hegar needle holders.*

Gingiva – the gum, a thick layer of *mucous membrane* covering the alveolar bone. See *Gingivitis.*

Gingivitis – inflammation of the gums, often seen as a red rim at the margin with the teeth. Commonly associated with dental disease. See also *Periodontitis*, *Tartar*.

Giving set – sterile tubing used to deliver intravenous fluids.

Gizzard – also called the *ventriculus*, the muscular grinding part of the stomach in birds. Important because birds are unable to mechanically grind food through mastication. Often contains grit and small stones, which the bird has swallowed and which enhances the grinding of the food.

Gland – an organ producing a substance for release directly into the bloodstream (*endocrine gland*, eg thyroid gland), or for release through a duct that opens into a body cavity or onto the body surface (*exocrine gland*, eg sweat gland). The pancreas is described as a *mixed* gland because it has both endocrine (eg insulin) and exocrine (eg pancreatic juice) functions.

Glandular epithelial tissue – a tissue type found in the body that secretes *hormones*, *enzymes* and specialised fluids. Can be *exocrine* (eg *mucus* gland, *sweat gland*, *mammary gland*, *salivary gland*, *lacrimal gland*) or *endocrine* (eg *adrenal gland*, *thyroid gland*, *pituitary gland*, *ovary*, *testicle* etc). See also *Pancreas*.

Glans penis – an expansion of erectile tissue near the tip of the penis.

Glass envelope – surrounds the cathode and anode within the tube head, supplying a vacuum.

G

Glaucoma – an ophthalmic emergency. Intra-ocular pressure becomes raised and is often accompanied by severe pain; can result in loss of vision as a result of the excess pressure on the *retina*. *First-aid* measures are usually limited to administering pain relief. See *Enucleation*.

Glenoid cavity – a depression on the *ventral* part of the *scapula*, the area that articulates with the head of the *humerus*.

Glial cell (neuroglia) – cells of the *central nervous system* that provide support and protection for the *neurone*.

Globe – the eyeball.

Globulin – a *plasma protein*; increased globulin levels can indicate *inflammation*, *infection* and some types of tumour. See also *Albumin*, *Immunoglobulins*.

G

Glomerular filtrate rate (GFR) – the amount of fluid filtered out of the blood at the glomerulus in all the nephrons of both kidneys in a specified time (usually measured in ml/minute). Nearly all of this filtrate is reabsorbed. The GFR may be used to assess renal function.

Glomerulonephritis – inflammation of the glomerulus and associated capillary beds; usually the results of deposits of immune complexes (clumps of antibodies and antigens). May be associated with feline infectious peritonitis in cats, or chronic infections in dogs. The immune complexes cause a change in permeability of the nephron so that protein can leak out into the urine.

Glomerulus – a cluster of blood vessels that sits inside *Bowman's capsule* at one end of a *nephron* in the *kidney*. Blood enters the glomerulus at high pressure and fluid (glomerular filtrate) is forced out into Bowman's capsule and into the renal tubule.

Glossal – relating to the tongue.

Glossopharyngeal nerve – *ninth cranial nerve* (IX), concerned with taste and swallowing. Also innervates the *pharynx*, tongue and *salivary glands*.

Glottis – part of the *larynx* that consists of the space between the *vocal folds*. It is here that sounds are produced, eg mewing/barking, as the inspired air passes through it.

Gloving-up – the aseptic procedure by which scrubbed theatre personnel put on sterile surgeons' gloves before surgery so that there is no contamination to the gloves from the hands or environment. Two techniques for gloving up – closed and open.

- ❧ During open gloving, the surgeon's hands are extended out of the long-sleeved gown and the gloves are pulled on.
- ❧ During closed gloving, the hands stay within the sleeves of the gown while the gloves are manoeuvred onto the hands.

Glucagon – a *hormone* produced by the alpha cells of the *pancreas* that stimulates the breakdown of *glycogen* into *glucose*. It has the opposite effect to *insulin*, ie it raises blood glucose levels.

Glucocorticoids – a group of steroid *hormones* such as *cortisol* which are produced in the *adrenal gland* and are important for enabling an animal to cope with physical and mental stress. Synthetic glucocorticoids such as prednisolone and methylprednisolone have widespread uses in veterinary medicine, as anti-inflammatories and immunosuppressive drugs.

Glucometer – a machine (usually hand-held) that is used to measure blood glucose levels rapidly from a drop of blood.

Gluconeogenesis – the production of glucose molecules from the breakdown products of fats or proteins; usually occurs in the liver.

Glucose – a simple sugar used by the body as an important energy source. Any glucose not required is stored by the body as *glycogen*. Blood glucose levels can be measured using a glucometer. An increase in blood glucose can be occur as the result of fear/excitement/stress, following a meal, or in *diabetes mellitus* or *hyperadrenocorticism*. A decrease can be the result of *hypoadrenocorticism*, starvation, an increase in *insulin* levels or *chronic malabsorption*.

Glucose saline (fluid therapy) –an isotonic crystalloid fluid, used for maintenance and for primary water deficits. Available in various concentrations, eg sodium chloride 0.9% and glucose 5%.

Gluteal muscle – group of *muscles* of the hindlimb that are used to *extend* the hip and *abduct* and *rotate* the limb.

Glycerol – a component of fat. When fats are broken down by enzymes (lipases) fatty acids and glycerol are produced.

G

Glycogen – any *glucose* not needed for energy is stored in the body as glycogen in the *liver* and *muscles*. Glycogen is broken down into glucose by the hormone *glucagon*.

Glycogenesis – the production of glycogen from glucose molecules; occurs in many different types of cells. Is stimulated by the hormone *insulin* when blood sugar levels are high.

Glycolysis – a metabolic pathway that produces energy in the form of ATP. Glycolysis does not require oxygen and occurs in the cytoplasm of cells.

Goblet cells – epithelial cells that secrete *mucus*; present on the epithelial lining of many systems including the gastrointestinal and respiratory tracts.

G

Golgi apparatus – *cell organelle* made up of membrane-bound sacs that receives lipids and proteins from the *endoplasmic reticulum* and then packages and dispatches them to a variety of destinations.

Gonad – the reproductive glands of the male and female animal which produce the *gametes*. See also *Ovary, Testis*.

Gonadotrophins – hormones secreted by the anterior pituitary gland and placenta that stimulate the reproductive organs and control the reproductive cycle, eg follicle stimulating hormone, luteinising hormone.

Gouge – a surgical instrument used during orthopaedic procedures to shave the bone when contouring is necessary; has a crescent-shaped tip and can easily be confused with an *osteotome* and *chisel*.

Gram-negative bacteria – bacteria that only take up the second dye in the *Gram stain* and appear pink/red under the microscope. The Gram-negative bacteria have a cell wall component (*endotoxin* or lipopolysaccharide) that prevents uptake of the first dye. Many Gram-negative bacteria are *pathogenic*, eg *Pseudomonas*, *Salmonella* and *E. coli*.

Gram-positive bacteria – bacteria that take up both dyes in the *Gram stain* and show up blue/purple under the microscope, eg *Staphylococcus*, *Streptococcus* and *Clostridium*.

Gram stain – a differential stain (one which contains a number of dye substances) used to stain and assist in the identification of bacteria under the microscope.

G

Granulation tissue – fragile tissue that is produced at the site of a wound during the healing process; contains connective tissue, macrophages and capillaries, and appears as moist pink tissue at the site of a wound.

Granulocyte – a type of *white blood cell*; on staining it can be seen that the *cytoplasm* contains granules. The three types of granulocytes are *neutrophils*, *eosinophils* and *basophils*. See also *Agranulocyte*.

Gravid – pregnant with young or eggs.

Grazing animal – an animal that feeds ad libitum throughout the day and night.

Greater trochanter – a large, rough projection near the head of the femur for muscle attachment.

Green gutter splint – see *Gutter splint*.

Green-sensitive film – radiographic film that is sensitive to both green and blue light; usually used with rare-earth intensifying screens.

Green-stick fracture – also known as an incomplete fracture; the bone cortex is only broken on one side. See also *Comminuted fracture, Compound (open) fracture, Depressed fracture*.

Grey matter – area of the *brain* and *spinal cord* containing the cell bodies of the *neurones*. See also *White matter*.

Grid – a device placed between the patient and the radiographic film to absorb scatter radiation, therefore increasing the quality of the radiograph; made of lead strips and interspaces and can be stationary or moving. Types of stationary grids: parallel, focused, pseudo-focused and crossed. Types of moving grids: *Potter–Bucky grid*.

Grid factor – the amount by which the exposure needs to be increased when a grid is being used during radiography.

Grid ratio – the ratio of the height of the lead strips to the distance of the radiolucent interspaces, the larger the ratio the more efficient is the grid at absorbing scatter radiation.

Grief – an emotion felt following the loss or death of a loved one.

Grit – an essential component of a bird's diet; stored in the gizzard and used to help break down hard foods such as seed. An important part of a bird's diet because, unlike other animals, they do not chew their food before swallowing.

Growth hormone (GH) – a hormone secreted by the anterior pituitary gland that stimulates growth and repair of tissues, and speeds the breakdown of fat stores. Lack of growth hormone is called *pituitary dwarfism*; excess growth hormone is known as *acromegaly*.

Growth plate – see *Epiphyseal plate*.

Guard hair – also known as a primary hair, these hairs are long and coarse and each one has an adjacent *arrector pili muscle* that erects the hair in cold weather to trap air and conserve heat.

Guide to professional conduct – the declaration veterinary surgeons make on admission to the RCVS in exchange for the right to practise veterinary surgery in the UK.

Gutter splint – a rigid green splint used to reduce flexibility in a bandage. Can be used during first-aid measures for fractures or in addition to internal fixation.

G

H

Haemangiosarcoma – a malignant tumour of vascular tissue, most commonly found in the spleen. If this is the case, the spleen often needs to be surgically removed (splenectomy).

Haematemesis – vomited material that contains either fresh or digested blood.

Haematochezia – faeces containing visible, fresh blood.

Haematocrit (Hct) – also known as the packed cell volume (PCV), the proportion of blood made up by erythrocytes (ie not including the leukocytes or platelets), usually expressed as a percentage. Normal ranges are 30–45% (cat) and 37–55% (dog). A raised PCV may indicate dehydration; a low PCV may indicate *anaemia* or *shock*. See also *Microhaematocrit*.

Haematology – the study of blood; haematology analysis involves assessing the number and types of cells and platelets, and also identifying abnormal cells and organisms within the blood.

Haematoma – a collection of blood under the skin; it can be caused by trauma or head shaking, eg aural haematoma.

Haematopoiesis – the production of blood cells.

Haematopoietic tissue – connective tissue involved with the production of blood cells, eg the *bone marrow* of *cancellous bones*, which produces *red* and *white blood cells*.

Haemobartonella felis – see *Mycoplasma haemofelis*.

Haemocytometer – a specially marked slide used for manual determination of cell counts in a blood sample using a microscope.

Haemoglobin (Hb) – a *protein* containing *iron* and found within *erythrocytes*. Has a high affinity for *oxygen* and binds with it to form oxyhaemoglobin. Carries oxygen from the *lungs* to the body tissues.

Haemolysis – lysis (rupture) of erythrocytes with the loss of *haemoglobin*. Plasma/serum of a haemolysed sample is pink to red in colour. Haemolysis may occur as a result of erythrocyte damage during blood sampling and may affect the results of laboratory tests. Haemolysis may also occur as a disease process in the body such as *immune-mediated haemolytic anaemia*, which results in anaemia.

Haemorrhage – bleeding or the loss of *blood* from the *circulation*. Can be caused by *trauma*, surgery, *neoplasia* and *parasites*; can be external (blood leaving the body via a wound or through the gut or urogenital tract) or internal (blood leaks out into body tissues and cavities). It can lead to *hypovolaemic shock*, unless it is controlled by digital pressure over the site, by *pressure bandaging* or by use of a *tourniquet*. See also *Clotting cascade*, *Coagulation*, *Haemostasis*.

Haemorrhagic viral disease (HVD) – see *Viral haemorrhagic disease*.

Haemostasis – surgical stopping of haemorrhage, also known as blood clotting or coagulation See also *Clotting cascade*.

Haemothorax – the presence of *blood* in the pleural space which causes respiratory distress; normally occurs as the result of *trauma*, a bleeding *tumour* or a *clotting* disorder. *Thoracocentesis* can be carried out to drain away the blood and to ease respiratory distress. See also *Chylothorax, Hydrothorax, Pyothorax*.

Halogen –

a) An ingredient used in some disinfectants eg hypochlorites
b) A special type of light bulb used in operating lights

Halstead mosquito forceps – small, fine-tipped artery forceps available in straight and curved versions, used during surgery for clamping small blood vessels to achieve *haemostasis*.

Hammondia hammondii – a tissue-cyst-forming coccidian parasite that can infect dogs and cats but is rarely pathogenic.

Hand feeding – placing food within the hand and offering it to patients, works well particularly in nervous, frightened or ill patients.

Haploid – describes a cell with only one set of *chromosomes*, ie half the number of the original parent cell. See also *Diploid, Gamete, Meiosis*.

Hard palate – the structure forming the roof of the mouth; made up of three bones: the palatine, the maxilla and the premaxilla. It is covered with a tough, ridged *mucous membrane*. The ridges point caudally and help direct the food towards the *oesophagus*. The *caudal* edge of the hard palate is continuous with the beginning of the *soft palate*.

Hardbills – birds with a beak designed to remove the tough outer coating from seeds and nuts. Most psittacines (parrot-like birds) and finches are hardbills.

Hardeners – **1.** added to developer for use with automatic processors, they prevent excessive swelling of the film emulsion and harden the film; **2.** in fixer: contain aluminium salt, they prevent excess swelling and softening of the emulsion and also shorten the drying time.

Hartman's solution – an isotonic crystalloid fluid, used for water and electrolyte loss, eg vomiting and diarrhoea, and pyometra.

Harvest mite – see *Trombicula antumnalis*.

Haversian canal – a central canal in an *osteon* in *cortical bone* that contains *nerves* and *blood vessels* to supply the bone tissue with nutrients. See also *Haversian system*.

Haversian system – also known as *osteons*; a structural unit of *cortical bone* consisting of layers of *osteocytes* around a central canal (*Haversian canal*) carrying the *nerves* and *blood vessels* to supply the bone.

Hazard symbols – various symbols designed to warn of potential danger, eg toxic, corrosive.

Head bandage – a type of bandage placed around the head, can be adapted to include the ears or eyes.

Health and Safety Executive (HSE) – body responsible for enforcing and advising on the *Health and Safety at Work Act*.

Health and Safety at Work Act 1974 – legislation drawn up with the objective of making the workplace a safe environment, so that no one, including the general public, is risking their health and safety. See also *Health and Safety Executive*.

Healthy carrier – an animal that has been exposed to an infectious disease and carries the agent without ever showing clinical signs. These animals are usually immune to the disease.

Heart – a muscular organ located in the *pericardial cavity* of the *mediastinum* in the *thorax*, responsible for pumping the *blood* round the body. Made up of four chambers, two *atria* and two *ventricles* which are separated from each other by *valves* and which contract rhythmically to propel the blood around the heart and body. See also *Aorta, Atrioventricular valve, Cardiac muscle, Heart beat, Mitral valve, Vena cava*.

Heart beat – consists of the first heart sound (lub) and the second heart sound (dub). Can be felt by placing fingers over ribs 5–6.

Heart rate – the number of heart beats in one minute.

Dog: 60–180 beats/min
Cat: 110–180 beats/min

Heat – see *Oestrus*.

Heat sterilisation – see *steam sterilisation* and *hot air oven.*

Heat stroke – see Hyperthermia.

Heavy-duty round hole plate – an implant used in internal fixation but that is stronger than most round hole plates.

Helminth – a description for *endoparasitic* worms, including *cestodes* and *nematodes.* See also *Cestode*, *Nematode.*

Hemicerclage wiring – see *Cerclage wire.*

Hemiparesis – weakness of the limbs on one side of the body.

Hemipene – a pair of organs found in male snakes and lizards that lie internally at the base of the tail and whose function is concerned with copulation.

Hemiplegia – loss of use of the limbs on one side of the body.

Heparin – an anticoagulant used in blood sampling tubes (these usually have an orange top), usually used for biochemistry analysis and for haematology in exotic species. Also occasionally used as a medical treatment for diseases in which there is a risk of blood clotting.

Hepatic – relating to the *liver.*

Hepatic encephalopathy – a serious condition caused by the build-up of toxic substances such as ammonia when the liver is not functioning properly. Clinical signs can include head-pressing, stupor and coma. May be seen in animals with *portosystemic shunts.*

Hepatic lipidosis – overload of the liver with fat. May occur particularly in overweight cats, which become suddenly anorexic, or in diabetic animals.

Hepatic portal vein – a blood vessel which delivers nutrient rich blood from the gut directly to the liver.

Hepatitis – generalised term meaning inflammation of the *liver*. Clinical signs can be varied but include *icterus* (jaundice), *anorexia*, *vomiting* and *diarrhoea*. May be caused by a bacterial or viral *infection* (eg *leptospirosis* or *infectious canine hepatitis*) or by the presence of toxins in the body, eg drugs. See also *Cirrhosis, Hepatic lipidosis*.

Herbal remedies – see *Alternative medicine*.

Herbivore – an animal that feeds only on plants and plant material. See also *Carnivore, Omnivore*.

Hereditary – a characteristic or feature passed on genetically from one generation to the next. See also *Chromosome, Gene, Genetics*.

Hernia – the protrusion of all or part of an organ through a defect in the wall of the cavity in which it lies; often a *congenital* defect. An acquired hernia, which is usually the result of *trauma*, is also called a rupture. Examples of common hernia sites include: *umbilical*, inguinal, *perineal*, *diaphragmatic*. Can normally be repaired surgically. See also *Irreducible hernia, Reducible, Strangulated hernia*.

Herpes virus – a *virus* causing the *disease* known as *feline upper respiratory tract disease* or 'cat flu'.

Heterozygous – when an animal carries two different copies (*alleles*) of a gene it is described as being heterozygous. For example, in dalmatians there are two colours: the black form of the spotting gene (**B**) and the liver-coloured spot form (**b**). A dalmation carrying **Bb** genes is described as heterozygous for that trait. See also *Homozygous*.

Hexagonal screwdriver – an instrument used to remove screws with hexagonal heads from internal implants.

Hiatus – an opening in a membrane, eg the oesophageal hiatus is the opening in the diaphragm through which the oesophagus passes.

Hierarchy – a group or series of people who are in order of rank.

Higginson's syringe – an instrument used to administer fluid into the rectum; generally used to perform enemas.

High-dose dexamethasone suppression test (HDDST) – a diagnostic test used to decide whether hyperadrenocorticism is caused by a tumour of the adrenal gland or a tumour of the pituitary gland.

Hilus – a depression in the surface of an organ where blood vessels or nerves enter, eg the hilus of the kidney is a depression in the surface of the kidney where the renal artery and vein and the ureter enter or leave.

Hindbrain – an area of the *brain* made up of the *pons*, *medulla oblongata* and *cerebellum*. See also *Forebrain*, *Midbrain*.

Hinge joint – a type of *joint* that allows *flexion* and *extension*. A hinge joint has limited rotational movement, eg elbow joint. See also *Cartilaginous joint, Fibrous joint, Synovial joint*.

Hip dysplasia – a variety of abnormal conditions, eg osteoarthritis in the young, that can affect the acetabulum and femoral head. Caused by genetic and environmental factors

Hip dysplasia scheme (hip score) – a scheme run by the BVA and the Kennel Club. By examining radiographs of the hips from dogs and bitches, a score (from a scale of 0 to 100) of their hips is given depending on the severity of hip dysplasia. The lower the score the fewer signs there are of hip dysplasia. This scheme is for breeding purposes, to try to reduce/control hip dysplasia.

Histamine – a chemical compound stored in the cytoplasmic granules of *basophils* and released during allergic reactions. See also *Antihistamine drugs*.

Histopathology – the examination of tissue sections (usually biopsy samples) under the microscope to assess for the presence and cause of disease.

History – previous treatment and care of the patient.

Hob – a male ferret. See also Jill.

Hock – also known as the *tarsus*, this is the *joint* in the hindlimb that corresponds to the human ankle. See also *Carpus*.

Hohmann retractor – a handheld retractor with a sharp point at the tip used during *orthopaedic* procedures for retraction within a joint.

Hoist – A mechanical device on wheels to assist with moving and handling patients. The patient is securely fastened into the seating area and may be transported or moved up or down.

Homeopathy – treatment of symptoms with an extremely dilute solution of a substance, which is itself capable of causing the same symptoms. See also *Alternative medicine*.

Homeostasis – the equilibrium or balance of the internal environment of the body. Many different systems and mechanisms contribute to homeostasis, such as thermoregulation, excretory systems, endocrinological (hormonal) systems, etc.

Homologous – having the same position or structure; a pair of chromosomes, one inherited from each parent, is said to be homologous because each one is alike.

Homozygous – when an animal carries two copies of a gene which are the same it is described as homozygous. For example, in dalmatians there are two colours: the black form of the spotting gene (**B**) and the liver-coloured spot form (**b**). A dalmation carrying **BB** or **bb** genes is described as homozygous for that trait. See also *Heterozygous*.

Hookworm – see *Uncinaria stenocephala*.

Horizontal beam – the primary beam is used horizontally instead of vertically. There are health and safety issues with this procedure; local rules and the radiation protection advisor or supervisor should be consulted.

Hormone – a chemical messenger that is released by an *endocrine gland* into the bloodstream, where it is carried to target cells in other tissues. When it reaches its target cells, it will bind to receptors there and initiate a response. Examples include luteinising hormone, *thyroxine* and *adrenaline.*

Horner's syndrome – a painless neurological condition where there is damage to the sympathetic nerve supply to the head. Clinical signs affect only one side and include a constricted pupil (*miosis*), drooping of the eyelid (*ptosis*), and protrusion of the third eyelid. Ear infections are a common cause of Horner's syndrome because the nerve passes close to the inner ear and is easily damaged.

Host – the animal upon which or within which a parasite lives, eg the cat is a host for the flea *Ctenocephalides felis.*

Hot-air oven – a piece of equipment used to carry out dry-heat *sterilisation* of glass, surgical instruments and powders. *Micro-organisms* are destroyed by the high temperatures reached (150–180°C is standard), although for this reason this method of sterilisation is not suitable for plastics, rubber or fabrics. See also *Autoclave, Ethylene oxide.*

Hot compress – used in wound care to aid healing; hot compresses or applications cause vasodilatation which in turn increases the blood supply to the wound and helps to drain fluid away from the area. Examples of heat applications include swabs soaked in hot water, hot-water bottles.

Howell–Jolly bodies – darkly staining, spherical inclusions seen within immature erythrocytes; remnants of the nuclear material.

Humerus – a *long bone* of the proximal forelimb, it articulates with the *glenoid cavity* of the *scapula*. Distally it forms the elbow joint with the *radius* and *ulna*.

Humidity – the amount of moisture or water vapour in the air.

Humphrey ADE system – an anaesthetic circuit that can be adapted to be a semi-closed circuit (for patients under 10 kg) or a re-breathing circuit incorporating soda lime (for patients over 10 kg). It uses low flow rates of fresh gas for all patients.

Hybrid – a cross between two different species, eg the mule is a cross between a female horse and a male donkey.

Hydatid cyst – the *metacestode* stage of some tapeworms including *Echinococcus granulosus*. The hydatid cyst is a fluid-filled bladder that may grow very large and contains many *scolices*; contents are often called hydatid sand.

Hydration – maintaining the correct balance of fluids within the body.

Hydrocephalus – a rare but serious condition, characterised by an abnormal accumulation of fluid in the *brain ventricles*, causing an enlargement of the head. Thought to occur when the *cerebrospinal fluid* is unable to drain away.

Hydrochloric acid (HCl) – keeps the contents of the stomach acid.

Hydrocolloid dressing – also known as interactive dressing; a self-adhesive gel held in place by a thin layer of plastic.

Hydrogel – also known as interactive dressing; amorphous hydrogel is applied directly into the wound and covered with a non-adhesive dressing.

Hydrolysis – a chemical reaction in which a compound reacts with water to produce another compound.

Hydrophobia – see *Rabies*.

Hydroquinone – a developer or reducing agent. See also *Developer.*

Hydrotherapy – a type of physiotherapy in which the patient exercises in water, resistance can be added in the form of whirlpools.

Hydrothorax – build-up of liquid in the pleural cavity. See also *Pleural effusion*.

Hyoid apparatus – a U-shaped structure made up of a series of small bones and cartilages which suspends the larynx and tongue.

Hypaxial muscle – the muscle lying ventral to the transverse processes of the vertebrae. The *flexor muscles* of the neck and tail. See also *Epaxial muscle.*

Hyperadrenocorticism – see *Cushing's disease*.

Hyperaemia – increase in blood supply to an area, eg hyperaemia of the conjunctiva can result in the eye appearing reddened.

Hypercalcaemia – abnormally high levels of *calcium ions* in the *blood*. Can be caused by among other things *hyperparathyroidism, renal failure* and *dehydration*. See also *Eclampsia*.

Hyperglobulinaemia – an increase in the level of globulins in the blood. Possible causes include inflammation and some types of tumour.

Hyperglycaemia – abnormally high levels of *glucose* in the *blood*, which is one of the clinical signs of *diabetes mellitus*. Mild hyperglycaemia can be caused by fear, excitement, stress or taking a blood sample soon after the animal has eaten. See also *Hypoglycaemia*.

Hyperimmune serum – serum containing large numbers of *antibodies* against a particular *disease*. Can be given to an animal in the face of an outbreak to give short-lasting *passive immunity* to that disease. See also *Vaccination*.

Hyperkalaemia – an increase in blood potassium levels; may occur as an artefact when the serum/plasma is not separated from the erythrocytes promptly. May also be associated with *hypoadrenocorticism* and *acute renal failure*.

Hyperkeratosis – colloquially known as 'hard pad', the *epidermis* of the skin becomes thickened and crusty, most obvious on the foot pads and nose. One of the clinical signs of *distemper* and is also caused by zinc deficiency.

Hypernatraemia – an increase in blood sodium levels; usually associated with dehydration.

Hyperparathyroidism – excessive secretion of parathyroid hormone. May be primary, or secondary as a result of poor diet or renal disease. Causes loss of calcium from the bones and hypercalcaemia.

Hyperphagia – see *Polyphagia*.

Hyperphosphataemia – an increase in blood phosphorus levels most commonly seen in animals with renal failure. Young animals have higher phosphorus levels than adults.

Hyperproteinaemia – an increase in total blood protein levels (either albumin, globulin, or both).

Hypersalivation – also known as *hyperptyalism*; the excess production of *saliva* causing the animal to drool. It can be a sign of *nausea*, ingestion of a toxin or caustic substance, dental disease or neuromuscular problems causing difficulties with the swallowing reflex. It is also seen in animals that have licked/picked up a toad in their mouth!

Hypersensitivity – an exaggerated response by the immune system to a substance such as pollen, insects or food.

Hypertension – abnormally increased blood pressure. Often associated with cardiac or renal disease, or hyperthyroidism.

Hyperthermia – the *core body temperature* increases to a high level, causing collapse. Can be fatal unless treated promptly. Treatment includes immersion of the animal in cold water, application of cold wet towels, administration of ice cold enemas, chilled intravenous fluids, etc. See also *Hypothermia*.

Hyperthyroidism – a condition in which the *thyroid glands* secrete excess thyroid hormones into the circulation. Usually caused by the growth of a *benign tumour* on the glands. It is most commonly seen in middle-aged/older cats. Symptoms include weight loss, hyperactivity, *polyphagia*, poor-quality coat, *tachycardia*, often with a murmur and a palpable enlargement of the thyroid glands. Treatment is by oral anti-thyroid drugs (methimazole) or by surgery in which one or both of the thyroid glands are removed. See also *Parathyroid gland*.

Hypertonic solution – a solution with a higher osmotic pressure than blood.

Hypertrophic cardiomyopathy – a disease of the heart in which the heart muscle becomes thickened so that the diameter of the chambers is reduced. More common in small dogs and cats.

Hyperventilation – increase in respiratory depth. Presents as deep and rapid breathing.

Hypervitaminosis A – excess levels of vitamin A, can cause liver damage and ankylosis of the joints especially the cervical vertebrae.

Hypervitaminosis D – excess levels of vitamin D, can cause depression and poor growth.

Hyphae – the filaments that are found in some species of fungi such as *Aspergillus* sp.

Hyphaemia – the presence of blood in the anterior chamber of the eye.

Hypoadrenocorticism – A life threatening medical condition which is fairly uncommon in dogs and rare in cats. The adrenal glands fail to secrete cortisol and minerals corticoids. Affected animals show vague clinical signs such as vomiting and diarrhoea. On blood tests they usually have azotaemia and hyperkalaemia among other changes. The hyperkalaemia can cause cardiac arrythmia and death if untreated. Treatment involves supplementing the steroids and mineralocorticoids and is life long but the prognosis is good if diagnosed in time. This condition is also called Addison's disease.

Hypoalbuminaemia – reduced levels of albumin in the blood. Possible causes include decreased synthesis in the liver, or increased losses through the kidneys or gastrointestinal tract, haemorrhage or burns.

Hypocalcaemia – reduced levels of calcium in the blood. Common causes include hypoalbuminaemia (as most calcium is bound to albumin), hypoparathyroidism and *eclampsia*.

Hypochromic – a term relating to erythrocytes with a reduced haemoglobin content, usually because of iron deficiency, or during regenerative anaemias.

Hypodermis – also called the subcutis, this is the *subcutaneous* layer of the skin. It is the layer below the *dermis*, made up of *loose connective tissue* and fat and it acts as an energy store and also as a layer of protection and insulation.

Hypoglossal nerve – twelfth (XII) *cranial nerve*, which innervates the tongue muscle.

Hypoglycaemia – abnormally low levels of *blood glucose*. Can occur as a result of starvation, *hypoadrenocorticism* and also *chronic malabsorption*. Can also occur in animals diagnosed with *diabetes mellitus* – if too much *insulin* is injected by mistake by the owner, or if the animal is *inappetant*, hypoglycaemia can be caused. Symptoms include weakness, lethargy, tremors, *ataxia*, collapse and death. *First-aid* treatment involves giving the animal sugary food if conscious and then taking it immediately for veterinary attention. See also *Hyperglycaemia*.

Hypokalaemia – decreased blood levels of potassium. Possible causes include reduced intake or increased losses in the kidney or gastrointestinal tract.

Hyponatraemia – decreased blood levels of sodium. Possible causes include overhydration and hypoadrenocorticism.

Hypophosphataemia – decreased blood levels of phosphorus. Possible causes include malabsorption and hyperparathyroidism.

Hypophysis – see *Pituitary gland*.

Hypoproteinaemia – a decrease in total blood protein levels; usually caused by hypoalbuminaemia with or without reduced globluins.

Hypopyon – pus in the anterior chamber of the eye.

Hypostatic congestion – can be seen in prolonged recoveries; pooling of blood occurs in the dependent lower body and lung, causing a certain degree of hypoxia through the pooling of *blood* and secretions in the *lungs* because of the patient having been lying in *lateral recumbency* on one side for a long period. Turning a recumbent patient every 2 hours, encouraging *sternal recumbency* where possible and carrying out *coupage* regularly will decrease the chance of the problem occurring.

Hypotension – low blood pressure.

Hypothalamus – an area of the *forebrain* situated below the *thalamus*, concerned with thermoregulation, emotion, regulation of the *pituitary gland* and control of the *autonomic nervous system*.

Hypothermia – an abnormally low core body temperature. It can occur post-operatively or if the patient is in shock. Treatment includes keeping the patient warm by use of blankets, foil, bubble wrap, incubators or heat pads, warming intravenous fluids and maintaining a warm room temperature. See also *Hyperthermia*.

Hypothyroidism – a deficiency in the production and release of thyroid hormones, usually caused by damage to the thyroid glands. Usually occurs in middle-aged dogs, and is rarely seen in the cat. Symptoms include *alopecia*, weight gain, *bradycardia*, exercise intolerance and weakness. Treatment is by *oral thyroxine* supplementation.

Hypotonic solution – a solution that has a lower osmotic pressure than blood.

Hypoventilation – decrease in respiratory depth. Presents as slow and rapid breathing.

Hypovolaemia – a decreased circulating blood volume. Possible causes include haemorrhage, dehydration and diuretic use.

Hypovolaemic shock – an abnormally low circulating *blood* volume causes a decrease in the perfusion of the tissues and the animal goes into hypovolaemic *shock*. Can be caused by extensive blood loss or severe *dehydration*. See also *Anaphylactic shock, Cardiogenic shock*.

Hypoxia, hypoxic – reduced levels of *oxygen* in the *blood* lead to reduced availability of oxygen to the tissues. If the *heart* muscles become hypoxic, *cardiac arrest* will follow. Hypoxia can result from reduced amounts of available *haemoglobin* (eg caused by *anaemia*), reduced lung efficiency (eg *pneumonia*), reduced oxygen in inspired air (eg empty oxygen cylinder during an anaesthetic) or insufficient cardiac output to deliver blood to tissues (eg as a result of anaesthetic overdose).

I

Iatrogenic – a condition caused by medication or a medical procedure, eg iatrogenic Cushing's disease may occur when a patient has been given steroids for a prolonged period to treat a skin complaint.

Ictal stage – the second stage of a *seizure*, in which the animal often loses consciousness. Paddling of the legs can occur, as can jerky *muscle* movements and urine and/or faeces may be passed. Owners should be warned that the animal may bite during a seizure, so should be handled with care. See also *Epilepsy, Status epilepticus*.

Icterus – also called jaundice. The yellow coloration of skin, sclera and mucous membranes caused by increased blood levels of bilirubin. Usually caused by liver disease, or occasionally haemolytic anaemia.

Identification of patients – system to ensure the correct procedures are carried out on the correct patients; can use identity tags/collars, cage labels.

Idiopathic – a condition or *disease* arising spontaneously and of which the cause is unknown.

Ileocaecocolic junction – the junction between the ileum, colon and caecum, ie where the small intestine joins the large intestine. Acts as a pacemaker for the gut.

Ileum – the part of the *small intestine* that follows the *jejunum*. This area of the small intestine is concerned with *digestion* and also the absorption of water and the products of digestion. The ileum eventually joins the *colon* (*large intestine*). See also *Duodenum*. Not to be confused with *ilium*.

Ilium – one of the bones which makes up each half of the *pelvis*. The wing of the ilium can be felt as the bony protuberance known as the hip. It is a useful landmark for positioning during *radiography*. See also *Ischium*.

Ilizarov fixator – a type of external fixation, useful in complicated and open fractures or where infection is present. See also *External fixation*.

Immune-mediated haemolytic anaemia (IMHA) – a life-threatening condition that occurs when the body makes antibodies that attack its own erythrocytes. The result is auto-agglutination (where the erythrocytes stick together), and destruction of the erythrocytes (haemolytic anaemia). Some breeds, such as cocker spaniels and poodles, are more commonly affected. Treatment usually involves immunosuppressive drug therapy.

Immune-mediated thrombocytopaenia (IMT) – a condition which occurs when the body's immune system attacks its own platelets (thrombocytes). As platelets are important for blood clotting the result is haemorrhage – usually petechiae on the skin and mucous membranes and mucosal bleeds. Treatment usually involves immunosuppressive drug therapy.

Immune system – the body system that detects and fights off infections and foreign substances. It is composed of cells (the white blood cells in the blood, as well as cells within many different tissues) and organs such as the lymph nodes and spleen.

Immunity – the ability of the body to resist *disease* caused by *pathogens*. Immunity can be natural or acquired. Natural immunity is passed on either from mother to offspring, via the placenta or through *antibodies* in the *colostrum* (see also *Maternally derived antibodies*), or by exposure to a disease, which allows the body to produce specific antibodies to that disease. Acquired immunity is achieved by *vaccination* or by administering *hyperimmune serum*.

Immunoglobulins – also called *antibodies*; these are protein molecules produced by plasma cells (activated B lymphocytes). They attack foreign antigens so that they can be removed by the immune system.

Immunosuppression – the inability of a body to mount a normal and effective immune response in the face of disease. May be the result of an overwhelming infection or a side-effect of certain drugs (eg *corticosteroids*).

Impaction – a condition where hard dry faeces become firmly wedged in the bowel and cannot be passed naturally.

Impregnated gauze dressings – gauze dressings impregnated with substances such as Vaseline or iodine; applied directly over the wound.

Inactivated (dead) vaccine – a vaccine containing *antigens* from a specific *pathogen*, but the antigens are not alive. Causes an active immune response but this tends to be shorter-lived than the response to a *live vaccine*. Inactivated vaccines usually contain an *adjuvant* that serves to enhance the immune response.

Inappetance – unwillingness to eat.

In-breeding – when an animal breeds with an immediate relative (brother/sister or parent/offspring breeding). Sometimes used by breeders to pass on desirable show features but undesirable because harmful genes are more likely to be passed on, and the health and welfare of the offspring are at risk.

Incised wound – a wound produced by sharp objects, eg glass; they are parallel to the skin.

Incision – a cut made on the body with a surgical instrument.

Incisional biopsy – a small sliver of the *tumour* is cut away surgically, often using a scalpel blade or scissors. An ideal incisional biopsy will include a border between normal and diseased tissue in the sample. It is then sent to the laboratory for *histopathology*.

Incisor – the most *rostral* teeth in the upper and lower jaws. Adult cats and dogs have six upper and six lower incisors. Have a single root and are mainly used for nibbling and for grooming. See also *Canine, Carnassial, Premolar*.

Incontinence – the inability of an animal to control urination. Can range in severity from mild (the animal dribbles small puddles of *urine* when asleep or lying down) to complete incontinence, where the animal has no control at all. The animal will show signs of urine scalding around the *perineum* and on the hindlimbs and the fur will become soiled. Causes include *urinary tract infection*, *ectopic ureters*, neurological impairment and *bladder* sphincter mechanism incompetence. To successfully treat incontinence, the underlying cause must first be identified.

Incubation period – the period of time between the body coming into contact with an *infectious agent* and the development of clinical signs. Incubation periods for different *diseases* vary in length.

Incus – the middle *auditory ossicle*, shaped like an anvil and found in the *middle ear*. Located between the *malleus* and *stapes*; together their function is to amplify sound-wave vibrations and carry them across the middle ear to the *oval window*.

Indigenous – meaning native, or occurring naturally in a country or area. It is illegal to release non-indigenous species into the wild in the UK. Non-indigenous species include grey squirrels and rabbits.

Indirect transmission – passing on of infectious disease where the animals are not in direct contact; instead the infection is spread by the environment, eg placing a healthy puppy in a poorly cleaned kennel where the previous resident had a parvovirus infection.

Induced ovulation – in cats ovulation is not spontaneous but is stimulated, or *induced*, by the act of mating. Female cats that are not mated while in season do not ovulate.

Induction (anaesthesia) – introducing a general anaesthetic either intravenously, using an intravenous agent, or by inhalation, using a volatile agent and face mask.

Indwelling catheter – urinary catheter inserted into the bladder and anchored. It can remain on a temporary or permanent basis.

Infection – the invasion of the body by a pathogenic *micro-organism*; after the *incubation period*, during which time the micro-organisms multiply in the host, the symptoms of the *disease* start to become apparent. Symptom severity depends on the *virulence* of the *pathogen*. See also *Infectious*.

Infectious – describes a *disease* that is able to spread from one animal to another, by direct contact, by a *fomite* such as bedding, or by a *vector*, such as an insect. See also *Contagious*.

Infectious canine hepatitis (ICH) – *infectious* disease caused by *adenovirus* 1; spread by direct and indirect contact and targets the *liver* and lymphoid tissue. Clinical signs include *jaundice*, enlarged liver, enlarged *lymph nodes*, *anorexia*, *pyrexia* and painful *cranial abdomen*. Sudden death is seen in young puppies.

Infertility – the inability to produce healthy offspring. Many factors may influence fertility such as age, health status, sexual behaviour, conformation and nutrition.

Infiltration (intradermal) anaesthesia – local anaesthestic is infiltrated into tissues close to nerves, or subcutaneously or between muscles. Can be applied as nerve block or line block.

Inflammation – reaction of tissues to injury. Can be acute or chronic. Signs include: swelling, redness, heat, loss of normal function, pain.

Infraspinatus – one of the *muscles* of the upper forelimb; runs from the *scapula* to the *humerus* and helps *extend/flex* and *abduct* the shoulder joint and also rotate the limb *laterally*.

Infundibulum – the funnel-shaped end of the oviduct that collects the ovum after ovulation.

Infusion pump – a device used to deliver set amounts of intravenous fluids.

Ingesta – foods and fluids that are eaten.

Ingestion – consumption of food and fluid through the mouth.

Inguinal – the area of the body between the *abdomen* and the hindlimb, also known as the groin. See also *Inguinal hernia*.

Inguinal hernia – a defect in the inguinal canal, allowing the protrusion of abdominal organs. See also *Hernia*.

Inguinal ring – the hole in the abdominal wall through which each testicle descends on its journey to the scrotum during fetal development.

Inhalation – breathing a substance into the lungs and body.

Inhalational anaesthesia – producing unconsciousness by delivering a volatile agent/gas, eg isoflurane, sevoflurane, halothane.

Inhibition – prevention or blocking of a process, eg an ACE inhibitor is a drug used to block the actions of *angiotensin-converting enzyme* (ACE) and is used to treat heart failure.

Injectable anaesthesia – see *Intravenous anaesthesia*

Injection – using a syringe and needle, substances such as drugs or fluids are administered into the body.

Inner ear – consists of a bony labyrinth in two parts, containing the organs of hearing (*cochlea* and *organ of Corti*) and of balance (*semicircular canals*). The space between the two labyrinths is filled with *perilymph*.

Inotrope – a drug that affects the strength of the contraction of the heart muscle. A positive inotrope (eg digoxin) increases the strength of each contraction, whereas a negative inotrope (eg diltiazem) decreases the strength.

In-patient – a patient who is admitted into the practice or hospital.

Insectivore – an animal whose diet consists of insects.

Insensible water losses – those losses that cannot be controlled: breathing/cutaneous loss is 20 ml/kg per day.

Insert sleeve (surgical nursing) – provides accurate positioning of holes for screws; various sizes are available to fit the appropriate drill bit.

Insertion – the *distal* point of attachment for a *muscle* or *tendon* attaching onto the *bone*. See also *Origin*.

Inspiration – the active process by which air flows into the respiratory tract from the atmosphere. The *diaphragm* and *intercostal muscles* contract, swinging the ribcage upwards and outwards, increasing the volume of the *thorax* and thus lowering the pressure. Air flows in until the pressure outside the body is equal to the pressure in the thorax. See also *Expiration*.

Inspiratory dyspnoea – difficulty breathing on inspiration.

Insulin – a *hormone* produced in the *pancreas* by the islets of Langerhans beta cells. Secreted in response to a rise in *blood glucose* levels, eg after a meal, it stimulates the production of *glycogen* from glucose and also aids the transport of glucose from the blood into respiring tissues. *Diabetes mellitus* occurs most commonly when the pancreas fails to produce enough insulin and blood glucose levels become elevated. Treatment involves injecting the animal with commercially produced insulin.

Insulinoma – a tumour of the beta cells in the *pancreas*; they produce excessive *insulin*, which causes *hypoglycaemia* and clinical signs including weakness and collapse.

Insurance – provides for reimbursement of the cost of veterinary treatment; however, there is an excess to pay for each claim, and practices are subject to the rules and regulations of the Financial Services Authority (FSA). A claim form is filled in both by the owner and the practice and sent to the insurance company for assessment.

Integument – the skin.

Intensifying screen – a sheet of plastic containing phosphor crystals, which convert part of the X-ray beam into visible light. They drastically reduce the amount of exposure needed to obtain a latent image. The phosphors used are either calcium tungstate (blue-emitting) or more commonly rare earth phosphors (green-emitting); usually fitted onto both sides of the cassette.

Inter – prefix meaning, in between.

Intercostal muscle – the external and internal intercostal muscles form part of the thoracic wall. They run from *rib* to rib and have an important role in drawing the ribs upwards and together during *inspiration*.

Interlocking nails – a method of internal fixation; the interlocking nail (similar to an intramedullary pin) is also anchored with screws at both the proximal and distal ends of the nail.

Intermediate host – term used in *parasitology* to describe the host (other than the *final host*) in/on which part of the development of the parasite takes place.

Intermittent positive pressure ventilation (IPPV) – an emergency procedure carried out when a patient shows signs of *apnoea* during *general anaesthesia*. The anaesthetic agent is immediately turned off and IPPV is carried out using 100% *oxygen*. The *reservoir bag* on the anaesthetic circuit needs to be squeezed 10–30 times a minute to mimic the patient's own *respiratory rate*. The valve on the circuit needs to be closed to allow the reservoir bag to fill with oxygen, and then opened to allow the gas to be delivered to the patient's *lungs*. See also *Cardiopulmonary resuscitation*.

Internal abdominal oblique – one of four groups of *muscles* that make up the abdominal wall. The fibres run cranioventrally underneath the *external abdominal obliques* and insert onto the *linea alba* via an *aponeurosis*.

Internal fixation – a method for repairing fractures using plates, screws and/or intramedullary pins; all the implants are applied directly into/onto the bone.

Interneurone – a small neurone that conducts a nervous signal between an *afferent* and *efferent* neurone during a *reflex* response. See also *Reflex arc*.

Interphase – a resting stage of cell division in both *mitosis* and *meiosis*. During this phase, *DNA* replication and synthesis of nuclear proteins occurs; the *centrioles* also divide.

Interrupted sutures – a suture pattern often used for *skin* and *midline* closures. Thought to be more secure than *continuous sutures* but take longer to place.

Interstitial fluid – fluid located in the spaces between cells, making up part of the *extracellular fluid* of an animal. Also known as *tissue fluid*.

Intertrigo – inflammation of the skin (*dermatitis*) in a fold of skin, eg dogs with heavily folded facial skin such as Boxers, Bulldogs and Shar peis may suffer from intertrigo between the skin folds.

Intervertebral disc – found between the bodies of adjacent *vertebrae*, intervertebral discs act as shock absorbers in the spine and also allow for movement between the vertebrae. Composed of a *nucleus pulposus* (semi-fluid centre) surrounded by a tough fibrous layer (*annulus pulposus*). In older animals, the discs can become calcified, making them less flexible and therefore more prone to damage.

Intra – prefix meaning inside or within.

Intracardiac injection – injection into the heart; this is painful and damaging, but is occasionally used for euthanasia of small animals.

Intracellular – located within a cell.

Intradermal (local anaesthesia) – see *Infiltration (intradermal) anaesthesia*.

Intradermal allergy testing – a diagnostic test used to assess which antigens cause allergy in an animal. Tiny amounts of different antigens are injected into the skin and the reaction (swelling, inflammation) is noted.

Intramedullary pin – metal orthopaedic implant used for internal fracture fixation; the pin is placed into the *medullary cavity* of a *long bone* and is used to stabilise fractures. Often left in place for the rest of the animal's life. See also *Kirschner wires*, *Rush pin*.

Intramembranous ossification – the formation of *bone* within a membrane of connective tissue, without the prior development of a cartilage model. *Flat bones* (eg those that make up the skull) are an example of bone formed by this method. See also *Endochondral ossification*.

Intramuscular (IM) – injection into a *muscle*; the most commonly used sites are the *lumbar* muscles and the muscles over the *scapula*.

Intraoral – inside the mouth.

Intraosseus – injection into a *bone*; this route is very occasionally used for administering fluids when placing intravenous catheters is not possible. It needs to be carried out by an experienced person as incorrect technique can result in infection.

Intraperitoneal (IP) – injection into the *peritoneal* cavity; this method is occasionally used to give fluids to puppies, kittens and small mammals.

Intrathecal injection – injection within the meninges of the spinal chord.

Intravascular – meaning into a blood vessel.

Intravenous (IV) – injection into a vein; the most commonly used sites are the *cephalic* and *saphenous veins*. The site should be *aseptically* prepared before the needle is introduced into the vein. See also *Venepuncture*.

Intravenous anaesthesia – producing unconsciousness by delivering an agent administered intravenously. Commonly used agents are: propofol (Rapinovet®, Schering Plough) thiopentone sodium (Thiovet), alphaxalone/alphadolone (Saffan®, Schering Plough).

Intravenous local anaesthesia – local anaesthetic is injected into a vein, a tourniquet is placed around the limb and the agent is injected below this.

Intravenous urography – contrast study of the kidneys and ureters. There are two ways to perform the study: low-volume, rapid injection – a small amount of contrast medium is rapidly introduced intravenously; high-volume, slow infusion – a larger amount of dilute contrast medium is infused intravenously over 10–15 min.

Intromission – placement of the penis into the vagina during mating.

Intubation – the act of placing an *endotracheal tube* into the *trachea* of an anaesthetised animal. Maintains a secure airway by protecting the airway from the entry of saliva and other fluids (eg water during a dental procedure) and allows maintenance of anaesthesia. However, the act of introducing a tube can cause trauma to the *larynx* if not carried out carefully and it is possible for the tube to become occluded or kinked, so careful monitoring is required.

Intussusception – a condition caused when a piece of gut is forced into the lumen of the next section of gut rather like a telescope. Commonest in young animals following a bout of diarrhoea. The blood vessels to the affected piece of gut become *occluded* and the damage may be irreversible. Clinical signs include vomiting, abdominal pain and diarrhoea.

Inverse square law – the intensity of the primary beam varies inversely as the square of the distance from the source.

Invertebrate – an animal without a backbone, eg insect, worm.

Involuntary muscle – a muscle whose action takes place without conscious will, eg *cardiac muscle* and *smooth (visceral) muscle*. Under the control of the *autonomic nervous system*.

Iodophore – an agent used in skin disinfection. It is found within the solution.

Ion – a charged particle formed when an atom gains or loses electrons, eg sodium ion (Na^+), potassium ion (K^+) and chloride ion (Cl^-).

Ionic contrast media –water-soluble positive contrast media; can be administered into the vascular system.

Ionising Radiation Regulations 1999 – guidelines regarding safety for personnel involved with ionising radiation such as X-rays.

Iris – the pigmented area of the *eye* containing *smooth muscle* fibres, which act to alter the diameter of the aperture within the iris, the *pupil*. This allows control over the amount of light entering the eye.

Iris scissors – small, sharp surgical instrument used during ophthalmic procedures for cutting the *iris* and *conjunctiva*.

Iritis – inflammation of the iris in the eye.

Iron – a micro-mineral required in the diet on a daily basis; a deficiency can lead to anaemia.

Irreducible hernia – also known as an incarcerated hernia; often seen in long-standing hernias. The hernia contents cannot easily be replaced because they have often developed fibrous adhesions holding them in place. See also *Hernia*.

Irregular bone – a classification of *bone* that includes the *vertebrae*, and *carpal* and *tarsal bones*.

Ischaemia – a reduced or insufficient blood supply to a tissue.

Ischium – one of the bones that make up each half of the *pelvis*. See also *Ilium*.

Islets of Langerhans – islands of endocrine tissue found in the pancreas that contain alpha, beta and delta cells. Alpha cells secrete glucagon, beta cells secrete insulin, and delta cells secrete somatostatin.

Isolation – being placed alone or apart from other patients. *Infectious* patients should be housed in an isolation unit, away from other patients, to minimise the risk of the infection spreading. See also *Barrier nursing*, *Quarantine*.

Isometric – a type of muscle contraction where the muscle tone increases without shortening the muscle. See also *Isotonic*.

Isosthenuria – a term which describes urine that has the same *specific gravity* as plasma (1.008–1.012). When plasma is filtered at the glomerulus the filtrate has the same specific gravity as the plasma. Normally this is concentrated or diluted along the tubule before it is excreted, depending on the hydration of the animal. When the kidney is not functioning correctly the filtrate is not modified and the urine is isosthenuric.

Isotonic – **1.** a type of muscle contraction where the muscle shortens. See also Isometric. **2.** describes a solution with equal *osmotic pressure* to the one to which it is being compared.

Ixodes ricinus – the commonest tick present in the UK that is commonly seen in dogs; may transmit diseases such as Lyme's disease.

J

Jackson's cat catheter – a urinary catheter used in cats, may be sutured in place so it becomes indwelling.

Jacob's chuck – a piece of surgical equipment used during *orthopaedic* procedures to introduce or extract *intramedullary pins*, eg *Kirschner wires* or *Steinmann pins*. It has a hole through the centre to allow the pin/wire to be securely held in place while being positioned. A guard can be screwed in the end to cover the pin to prevent injury to the surgeon.

Jacobson's organ – also known as the *vomeronasal organ*; acts as a sensory organ that contributes to a snake's keen sense of smell. Found in the roof of the mouth and is thought to detect scent particles picked up by the snake's tongue.

Jaundice – also known as *icterus*; describes a yellow discoloration of the skin and mucous membranes caused by an increase in *plasma bilirubin* levels. See also *Hepatitis*, *Icterus*.

Jaw tone – the tension felt when the upper and lower jaws are separated, eg diminishes with general anaesthesia.

Jejunostomy tube feeding – a feeding tube placed into the jejunum to enable artificial feeding.

Jejunum – the longest portion of the small intestine, extending from the duodenum to the ileum.

Jill – a female ferret; see also *Hob*.

Jird – a gerbil-like rodent, larger in size, occasionally kept as a pet.

Joint fluid – also called *synovial fluid*; it is similar to *plasma* but with added lubrication. Occurs in *synovial joint* spaces and lubricates the joints and provides nourishment for the *articular cartilage*.

Jugular vein – a pair of large *veins* found running either side of the neck. Blood from the head is carried in the jugular veins. The jugular, along with the *cephalic vein* in the foreleg, is one of the most commonly used veins for *venepuncture* to obtain a blood sample.

K

K – the chemical symbol for potassium.

Keel – a large ventral part of a bird's *sternum* that has been modified to form the keel. The *pectoral (flight) muscles* attach here and the depth of keel varies with the ability of that species to fly.

Kennel Club (KC) – an organisation that promotes responsibility of canine ownership and canine health. They hold a list of all registered breeders and breeds that are recognised by the Kennel Club. The Kennel Club is the governing body for all dog trials, competitions and official shows.

Keratin – a structural protein found in hair, claws and the epidermis.

Keratitis – inflammation of the cornea. See also *Conjunctivitis, Uveitis*.

Keratoconjunctivitis sicca (KCS) – also known as *dry eye*; deficiency of tear production, which causes drying of the corneal surface. Usually caused by immune-mediated destruction of the lacrimal gland. Clinical signs include thick ocular discharge, a dull appearance to the cornea and keratitis. Diagnosed using a *Schirmer tear test*.

Ketamine – a dissociative anaesthetic agent; can be used alone or, more commonly, alongside other agents.

Ketones – breakdown products of fat metabolism that are produced when the body uses fat instead of carbohydrate for energy. Produced in larger quantities during starvation or in diabetes mellitus. They are acidic and can cause acidosis. See also *Diabetic ketoacidosis*.

Ketonuria – the presence of *ketones* in the urine, usually associated with *diabetic ketoacidosis* or starvation.

Kidney – a pair of organs lying either side of the vertebral column pressed to the dorsal wall of the abdominal cavity in a *retroperitoneal* position. The right kidney lies more cranially than the left. Each kidney is made up of three regions, the *cortex*, *medulla* and *renal pelvis*. The cortex and medulla are made up of a large number of tubules called *nephrons*, which are the functional units of the kidney. The kidney's main function is to remove *urea* from the blood and to excrete it in *urine*. *Antidiuretic hormone* (ADH) acts on the kidney to control how concentrated the urine is (see also *Specific gravity*). Kidneys also secrete the hormones *renin* and *erythropoietin*.

Kidney dish – a stainless-steel or plastic dish shaped like a kidney, used in veterinary practices and hospitals as a multi-purpose receptacle.

Kilo- – suffix meaning a thousand, eg there are 1000 g in 1 kg and 1000 volts in a kilovolt (kV).

Kilovoltage – the penetrating power of the primary beam, ie how fast the electrons are accelerated from the cathode to the anode. Can be controlled on the control panel; as rule of thumb the higher the density and atomic number of the tissue the higher the kilovoltage required.

Kirschner–Ehmer apparatus – see *Ilizarov fixator*.

Kirschner wires – look similar to intramedullary pins but one end is blunt and the other is flattened in a diamond shape. Used to repair fractures of the epiphysis and other small fractures.

Kit – a young ferret. See also *Hob, Jill*.

Kreb's cycle – also known as the tricarboxylic acid (TCA) cycle or citric acid cycle; a series of chemical reactions that break down carbohydrates, fats and proteins to carbon dioxide and water to produce energy. The cycle is *aerobic* and occurs within the *mitochondria* of the cell; produces more energy than *glycolysis*.

Küpffer cells – phagocytic cells in the liver that remove old or damaged erythrocytes from the circulation.

Kyphosis – dorsal curvature of the spine and ventroflexion of the neck. Imagine the back in a slouching position with the chin tucked towards the chest.

Laceration – also known as a *degloving injury*, a lacerated wound is one where the skin has been torn away from the tissue, the wound edges are jagged and the risk of infection is high because of contamination with dirt and bacteria. This type of wound is commonly seen after road traffic accidents where the animal has been dragged along the rough surface of the road by the vehicle.

Lachrymal gland – see *Lacrimal gland*.

Lack anaesthetic circuit – a non re-breathing anaesthetic circuit used to deliver and maintain anaesthesia and also to remove waste gases. Can be parallel (two pieces of tubing alongside each other) or co-axial (two pieces of tubing inside each other). In co-axial circuits fresh gas enters the patient via the outer tube and waste gas is breathed out into and removed by the inner tube. The Lack uses lower flow rates than the Bain circuit but cannot be used for intermittent positive pressure ventilation. Used in patients over 7 kg.

Lacrimal apparatus – a structure found in the *eye* made up of the *lacrimal glands*, *sac* and *ducts*, it provides and distributes the *tear film* across the *cornea*.

Lacrimal gland – also known as the tear gland and part of the *lacrimal apparatus* of the *eye*; it provides the *tear film* that lubricates, protects and nourishes the *cornea*.

Lacrimal sac – part of the *lacrimal apparatus* of the *eye*, located at the end of the *nasolacrimal ducts* near the *medial canthus*. The lacrimal ducts empty into the lacrimal sacs.

Lacrimation – the act of *tear* production. See also *Schirmer tear test*.

Lactated Ringer's solution – see *Hartmann's solution*.

Lactation – the production of *colostrum* and milk that occurs following *parturition* (and during phantom pregnancy), and continues until the offspring are *weaned*.

Lacteal – see *Lymph vessel*.

Lactose – made from one glucose molecule and one galactose molecule, an example of a disaccharide; a sugar commonly found in milk or dairy products.

Lacuna (pl. **lacunae)** – a small cavity between the *lamellae* in the matrix of *compact bone*. *Osteocytes* are found within the *lacunae*.

Lagomorph – a classification of exotic species that includes rabbits and hares.

Lamella (pl. **lamellae)** – a thin layer of bone matrix in *cortical bone*. See also *Lacuna*.

Lance – making a ventral incision over a wound, usually an abscess, to allow drainage.

Langenbeck retractor – hand-held, L-shaped retractor used during surgery for retracting soft tissue to expose other structures underneath.

Laparotomy – a surgical incision into the abdomen exposing the abdominal cavity.

Large-breed puppy diets – a complete puppy food fed to puppies that will be over 25 kg when adult. Fat and calories are altered in this type of diet compared to a standard puppy food, and calcium levels are controlled. This aids growth at the correct rate and may reduce future problems of joint disease; should be fed until the puppy is 12 months (some large breed puppy foods say up to 18 months) old.

Large intestine – the *distal* part of the digestive tract, made up of the *colon, caecum, rectum* and *anus*. See also *Anal glands, Defecation, Faeces*.

Larva – the immature stage that follows hatching from the egg in many insects, worms and arachnids. The larval stage is followed by the pupal stage in insects.

Laryngitis – inflammation of the larynx that may be caused by infectious agents, trauma, foreign bodies and excessive coughing.

Laryngospasm – a post-operative emergency where the *larynx* goes into spasm, causing the airway to occlude. Treatment includes keeping the *endotracheal tube* in place (if not already removed) and administering steroids to reduce the inflammation. A *tracheotomy* can be carried out if required.

Larynx – an area of the airway that connects the *nasopharynx* to the *trachea*. The *hyoid apparatus* is found here. Involved in vocalisation and in the prevention of food particles being inhaled into the trachea (see also *Cough reflex*, *Epiglottis*, *Vocal folds*.

Latent carrier – also known as a convalescent carrier; an animal that has recovered from a specific *disease*, so will no longer be showing clinical signs, but who may still be harbouring the *infectious* agent and be able to pass it onto others. See also *Convalescent carrier*.

Lateral – towards the side, away from the *midline* or *medial* plane.

Lateral canthus – the outer edge of the eyelids where the upper and lower lids join. See also *Medial canthus*.

Lateral recumbency – a patient lying on its side.

Lateral wall resection – surgery to remove the lateral wall of the *external ear canal* so that the vertical canal opens directly to the skin. Used to treat *chronic* persistent *otitis externa* in animals with stenosed ear canals. See also *Total ear canal ablation*, *Vertical canal ablation*.

Latissimus dorsi – one of the *muscles* of the shoulder, it draws the forelimb *caudally* and flexes the shoulder joint.

Lavage – the flushing of a cavity or *wound* using large volumes of *sterile* saline. High pressure lavage is a technique often used on *contaminated wounds* (eg a *lacerated wound*) where sterile saline is squirted onto the wound from a 20-ml syringe through a hypodermic needle. The fluid under pressure flushes out debris and bacteria from the wound.

Laxative – a drug or substance used to treat constipation, can be given orally or rectally depending on the type.

Laxity – loosening or lack of stability of a joint.

Lead – see *Protective clothing*.

Leading question – a type of questioning that leads the client or owner into making a certain response, eg so has he been drinking more?

Left shift – a term used to describe the release of increased numbers of immature (band) neutrophils from the bone marrow. Usually occurs during acute inflammation.

Legal accountability – that of the veterinary nurse is the responsibility of the veterinary surgeon.

Legibility – how easily another person's writing can be read.

Leiomyosarcoma – a tumour of the smooth muscle that may occur anywhere where there is smooth muscle, eg the uterus and gastrointestinal tract.

Leishman's stain – a stain for blood films that is useful for identifying some blood parasites, including *Leishmania*.

Leishmania – a flagellate protozoan parasite which is transmitted by sandflies; not present naturally in the UK but may be seen in animals that have travelled abroad. Clinical signs include anorexia, weight loss, lethargy, lymphadenopathy and skin lesions. Treatment is difficult and relapses may occur.

Lempert rongeur – used for 'nibbling' bone, this type of rongeur is particularly useful in spinal surgery.

Lens – a transparent structure located between the *anterior* and *posterior chambers of the eye*, supported by the *suspensory ligaments*. Its shape can be altered, controlled by *smooth muscle*; changing the lens shape causes light rays to be bent and focused onto the *retina*, allowing the eye to focus on near and distant objects. This process is called *accommodation*.

Lentivirus – causal agent of *feline immunodeficiency disease*.

Leptospira canicola – bacterium causing an *infectious*, *zoonotic disease* of the dog; spread by direct contact with the *urine* of infected dogs and rats. Clinical signs include *polydipsia*, *vomiting*, renal and hepatic damage. See also *Leptospira icterohaemorrhagiae*, Leptospirosis.

Leptospira icterohaemorrhagiae – bacterium causing an *infectious*, *zoonotic* disease of the dog; spread by direct contact with the *urine* of infected dogs and rats. Clinical signs include *vomiting* and *haemorrhagic diarrhoea*. See also *Leptospira canicola*, Leptospirosis.

Leptospirosis – *zoonotic* disease of dogs, caused by infection with *Leptospira canicola* or *Leptospira icterohaemorrhagiae*.

Lethargy – abnormal tiredness, sluggishness or lack of energy; a common symptom of many diseases.

Leucocyte (leukocyte) – a white blood cell; five types: the granulocytes (cytoplasm contains granules) are the *neutrophils*, *eosinophils* and *basophils*, and the agranulocytes (no granules in cytoplasm) are the *lymphocytes* and *monocytes*. They are an important part of the immune system.

Leucocytosis (leukocytosis) – an increase in the overall number of circulating leucocytes in the blood; may occur in many inflammatory diseases, during steroid treatment and in leukaemia.

Leucopenia (leukopenia) – a decrease in the overall number of circulating leucocytes in the blood; may occur in bone marrow disease, and in severe bacterial or viral infections (such as parvovirus).

Leukaemia – neoplasia of the haematopoietic system during which there are increased numbers of circulating neoplastic erythrocytes or leucocytes in the blood. Classified according to the affected cell line (*lymphoid*, *myeloid* or *erythroid*) and may be acute or chronic.

Levator nasolabialis – one of the muscles of facial expression, innervated by *cranial nerve VII* – the *facial nerve*.

Leydig cells – also called interstitial cells; found within the testes and produce the male sex hormone *testosterone*.

Libel – false written or defamatory information.

Libido – the drive for sexual behaviour; in male animals the hormone *testosterone* is responsible for libido.

Lichenification – thickening and hardening of the skin caused by persistent irritation and scratching; often occurs in dogs with chronic *pruritic* skin disease such as *atopy*.

Life cycle – the stages through which an organism passes during its life, eg the life cycle of a flea involves egg → larva → pupa → adult, the adult lays eggs and completes the cycle.

Ligament – a tough, fibrous band that joins two bones. See also *Tendon*.

Ligature – a length of sterile *suture* material that the surgeon ties tightly round a *blood vessel* to control *haemorrhage*.

Light beam diaphragm – a method of reducing and collimating the primary beam by illumination of the field of the primary beam.

Light marker – a piece of equipment used for labelling radiographic film; it is placed on after the exposure but before processing.

Lignocaine – a local anaesthetic available as an injection, a spray or a gel; takes effect quickly, usually within 3– 5 minutes, and can last up to $1\frac{1}{2}$ hours. Ideally used for short surgical procedures, or when a patient is not well enough to undergo a general anaesthetic; also for large-animal work, eg cow *Caesarean sections*.

Limb – an arm, leg or wing.

Limbus – the junction between the *sclera* and the *cornea* in the *eye*.

Line-breeding – when an animal breeds with a more distant relative such as a grandparent or cousin; undesirable for similar reasons to *in-breeding*.

Line-voltage compensator – maintains the voltage so that it remains constant by adjusting the incoming voltage.

Linea alba – meaning 'white line', a fibrous band that runs along the *midline* from the *xiphoid process* of the *sternum* to the *pubic symphysis*. The *internal* and *external oblique* and *transverse abdominal muscles* all insert here. Surgical incisions made through the linea alba to gain access to the *abdominal* cavity cause much less tissue damage than an incision through the abdominal muscles.

Linear foreign body – a foreign body in the gastrointestinal system that is elongated, such as a piece of string. May initially only cause partial obstruction and may be difficult to diagnose. Eventually the foreign body causes damage and 'bunching' of the gut and surgery is usually necessary to remove it and repair the gut.

Lingual – relating to the tongue.

Linognathus setosus – a sucking louse that occurs on the dog.

Linoleic acid – one of the three essential fatty acids.

Lint – an absorbent material with raised fibres on one side, often used in dressings or as surgical swabs.

Lipaemia – the turbid or opaque appearance of serum/plasma that occurs when there is an increase in fats (*triglycerides, cholesterol*, etc) in the blood; occurs normally following a meal, but fasting lipaemia may occur in diseases such as *hypothyroidism, diabetes mellitus* and *hepatic* disease.

Lipase – an enzyme produced by the pancreas and involved in digestion of fats; commonly measured on blood biochemistry profile. Increased blood lipase levels occur with pancreatitis.

Lipid – also known as fat; an organic compound consisting of *fatty acids* and *glycerol*. See also *Lipoma*.

Lipoma – a fatty lump or *benign tumour* of *adipose* cells, found in the *subcutaneous* tissue, very commonly seen in older, overweight dogs. Can grow quite large and start to hinder the animal's movement, in which case surgical removal is recommended.

Liquid paraffin – an oil-based liquid useful in treating constipation or as an agent (mixed with water) to perform an enema.

Lister scissors – scissors that are angled beyond the joint with a distinctive flattened tip used for cutting/removing bandages. The flattened tip prevents injury to the patient while the bandage is being removed.

Liston bone cutters – an instrument used for cutting bone.

Live vaccine – a *vaccine* containing a living, but harmless, strain of the *pathogen*. Once injected, these multiply in the host and create a long-lasting *active immune* response. See also *Inactivated (dead) vaccine*.

Liver – a large, firm, red/brown, lobed organ found in the cranial abdomen; has a dual blood supply from the hepatic artery and the *hepatic portal vein*. Has many functions, some of which include metabolism of proteins, fats and carbohydrates, detoxification, vitamin storage, production of *bile* and metabolism of *haemoglobin*. See also *Gall bladder*.

Lobe – a subdivision of an organ within the body, eg the *lungs* are divided into lobes – the left lung into cranial and caudal lobes, the right into cranial, middle and caudal lobes; the *liver* is divided into lobes that are then further subdivided into lobules.

Local anaesthetic – drug or agent used to provide local anaesthesia, eg lignocaine, bupivicaine, procaine.

Localised – describes a condition which affects only a small area of the body or system, eg *demodicosis* may be localised (affecting just a small area) or *generalised* (affecting the whole skin).

Locomotion – the act of walking/moving.

Long bone – a classification of bone that is characterised by a shaft and two ends and a medullary cavity. It has an outer layer (cortex) of *compact bone* and *spongy bone* at the ends, eg the *femur, tibia, humerus, radius*, etc. See also *Diaphysis, Epiphysis*.

Loop of Henlé – a loop in the renal tubule between the proximal and distal convoluted tubules; this part of the nephron is important for determining the concentration of urine.

Loose connective tissue – also known as *areolar tissue*; found between organs in the body and in the *subcutaneous* layer of the *skin*.

Lordosis – arching of the spine, eg this occurs in the female cat during mating.

Lymphadenopathy – disease or swelling of the *lymph nodes*.

Lymphangiectasia – dilation of the lymphatic vessels, which causes obstruction to lymph flow; may occur in the lymphatic vessels of the intestine and is a cause of chronic diarrhoea and protein-losing enteropathy.

Lymphatic system – consists of the *lymphatic vessels* and *lymph nodes*. The *thoracic duct* is the largest duct of the lymphatic system, starting as a small pouch in the *cisterna chyli*.

Lymphatic vessel – part of the lymphatic system, consisting of capillaries and veins which collect excess tissue fluid (*lymph*) and *chyle* from the gut. Those from the gut and caudal part of the body converge to form the *cisterna chyli*. Fluid from the lymphatic circulation drains back into the blood via the *thoracic duct*. Lymphatic vessels are similar in structure to *veins*, having thin walls and *valves* to prevent backflow of lymph.

Lymphocyte – an *agranulocyte* produced in the *bone marrow* (and thymus of young animals), makes up around 20–30% of the total *white blood cell* count. Occurs in two forms, *B* and *T lymphocytes*, and forms an important component of the immune response. T lymphocytes travel to the lymph nodes and attack invading cells directly. B lymphocytes circulate in the blood and produce *antibodies*.

Lymphocytosis – increase in the number of circulating lymphocytes; may occur in young animals, with adrenaline release (fear, excitement), in viral infections and with lymphoid disease such as lymphosarcoma.

Lymphoid – relating to the lymphatic system.

Lymphopenia – a decrease in the number of circulating lymphocytes; may occur with stress, steroid therapy, inflammation, immune suppression, renal failure and loss of lymph.

Lymphosarcoma – a *malignant tumour* of the *lymph nodes*; quite common in dogs and is also often seen in association with *feline leukaemia virus* in cats.

Lysis – rupture and breakdown of a cell by damaging the cell membrane.

Lysoenzyme – an enzyme that causes lysis of cells and breakdown of large molecules.

Lysosome – a vesicle within the *cell cytoplasm* that contains digestive *enzymes* used for breaking down worn-out cell components and foreign particles.

Macrocytic – literally means large cell; macrocytosis describes erythrocytes that are larger than usual, eg immature erythrocytes (reticulocytes) are macrocytic.

Macrophage – also known as a histiocyte; a large phagocytotic cell, usually found in connective tissue, that is involved with *inflammation* and with fighting *infection*. See also *Monocyte*, *Phagocytosis*.

Magill anaesthetic circuit – a non-re-breathing anaesthetic circuit, used to deliver and maintain anaesthesia and also to remove waste gases. It is a single tube with the valve and reservoir bag near the patient end, which can make it awkward to use. The Magill uses lower flow rates than the Bain circuit but cannot be used for intermittent positive pressure ventilation. Used in patients over 10 kg.

Magnesium (Mg^{2+}) – an electrolyte involved in the maintenance of muscles, bones and nerves; sometimes measured as part of a biochemistry profile.

Magnetic resonance imaging (MRI) – uses magnetism and radio waves. The patient is placed in a magnetic field, which enables the protons to spin (the speed depends on the strength of the magnetic field), radio waves then disrupt the protons, after which they retreat back to their original position. In doing so each proton produces a radio signal for each part of the body being examined. A computer then coverts these signals to a visible image. The patient has to be anaesthetised because they need to be still for the whole procedure.

Magnify, magnification – to increase or enlarge the size of the original object or image.

Malabsorption – a condition that occurs when there is damage to the intestinal mucosa and villi (or an inherited lack of receptors) so that products of digestion cannot be absorbed into the body. Clinical signs depend on which nutrient(s) cannot be absorbed, and may include diarrhoea and chronic weight loss.

Malassezia pachydermatis – A yeast organism which is commonly found on the skin. In healthy skin it does not cause disease but when the environment of the skin is altered *malassezia* can cause severe dermatitis. It is most commonly in ear canals and skin folds.

Maldigestion – a condition occurring when the ingesta cannot be digested properly because of a lack of digestive enzymes, eg *exocrine pancreatic insufficiency*.

Malformation – abnormal development affecting physical structure.

Malignant – a classification of a neoplastic *tumour* that is fast growing, aggressive, uncontrollable. It invades and destroys the tissue from which it originates and may also spread to other sites in the body. See also *Benign*, *Metastasis*.

Malleus – hammer-shaped *auditory ossicle* located in the *middle ear*. Situated next to the *incus* and *stapes*, the function of these three ossicles is to amplify sound-wave vibrations and carry them across the *middle ear* to the *oval window*.

Malocclusion – commonly seen in rabbits; a dental condition where one tooth does not correctly meet the corresponding tooth in the opposite jaw, leading to difficulties eating and grooming and to uneven wear/growth of the teeth.

Malunion – a fracture that has not healed in the correct alignment.

Mammary gland – a modified *sweat gland*; usually five pairs of mammary glands in the dog and four pairs in the cat. During *pregnancy*, the *hormone prolactin* stimulates the gland to produce milk and *oxytocin* stimulates milk letdown. The act of suckling by the offspring is the main stimulus for further milk production.

Mandible – the lower jaw, made up of two bones that are fused at the *mandibular symphysis*; forms a *synovial joint* with the *temporal bone* of the skull, known as the *tempromandibular joint*. See also *Maxilla*.

Mandibular symphysis – the point of the chin at which the two *mandible* bones are fused; a point of weakness in the jaw and a common site for fractures, especially in cats, following direct trauma, eg road traffic accident.

Mange – infection with mites; infection with *Sarcoptes* is called sarcoptic mange, infection with *Demodex* is called demodectic mange.

Manual expression of bladder – application of digital pressure on the caudal abdomen to empty the bladder or obtain a urine sample.

Manual Handling Regulations Act 1992 – a set of regulations governing the safe lifting, moving and handling of heavy objects. Aims to reduce the risk of injury by providing guidelines on safe lifting techniques and by encouraging a *risk assessment* to be carried out, before manual handling operations take place.

Manual restraint – the patient is given no drugs; the following aids can be used to help restrain the patient – cradles, sandbags, foam pads/wedges, rope ties, physical positioning (moving the patient).

Manubrium – a bony prominence on the *cranial* end of the first *sternebra*. See also *Xiphoid process*.

Manx cat – a breed of cat that has no tail as part of its genetic make-up.

Mapleson system – a classification system of non-re-breathing anaesthetic circuits.

Marginal ear vein – a *vein* running along the lateral edge of the *pinna*; usually the easiest site for *venepuncture* in a rabbit.

Marie's disease – see *Pulmonary osteopathy*.

Maslow's hierarchy of needs – a theory that each of the needs below needs to be achieved before moving to the next level. Once a person is 'self-actualised' he/she believes he/she is content. The needs are: body needs, security needs, social needs, ego needs, self-actualisation.

Masseter – one of the masticatory muscles, it runs from the *zygomatic arch* to the lateral side of the vertical ramus of the *mandible*; its function is to close the jaw.

Mast cell – a type of cell that is present in many body tissues (but not the blood) and is involved in allergic response and histamine release.

Mast cell tumour – a tumour composed of neoplastic *mast cells* that usually affects the skin. Mast cell tumours vary greatly in their behaviour from relatively *benign* to *malignant* tumours that may *metastasise*.

Mastication – the act of chewing.

Masticatory muscle myositis – a painful immune-mediated condition causing inflammation of the masticatory (chewing) muscles. Clinical signs include pain and restriction of movement when opening the mouth.

Mastitis – inflammation of the mammary gland. This may be caused by bacterial infection and usually occurs during lactation. Clinical signs include pain, firmness and increased warmth of the affected gland(s) and occasionally discoloration or lumps in the milk.

Maternally derived antibodies (MDA) – found in *colostrum* and absorbed by the *neonate* during the first 24 hours of life. Those neonates who drink plenty of colostrum during the first hours of their life will develop greater protection against *disease*. Weaker neonates who receive less colostrum tend to be more prone to *infection*.

Mating – when a male and female animal are brought together to breed.

Maturation – reaching maturity.

Maxilla – one of the bones of the *skull* that forms the upper jaw and contains the nasal chambers. See also *Mandible*.

Maximum exposure limit – a set of regulations approved by the *Health and Safety Executive* to limit the length of time employees can come into contact with hazardous substances to keep their exposure to the substance within safe levels. See also *Health and Safety at Work Act 1974*.

Mayo scissors – surgical scissors with smooth tips used for soft-tissue dissection and cutting; can have either straight or curved blades. See also *Metzenbaum scissors*.

McPhail needle holders – distinctive-looking, self-retaining needle holders with copper-lined jaws and pear-shaped handles. See also *Olsen–Hegar needle holders*.

Mechanoreceptors – receptors that measure the tension in the *lungs*. When there is an increase in tension, eg during inspiration, impulses are sent to the *respiratory centre* in the *brain*. This then inhibits *inspiration* so that *expiration* can occur, thus preventing overstretching of the lung tissue. See also *Hering–Breuer reflex*.

Meconium – the fetal gut contents that may sometimes be passed while the fetus is still in the uterus, particularly if there is a delay in parturition such as in *dystocia*.

Medial – toward the medial plane or midline; opposite to *lateral*.

Medial canthus – area on the *medial* aspect of the *eye* where the upper and lower eyelids meet. The *third eyelid* is also located here. See also *Lateral canthus*.

Mediastinal – relating to the *mediastinum*.

Mediastinum – the partition between the two pleural cavities in the thorax; within the mediastinal space the *heart*, *trachea*, *oesophagus*, *thymus*, *aorta* and various other *nerves* and vessels are located.

Medium (pl. **media)** – a term used in microbiology to describe the material used to transport and grow bacteria, fungi and viruses. *Simple media* contain a mixture of substances that provide the basic requirements for survival of undemanding species such as the bacteria *Escherichia coli. Complex media* are used to encourage the growth of more sensitive organisms, or to inhibit the growth of certain organisms.

Medulla – a term used to describe the innermost portion of an organ, eg the adrenal medulla, the renal medulla, or the medulla of bone and hair.

Medulla oblongata – an area in the *hindbrain* that is continuous with the *spinal cord*; it controls involuntary processes such a *respiration, heart rate* and *digestion*. See also *Respiratory centre*.

Medullary cavity – also known as the *bone marrow cavity* in *long bones*.

Megakaryocyte – a large cell found in the *bone marrow* that produces *thrombocytes*.

Megaoesophagus – dilation of part of the oesophagus; can be caused by diseases including hypothyroidism and myasthenia gravis and usually results in dysphagia and regurgitation.

Meibomian gland – also known as the tarsal gland; found along the edge of the eyelid. Secretes a fatty material that contributes to the *tear film*, which helps to lubricate the *cornea*.

Meiosis – the process by which cells divide to produce *gametes* (*spermatozoa* and *ova*). There are two phases of division that take place, each in five stages: *interphase*, *prophase*, *metaphase*, *anaphase* and *telophase*. Four daughter cells are produced, each containing the *haploid* number of *chromosomes* and each one contains a different mix of genetic material (genetic variation). See also *Mitosis*.

Melaena – partially digested blood in the faeces, which is visible; the faeces appear dark and tarry.

Melanin – a dark pigment present in the *skin*, hair and *iris* of the eye. See also *Melanocyte*.

Melanocyte – a specialised cell found in the *epidermis* of pigmented skin that produces the pigment *melanin*.

Melanoma – a tumour of the *melanocytes* in the *skin* and *mucous membranes* that is usually *malignant*.

Melatonin – a hormone produced by the pineal gland in the brain; its production is affected by light and it is involved in the body's natural clock.

Meninges – these membranes surround and protect the *brain* and *spinal cord*; made up of three layers, the *dura mater*, *arachnoid* and *pia mater*. See also *Meningitis*.

Meningitis – inflammation of the *meninges*, often resulting from bacterial infection. The disease can be diagnosed by analysing a sample of *cerebrospinal fluid*, usually taken from the *cisterna magna*.

Meniscus (pl. **menisci) – 1.** the curved upper surface of a liquid standing in a tube, produced by surface tension. **2.** a disc-shaped structure found in the *stifle joint* between the *femur* and the *tibia*. Injury to the stifle joint often occurs when the attachments of the menisci tear, leading to joint instability.

Mesentery – a layer of membranes in the *abdomen* and *pelvis* that suspends the gut from the body wall; also holds organs in place and provides a route for blood vessels and nerves to get to the organs. See also *Omentum*.

Mesocephalic – a description of skull shape; the 'normal' skull shape, as seen in Beagles, Labradors and Springer Spaniels. See also *Brachycephalic*, *Dolichocephalic*.

Mesoderm – a layer of tissue formed in an *embryo* that goes on to develop into the circulatory, musculoskeletal, reproductive and urinary systems.

Mesometrium – see *Broad ligament*.

Mesovarium – see *Broad ligament*.

Metabolic acidosis – see *Acidosis*.

Metabolic alkalosis – see *Alkalosis*.

Metabolic bone disease (MBD) – a nutritional disorder also known as *nutritional secondary hyperparathyroidism* commonly seen in captive reptiles; caused by the animal being given an unbalanced diet containing incorrect proportions of *calcium* and *phosphorus*, as well as inadequate exposure to ultraviolet B rays, leading to a deficiency of *vitamin D*. This causes uneven bone and shell formation, pathological fractures, soft, weak bones and, in severe cases, limb deformity. The condition known as 'rubber jaw' is seen when the bones of the mandible are so soft and malleable that the animal is unable to eat. See also *Rickets*.

Metabolism – the total amount of internal chemical and physical processes that occur within the animal and result in growth, energy production and waste elimination. See also *Basal metabolic rate*.

Metacarpus – the skeletal structure beyond the *carpus* of the forelimb, it consists of four parallel metacarpal bones that go on to connect to the *phalanges*. See also *Metatarsus*.

Metacestode – the larval stage of a tapeworm (cestode) that takes place in the intermediate host. There are a number of different types of metacestode, such as the *cysticercus*, *cysticercoid*, *coenurus* and *hydatid cyst*.

Metal bitch catheter – a type of urinary catheter specifically for bitches. Not often used.

Metal-frame splints – a splint applied to the distal end of the limb. The limb is slotted into the middle of the metal framework including the elbow. Not often used.

Metaldehyde – an agent found in slug bait that is poisonous if eaten by animals.

Metaphase – second stage of cell division (*mitosis* and *meiosis*) where the nuclear membrane breaks down and the *chromosomes* become attached to the *spindle* by their *centromeres*; followed by the third stage, *anaphase*.

Metaphyseal osteopathy – also called hypertrophic osteodystrophy; an *idiopathic* disease that mainly affects young large-breed dogs. Clinical signs include lameness and pyrexia. Radiography shows areas of lucency (reduced bone density) or extra bone formation in the metaphyses. Treatment involves pain relief and controlling the dog's growth rate.

Metaphysis – the part of a bone where bone growth occurs; located towards the end of the bone between the diaphysis and the epiphysis.

Metastasis – the spread of *tumour* cells via the *blood* and *lymphatic systems* into other organs or structure, often distant to the original tumour site. See also *Neoplasia*.

Metatarsus – bones of the hindlimb beyond the *tarsus*; the structure consists of four parallel metatarsus bones distal to the row of tarsal bones that go on to connect to the *phalanges*. See also *Metacarpus*.

Methicillin-resistant *Staphylococcus aureus*
  (MRSA) – a bacterium that has developed resistance to
  many antibiotics and is a serious problem in human
  medicine; can cause infections that are very difficult to treat.
  Transmission from human to human is thought to occur
  occasionally.

Metoestrus – the part of the reproductive cycle that follows
  oestrus in the bitch if fertilisation has not occurred. The
  hormones are similar to those during pregnancy and
  pseudopregnancy (false pregnancy) may occur.

Metritis – inflammation of the uterus, usually caused by
  bacterial infection; may occur following parturition.

Metzenbaum scissors – surgical scissors used for delicate
  soft-tissue dissection; characterised by their long handles
  and short blades. See also *Mayo scissors*.

Micelle – a water-soluble, lipid-containing structure that is
  made from fatty acids, cholesterol and fat-soluble vitamins;
  produced following fat digestion in the gut.

Micro- – meaning one-millionth, ie 1 g is 1,000,000 µg;
  1 litre is 1,000,000 µl.

Microaerophil – bacteria that require a lower concentration of
  oxygen than is found in air but that cannot survive in the
  absence of oxygen.

Microcytic – literally means small cell; describes erythrocytes
  that are smaller than usual, eg in iron-deficiency anaemia
  less haemoglobin is available and erythrocytes become
  microcytic.

Microfracture – very small fractures that can occur during fixation, particularly if a poor technique is used.

Microhaematocrit – a small capillary tube placed in a centrifuge and used to measure *haematocrit* in blood samples.

Microminerals – required by the body to maintain metabolic processes.

Micro-organism – any organism of microscopic size, eg *virus*, *bacteria*, *fungi*, *protozoa*.

Microscope – an essential piece of equipment in the veterinary laboratory, allowing the examination of biological samples such as blood smears or hair plucks by magnifying microscopic objects so they become visible. A moving stage is used to locate the specimen on the microscope slide, while the substage condenser focuses the light onto the specimen and the iris *diaphragm* regulates the amount of light on the stage. The *objective lenses* allow the specimen to be viewed at different magnifications, usually 4×, 10×, 40× and 100× (*oil immersion*). Types of microscope include light, compound, scanning electron and transmission electron. See also *Vernier scales*.

Microsporum canis – a fungal pathogen that is a common cause of *dermatophytosis* (ringworm) in cats and dogs.

Micturition – urination.

Midbrain – the area of the brain between the *thalamus* and the *pons*; contains two *ventricles*. Its primary job is to pass information regarding *vision* and hearing to the *forebrain*.

Middle ear – an air-filled cavity that lies within the *tympanic bulla* of the *temporal bone* of the *skull*; communicates with the *nasopharynx* via the *Eustachian tube* to ensure the pressure in the middle ear stays the same as the outer air pressure. The three auditory ossicles (*malleus, incus and stapes*) are located here. The function of the middle ear is to amplify sound waves and to pass them on to the *inner ear*. See also *Otitis media.*

Milli- – meaning one-thousandth, ie 1 g is 1000 mg; 1 litre is 1000 ml, etc.

Milliamperage (mA) – the number of electrons produced at the cathode, which determines the number of X-rays.

Mineral (ash) – a non-combustible residue. All animals require these essential minerals, which are divided into macrominerals and microminerals

Mineralocorticoids – steroid hormones, such as aldosterone, that are produced in the *adrenal* cortex and act on the kidney, regulating *electrolyte* and water balance in the body. Lack of mineralocorticoids occurs during *hypoadrenocorticism.*

Mini Lack anaesthetic circuit – a non-re-breathing anaesthetic circuit, used to deliver and maintain anaesthesia and also to remove waste gases. It uses lower flow rates than the standard Lack circuit

Minimum alveolar concentration (MAC) – the lowest concentration of an anaesthetic agent that produces no response in 50% of the patients exposed to a painful stimulus, ie those with a low MAC are potent anaesthetic agents, those with a high MAC are less potent, therefore more of the volatile gas will be needed.

Minute volume – the volume of air or gas inhaled in 1 minute; calculated by multiplying the *tidal volume* by the animal's body weight by the *respiration rate* (number of breaths per minute). The minute volume determines the amount of gas the patient will need when using an anaesthetic circuit. See also Flow rate calculations.

Miosis – constriction of the pupil to reduce the amount of light entering the eye; occurs in bright light, and also in conditions such as *Horner's syndrome*. Medication can be used to cause miosis, for example in the treatment of *glaucoma*.

Misalliance – mismating that can result in an unwanted pregnancy. It may occur in entire females that are not intended for breeding, or in breeding animals that are accidentally mated by the wrong dog or tom.

Misuse of Drugs Act 1971 – legislation, along with the *Misuse of Drugs Regulations 1985*, controlling the production, supply, possession, storage and dispensing of certain *controlled drugs* where the potential exists for abuse by humans. It states, among other things, that these drugs must be stored in a locked cupboard, which is attached to the wall and which is out of sight of the general public. A written record of all transactions involving Schedule 2 drugs must be kept.

Misuse of Drugs Regulations 1985 – legislation, along with the *Misuse of Drugs Act 1971*, controlling the production, supply, possession, storage and dispensing of certain *controlled drugs* where the potential exists for abuse by humans.

Mite – a type of arachnid (possessing eight legs) which may be parasitic. Common parasitic mites include *Sarcopes scabei, Demodex canis, Cheyletiella parasitivorax* and *Otodectes cynotis.*

Mitochondrion – cell *organelle* found in the *cytoplasm* that produces *adenosine triphosphate* (ATP), which generates energy to drive cellular reactions.

Mitosis – process by which body cells divide during periods of growth or when the body needs to replace cells that are damaged. There are five stages of division: *interphase, prophase, metaphase, anaphase* and *telophase.* Two identical daughter cells are produced, each containing the *diploid* number of *chromosomes.* See also *Meiosis.*

Mitral valve – see *Atrioventricular valves.*

Mixed dyspnoea – difficulty breathing on both expiration and inspiration.

M-mode (time-motion) – a type of image display used in ultrasound, commonly used in cardiology.

Mobility – the patient's ability to move.

Modified transudate – a type of effusion with a protein content and cell count between that of a transudate and an exudate; a non-specific finding and may be associated with many inflammatory, non-inflammatory and neoplastic diseases. Examination of the cells in the effusion may provide further information about the cause.

Molar – a type of tooth with multiple roots and a broad surface designed for crushing and chewing food. See also *Carnassial, Premolar.*

Molybdenum (Mo) – a metal that has a high melting point and is a poor conductor of heat, eg focusing cups are made of this.

Monochromatic film – used in radiography, sensitive to blue light and used with calcium tungstate intensifying screens.

Monocyte – an *agranulocyte* making up less than 5% of the total *white blood cell* count. When required, it leaves the *blood* to enter the *tissues* and acts as a *macrophage* dealing with *pathogens* by engulfing them by *phagocytosis* at the site of injury or infection.

Monocytosis – an increase in the number of circulating monocytes; may occur with stress, steroid therapy and infections.

Monoestrous – having one season or heat per year or breeding season.

Monorchid – an animal born with a testicle that is missing completely; this is very rare.

Monosaccharide – an individual sugar molecule.

Morbidity – refers to illness and disease and the extent of the individual illness or disease.

Morbillivirus – the causal agent of canine distemper.

Mordant – an iodine solution that causes the crystal violet stain to become chemically bound to the cell.

Morphine – an analgesic belonging to the opiate group; a full agonist.

Morphology – the shape, size and features of a cell or organism.

Mortality – death rate.

Morula – the stage of development when the conceptus has developed into a ball of cells and is ready for implantation into the uterus; follows the zygote stage.

Motivation – the feeling that drives a person to reach his/her goals or targets.

Motor neurone – an *efferent neurone* associated with movement and carrying *nervous impulses* from the *central nervous system* to *skeletal muscle* or to muscles within organs (*smooth muscle*).

Mouth breathing – breathing through an open mouth not the nose; a sign of distress or dyspnoea.

Movement blur – caused by movement of the patient, X-ray table, tube head or cassette; causes blurring of the image on the radiograph.

Mucolytic – a drug used to reduce the viscosity of mucus in the airways, eg bromhexine.

Mucometra – the build up of mucus inside the uterus; often occurs as a result of irritation and inflammation of the lining of the uterus (endometrium) and may develop into pyometra if there is bacterial infection.

Mucopurulent – used to describe any discharge caused by an infection consisting of mucus mixed with pus.

Mucosa – an alternative word for *mucous membrane*.

Mucous membrane – the moist mucus-secreting tissue lining the internal surface of many organs such as the gastrointestinal tract, reproductive tract, respiratory tract and also the orbit of the eye. Some mucosa are ciliated to waft the mucus along with waves of propulsion.

Mucus – a slimy, protective secretion of the *mucous membranes*; produced by *goblet cells* in the *epithelial* layer of the *skin*. See also *Mucopurulent*.

Multigravid – having had two or more pregnancies.

Multiparous – having produced live offspring from at least two pregnancies. See also *multigravid* and *primagravid*.

Multipolar – a type of *neurone* with one *axon* running from the *cell body* with several *dendrites* coming in, eg a *motor neurone*. It is the most common type of neurone in the *central nervous system*. See also *Bipolar, Unipolar*.

Muscle – contractile tissue that controls movement and locomotion. Made up of *actin* and *myosin* fibres. There are three types of muscle: *smooth, striated and cardiac*. Muscles are attached to bones by *tendons* and the action of muscles on *bones* allows movement to occur. Each muscle fibre is stimulated by a *nervous impulse* from a *motor neurone* to contract. The strength of contraction depends on how many motor neurones are stimulating the muscle fibres. See also *Muscle tone*.

Muscle relaxant drugs – see Depolarising neuromuscular blocking drugs, Non-depolarising neuromuscular blocking drugs.

Muscle tone – the degree of tension in a *muscle* while it is contracting. See also *Isometric, Isotonic*.

Muscular dystrophy – a rare inherited disease causing progressive muscle wasting and weakness; seen most commonly in Golden Retrievers and carries a guarded prognosis.

Musculoskeletal system – a system of the body made up of the *bones* of the *skeleton* and the *muscles* that attach to them, supporting the animal and allowing movement to take place.

Mutualistic relationship – a symbiotic relationship where both parties benefit, often they cannot live without each other.

Muzzle – **1.** the projecting part of a dog's face, the jaws and nose. **2.** a device made of plastic or strong material that is placed over a dog's nose and jaws to prevent it biting, eg while restraining the animal to take a blood sample.

Myasthenia gravis – an immune-mediated disorder that affects the *neuromuscular junction* and prevents transmission of nerve impulses; caused by antibodies attacking the acetylcholine (ACh) receptors. Clinical signs are generalised weakness and exercise intolerance; *megaoesophagus* may be a complication of this disease.

Mycoplasma haemofelis – previously known as *Haemobaronella felis*; a bacterium causing *feline infectious anaemia*. The organisms attach to the surface of *erythrocytes* and cause *haemolytic anaemia*.

Mydriasis – dilation of the pupil. See also *Miosis*.

Myelin sheath – a phospholipid layer produced by *Schwann cells* that is found wrapped round the *axon* of a *nerve* to increase the speed of conduction of the *nervous impulse*. Gaps in the myelin sheath (called the *nodes of Ranvier*) allow the impulse to travel even more quickly as it jumps from one gap to the next.

Myelography – a contrast study of the spine.

Myeloid – relating to cells and cell products that originate from the bone marrow, such as monocytes, neutrophils, platelets and erythrocytes (but not lymphocytes, See Lymphoid).

Myiasis – see *Fly strike*.

Myocarditis – inflammation of the *myocardium*. It is associated with *infectious diseases* such as *parvovirus*.

Myocardium – the muscular wall of the heart. See also Cardiac muscle.

Myoepithelial cells – specialised epithelial cells that can contract in a similar way to muscle cells. Their function is to squeeze the secretions out of glands, including mammary, sweat and salivary glands.

Myometrium – the thick muscular layer of the uterine wall that contracts to expel the fetus and fetal membranes during *parturition*.

Myopathy – a term used to describe non-inflammatory diseases of the muscles, eg *cardiomyopathy* (disease of the heart muscle), and myopathies which occur with *metabolic* diseases such as *hyperadrenocorticism* and *hypothyroidism*.

Myosin – one of the two *proteins* making up *muscle* fibres, playing an important role in muscle contraction. See also Actin.

Myositis – inflammation of the muscle, eg *masticatory muscle myositis* is inflammation of the masticatory (chewing) muscles. Generalised inflammation of the muscles is called *polymyositis*.

Myxoedema – a skin condition usually associated with hypothyroidism; skin appears thickened and puffy as a result of the presence of excessive fluid and proteins.

Myxomatosis – an infectious and usually fatal viral disease of rabbits causing swelling to the head, eyes and genitalia and a profuse *mucopurulent* discharge from the eyes and nose. There is a vaccine available that is given by a combination of subcutaneous and intradermal injections. It can be given from the age of 6 weeks and the animal will require an annual *booster*. See also *Viral haemorrhagic disease*.

N

Na – the chemical symbol for sodium.

Narcolepsy – a rare neurological condition in which the patient has excessive and overwhelming sleeping patterns.

Nares – the external nostrils, the opening to the *nasal cavity*.

Nasal cavity – extends from the external to the internal *nares*, where the air enters the *pharynx*; cavity is divided into left and right chambers by the *nasal septum*. In each chamber there are nasal turbinates, which are scroll-shaped bones covered in *ciliated mucous membranes* to moisten, warm and filter the air before it enters the respiratory tract.

Nasogastric tube – a feeding tube passed via the central meatus into the oesophagus to enable artificial feeding.

Nasolacrimal duct – the *duct* that carries *tears* from the *nasolacrimal sac* to the nasal cavity. See also *Fluorescein*.

Nasopharynx – part of the *pharynx* located above the *soft palate*.

Nausea – the sensation of feeling sick, of needing to *vomit*. Animals will sometimes lick their lips repeatedly when they are experiencing a feeling of nausea. See also *Anti-emetic drugs*, *Emetic*.

Neck lesion – see *Feline odontoclastic resorptive lesions*.

Necropsy – see *Post mortem*.

Necrosis – cell or tissue death.

Negative contrast – contrast medium that is more radiolucent than the surrounding tissue, eg oxygen, room air.

Negative feedback – a control mechanism used widely in the body where the product of a process inhibits further production of that product, eg thyroid hormones: the presence of high levels of thyroid hormones in the blood inhibits further production of thyroid-releasing hormone in the hypothalamus and thyroid-stimulating hormone in the pituitary gland, thereby inhibiting further production of the thyroid hormones in the thyroid gland.

Negligence – carelessness, want of proper care and attention; the failure to exercise the normal level of skill and judgment that would be expected.

Nematode – roundworm; there are a number of important nematode parasites that affect animals in the UK including *Toxocara*, *Toxascaris*, *Uncinaria*, *Trichuris*, *Aelurostrongylus*, *Filaroides* and *Angiostrongylus*.

Neonate – describes a newly born animal. See also *Caesarean section*, *Colostrum*, *Congenital*, *Fading puppy/kitten syndrome*, *Weaning*.

Neoplasia – literally meaning 'new growth'; describes purposeless uncontrolled growth and proliferation of new cells, can be *malignant* or *benign*. See also *Tumour*.

Neospora caninum – a tissue-cyst-forming coccidian parasite that causes neuromuscular disorders, particularly in puppies and young dogs.

Nephrectomy – surgical removal of a kidney.

Nephritis – a generalised term meaning inflammation of the *kidney*; does not indicate which parts of the kidney are affected. See also *Glomerulonephritis, Nephrosis, Pyelonephritis.*

Nephron – a urinary tubule found in the *kidney*; consists of the *glomerulus, Bowman's capsule, proximal convoluted tubule, loop of Henlé, distal convoluted tubule* and *collecting duct.* Blood enters the glomerulus at high pressure so that some fluid passes out into the tubule. As the fluid passes along the nephron, water and *electrolytes* are selectively reabsorbed and *urea* is excreted into the tubule. By the time it reaches the collecting duct, the fluid is called *urine.* It is then passed out of the kidney to the *bladder* via the *ureters.*

Nephrosis – non-inflammatory damage to the renal tubules, often caused by ischaemia (lack of oxygen) or toxicity (drugs, anti-freeze, heavy metals, non-steroidal anti-inflammatories).

Nephrotic syndrome – a condition resulting from chronic protein leakage into the urine from damaged *nephrons* (eg in *glomerulonephritis*). Chronic protein loss causes *hypoproteinaemia*. The clinical signs include weight loss, *oedema* and *ascites* (as a result of hypoproteinaemia); *chronic renal failure* and *uraemia* (if a significant portion of renal tissue is damaged); and sudden death/respiratory compromise from *pulmonary thromboembolism*.

Nephrotomy – a surgical incision into a kidney.

Nerve – a bundle of nerve fibres (*axons*) which connect the *brain* and *spinal cord* to various parts of the body and along which *nervous impulses* pass. The fibres are either *afferent* (leading toward the brain and conveying sensory information or *efferent* (leading away from the brain and conveying sensor function information. See also *nervous system*.

Nervous impulse – a nervous impulse starts at the *dendrites* of the *cell body* and is then passed down the *axon* to the nerve endings. From there, it must either pass onto another *neurone*, or to a *muscle* fibre. See also *Neuromuscular junction*, *Synapse*.

Nervous system – a system made up of two parts, the c*entral nervous system* (CNS) comprising the *brain* and *spinal cord*, and the *peripheral nervous system* (PNS) made up of *cranial,* spinal and *autonomic* nerves. The nervous system allows the body to react to the external environment. It does this by receiving and interpreting internal and external stimuli and then reacting accordingly. It is the most complex system in the body.

Neurogenic shock – this occurs when there is serious damage to the central nervous system, for example spinal or brain injury.

Neuroglia – see *Glial cells*.

Neurohypophysis – or posterior hypophysis; the posterior lobe of the *pituitary gland* in the brain. Secretes the hormones *oxytocin* and *antidiuretic hormone* (ADH).

Neuroleptic anaesthesia – a combination of a sedative (phenothiazine or benzodiazepine) and an opioid drug, eg acepromazine and buprenorphine.

Neurological – relating to the *nervous system*.

Neuromuscular junction – the point at which the *nervous impulse* is transmitted from the *neurone* to its *muscle* fibre, stimulating the muscle to contract. See also *Motor neurone*, *Synapse*.

Neurone – a nerve cell specialising in the transmission of *nervous impulses*. A neurone is made up of a *cell body*, *dendrites* and an *axon*. A neuron can be *unipolar*, *bipolar* or *multipolar*. See also *Afferent*, *Efferent*, *Motor neurones*.

Neurotransmitter – a chemical substance (eg *acetylcholine* or *noradrenaline*) released by a *neurone* at a *synapse* to allow the *nervous impulse* to travel across the synapse. The transmitter moves across the synapse and attaches to receptors on the second neurone. There it can stimulate an *action potential* in the second neurone, so that the nervous impulse is continued.

Neutering – surgically preventing reproduction, eg castration.

Neutral-buffered formalin – a 10% solution of formalin in saline that is buffered to protect against changes in pH. Protects the sample from damage caused by changing acidity.

Neutralisation plate – used in internal fixation, when a fracture has been repaired with lag screws; it supports the screws to prevent refractures.

Neutron – a particle carrying no charge; found in the nucleus of the atom.

Neutropenia – a decrease in the number of circulating *neutrophils*; may be caused by overwhelming viral infections (such as *parvovirus*), severe acute bacterial infection, bone marrow disorders and *autoimmune* disease.

Neutrophil – the most commonly seen *granulocyte*, makes up around 60% of the total *white blood cell* count. Produced in the *bone marrow* and its role is *phagocytosis* and destruction of *bacteria*. Immature (*band*) *neutrophils* are released into the blood in cases of overwhelming bacterial infection.

Neutrophilia – an increase in the number of circulating *neutrophils*; may be caused by stress, steroids (including hyperadrenocorticism), inflammation and fear or excitement.

Nictitans gland – a structure at the *medial canthus* of the *eye* that secretes a lubricating fluid onto the *cornea*. See also *Cherry eye*.

Nictitating membrane – also known as the *third eyelid*, this is a protective fold of *conjunctiva* supported by a piece of *cartilage* and attached to the *medial canthus*. It moves across the eye when the eyelids are closed, providing additional protection. Failure of the third eyelid to retract fully when the eye is open can be a sign of trauma or of illness.

Nit – the eggs produced by *lice*; they are cemented to the animal's hair.

Nitrites (in urine) – often tested for in urine samples using the commercially available urine dipsticks; their presence indicates Gram-negative bacteria in the urine. This test is not particularly reliable in dogs and cats.

Nitrous oxide (N_2O) – a gas used to help maintain anaesthetics; itself a weak anaesthetic agent, it also possesses good analgesic properties.

Nocturnal – animals that are naturally active at night and that sleep during the day. See also *Diurnal*.

Node of Ranvier – a small gap between the adjacent *Schwann cells* on the *nerve axon*. The *nervous impulse* is said to jump from one node of Ranvier to another and this type of impulse transmission occurs much quicker than in non-myelinated axons.

Non-adhesive dressings – dressings that do not stick to the wound; they have good absorptive properties and maintain a moist environment.

Non-depolarising neuromuscular blocking drug (NMBDs) – used in anaesthesia to achieve a high level of muscle relaxation, eg vecuronium.

Non-direct trauma – damage caused by excessive force on the bone.

Non-essential amino acids – proteins are formed from amino acids joined together by peptide bonds; there are 12 non-essential amino acids. See also *Essential amino acids*.

Non-ionic contrast media – water-soluble positive contrast media, of a lower osmolar concentration than ionic contrast media (to reduce side-effects); suitable for myelography and intravascular use.

Non-obstructive dystocia (primary uterine inertia) – the uterus is unable to contract strongly enough to expel the fetuses.

Non-re-breathing anaesthetic circuits – classification of anaesthetic circuits. Expired gases are transported to the atmosphere and cannot be re-breathed. These include the Bain, Lack, T-piece (with or without the Jackson–Rees modification) and Magill circuits.

Non-screen film – radiographic film used with cassettes but no intensifying screens; used when finer detail is required.

Non-steroidal anti-inflammatory drug (NSAID) – used to treat pain, inflammation and pyrexia by blocking the release of substances that cause inflammation, eg meloxicam, carprofen and tepoxalin.

Non-union (surgical nursing) – complete failure of the fractured ends of a bone to unite.

Non-verbal communication – affects the way in which you are perceived, eg facial expression, posture, gestures, eye contact. Can also include sign language, Braille and images.

Noradrenaline – *hormone* secreted by the adrenal medulla and used by the *synspathetic nervous system*. It is involved in the 'fight or flight' reaction, causing among other things a quickening of the *heart* beat, an increase in the force of the hearts contraction and an opening of the airways in the *lungs*. See also *adrenaline*.

Normochromic – describes erythrocytes that contain a normal amount of haemoglobin. See also *Hypochromic*.

Normocytic – describes erythrocytes of a normal size. See also *Macrocytic*, *Microcytic*.

Notoedres cati – a parasitic mite that is rare in the UK, tends to affect cats and rabbits. Similar to *Sarcoptes* in appearance and has a characteristic thumbprint pattern on the dorsum.

Nucleated red blood cell (nRBC) – also called metarubricytes or late normoblasts; immature *erythrocytes* that have been released from the bone marrow before they have lost their nucleus. Represent the stage before *reticulocytes* in the maturation process and are rare in the blood of normal animals. The presence of increased nucleated red blood cells indicates a strongly *regenerative anaemia*. Other causes may include disorders in erythrocyte production in the bone marrow (often associated with feline leukaemia virus infection), lead poisoning and animals that have had their spleen removed.

Nucleolus (pl. **nucleoli)** – region in the *nucleus* containing ribonucleic acid (RNA) and *ribosomes*.

Nucleus (pl. **nuclei)** – part of the cell containing the genetic material in the form of *deoxyribonucleic acid* (DNA); also contains one or more *nucleoli*.

Nucleus pulposus – the semi-fluid centre of an *intervertebral disc*. See also *Annulus fibrosus*.

Nulliparous – a term used to describe an animal that has never given birth.

Nursing clinics – consultations with nurses who create awareness and promote animal care, eg puppy parties, senior health clinics, dental advice.

Nutrition – food and fluid that is essential to maintain life, growth and good health.

Nymph – the second stage of the life cycle of some parasites.

Nystagmus – abnormal flicking movements of the eyeballs; may suggest that the animal has received trauma to the head and is suffering from some degree of brain damage.

O

Obesity – severely overweight, can be the result of overfeeding or a medical condition.

Objective (microscope) – the objective is a lens that gathers light once it has passed through a specimen on a microscope stage; usually a range of objective lenses on each microscope of different strengths, allowing the specimen to be observed at different magnifications.

Objectivity (communication) – speaking or recording of factual information only and avoiding making personal comments.

Obstetrics – the branch of medicine concerned with caring for a patient during *pregnancy*, the birth and the weeks immediately after the birth.

Obstipation – constipation resulting from an obstruction.

Obstructive dystocia – when a puppy or kitten becomes stuck in the birth canal, often as the result of an oversized fetus or a narrow birth canal.

Occipital bone – the *flat bone* at the back of the *skull* surrounding the *foramen magnum*. The muscles that support the head and neck attach here. See also *Temporal bone*.

Occlusion – **1.** blockage within an opening or passage. **2.** refers to the alignment and relationship between the upper and lower teeth and jaws.

Occult blood – blood that is not visible to the naked eye. Faecal samples may be tested for occult blood if there is suspicion of chronic haemorrhage from the gut. Patient must have a minimum of 5 days on a red-meat-free diet before testing to avoid false-positive results.

Occupational Exposure Standard – legislation used to control the exposure of personnel to *inhalational anaesthetic agents*. If the level is exceeded, the employer must identify the reason for this and take the appropriate action to rectify the problem.

Ocular larval migrans – *nematode* larvae that migrate to the eye and cause damage to the vision in the affected eye. *Toxocara canis* is a potentially *zoonotic* nematode parasite which can have this affect in humans.

Oculomotor nerve – *cranial nerve III*; concerned with the innervation of the muscles of the eyeball and *iris*.

Odour – a noticeable smell.

Oedema – an abnormal accumulation of fluid within the tissues or a body cavity. See also *Ascites*, *Hydrothorax*.

Oesophageal hiatus – one of three holes in the *diaphragm*; allows the *oesophagus* and vagal nerves to pass through. See also *Aortic hiatus*.

Oesophageal stethoscope – a piece of anaesthetic monitoring equipment; a plastic tube attached to an earpiece that is carefully fed down into the oesophagus. Once it is positioned correctly, it allows heart and lung sounds to be heard and therefore heart and respiration rate to be monitored.

Oesophagus – part of the *digestive system*; a muscular tube linking the *pharynx* to the *stomach*, lined with *stratified squamous epithelium*. The circular and longitudinal muscle fibres in the oesophagus wall propel food particles to the stomach. See also *Oesophageal stethoscope, Trachea*.

Oestradiol – the main oestrogen hormone; produced mainly in the ovaries but also in the placenta and testes.

Oestrogens – a group of steroid hormones (the most important being oestradiol) that are the female sex hormones; mainly secreted by the ovary and are important in controlling the oestrus cycle.

Oestrous cycle – the reproductive cycle; different phases in the cycle (*anoestrus, pro-oestrus, oestrus, metoestrus, dioestrus*) are dictated by the reproductive hormones *progesterone, oestrogens, follicle stimulating hormone, luteinising hormone* and *prolactin*.

Oestrus – also called heat or season; the period during the *oestrous cycle* when the female will accept the male and allow mating.

Off-loading – passing responsibility onto a third party, often blaming the third party.

Oil immersion – a special oil used in microscopy to improve the clarity and examination of samples such as blood smears. Always use the oil immersion lens on the microscope.

Olecranon – a bony projection on the *proximal* end of the *ulna* that helps to stabilise the elbow joint.

Olfaction – the sensation of smelling; the most highly developed sense in the dog and cat because it plays an important role in hunting, recognition of other animals and territory demarcation. See also *Olfactory bulb, Olfactory nerve*.

Olfactory bulb – area of the *brain* that lies under the *cerebrum*; receives sensory input from the *olfactory nerves*.

Olfactory nerve – *cranial nerve I*; originating from the *olfactory bulb* and concerned with the sense of smell.

Oligosaccharide – a short chain of sugar molecules.

Oliguria – the production of an unusually small quantity of urine (ie less than 7 ml/kg per day); can be caused by early-stage *acute renal failure* or end-stage *chronic renal failure*. See also *Anuria, Urination, Urine*.

Olsen–Hegar needle holders – self-retaining needle holders with incorporated scissors below the needle-holding tips to allow sutures to be cut. See also *McPhail needle holders* and *Gillies*.

Omentum – a double-layered sheet of *peritoneum* in the *abdominal* cavity with a lace-like structure. It is also known as the 'abdominal policeman' because it protects the organs and can help them to heal/repair themselves after surgery. See also *Mesentery*.

Omnivores – an animal that eats a wide range of foodstuffs, including animal and plant material. See also *Carnivore, Herbivore*.

Omotransversarius muscle – one of the muscles of the shoulder and neck, it acts to advance the forelimb.

Oncotic pressure – also called colloidal osmotic pressure; in the blood large molecules such as plasma proteins prevent fluid from leaving the blood and passing into tissues – this is oncotic pressure. Most of it is provided by albumin. Loss of plasma proteins (for example protein-losing enteropathy) causes a loss of oncotic pressure and can result in tissue oedema and ascites.

Oocysts – a stage in the life cycle of coccidian parasites such as *Toxoplasma, Neospora* and *Eimeria*; the infectious stage, usually shed in the faeces and ingested by the intermediate host, where they undergo further development.

Open anaesthetic circuits – this term of classification has been largely superseded by non-re-breathing circuits; however, it referred to a method of applying a volatile agent (eg chloroform) on a wad of material and the patient inhaling the agent.

Open question – encourages clients/colleagues to talk. The answer to an open question is left entirely to the client/colleague, eg what's his drinking like? See also *closed question/leading question*.

Ophthalmic – relating to the eyes.

Ophthalmology – the study of the structure and function of the eye; deals with disease and disorders of the eyes.

Ophthalmoscope – an illuminating instrument for examining the retina of the eye.

Opioid analgesics – potent analgesics derived from opium, although there are a range of synthetic and natural versions available. Side-effects include respiratory depression and decreased motility of the gastrointestinal tract; these products are also addictive. Pethadine is the only one licensed for use in animals.

Opportunistic pathogen – a commensal organism that can cause disease if present in high numbers or if the host's immune system is compromised.

Optic chiasma – an area in the ventral *forebrain* where the *optic nerves* cross over, distributing nerve fibres to both sides of the *brain* and to both *eyes*.

Optic disc – also known as the blind spot; the area on the retina where all the optic nerves leave the eye. There are no *photoreceptor cells* in the optic disc. See also *Fovea*.

Optic nerve – *cranial nerve II*; concerned with vision.

Oral – relating to the mouth.

Oral cavity – the area inside the mouth behind the lips. See also *Oral*.

Orbicularis oculi – a superficial facial muscle that acts to close the eye.

Orbicularis oris – a superficial facial muscle that acts to close the mouth.

Orbit – the pair of bony cavities in the skull in which the *globe* (eyeball) and associated muscles are housed; protected on the lateral side by the *zygomatic arch*.

Organ – an independent structure in the body made up of specific tissue and adapted to perform a particular function, eg *heart*, *lungs*.

Organ of Corti – part of the *cochlea* in the *inner ear* that contains sensory hairs, which detect the vibrations from sound waves in the *perilymph* and provide the sensation of hearing. See also *Semi-circular canals*.

Organelle – a microscopic membrane-bound structure within a cell, eg *mitochondria*, *Golgi body*, *endoplasmic reticulum*.

Organophosphate (OP) – chemicals that were commonly used in the past to treat ectoparasite infections such as sarcoptic and demodectic mange, eg amitraz. Now used infrequently because they can have toxic side-effects, and can cause serious environmental damage if released into waterways. Clinical signs of OP toxicity include drooling, dilated pupils, lack of co-ordination and seizures. The antidote is *atropine*.

Orifice – an opening onto the outside of the body.

Origin (relating to muscles) – the point of attachment of a *muscle* to a *bone* that is least moveable during muscle contraction. See also *Insertion*.

Oropharynx – the area of the *pharynx* between the *soft palate* and the *epiglottis*. The oropharynx is in contrast to the *rasopharynx*, the part of the throat that lies behind the nose.

Orphan – a very young animal with no mother.

Orthochromatic film – has dye added to the emulsion to include green and yellow parts of the visible spectrum. It is used with green-emitting, rare-earth intensifying screens.

Orthopaedic ruler – a metal ruler used to measure pins, wire and screws.

Orthopaedic wire – see *Cerclage wire*.

Orthopaedics – the field of veterinary science concerned with surgically correcting disorders and deformities of bones and joints.

Orthopnoea – difficulty breathing when the patient is lying down.

Os penis – a bone found running along the centre of the penis of the dog and cat (although it is very short in the cat); contributes to the rigidity of the penis when erect and is part of the *splanchnic skeleton*. If there are urinary *calculi* present in the *urethra*, a common site of obstruction is just caudal to the os penis because the urethra narrows here. A *urethrotomy* can be carried out to remove the calculi blocking the urethra.

Oscillating saw – a piece of equipment with a moving blade to remove casts.

Osmoreceptors – sensory receptors found in the *hypothalamus* that detect changes in osmotic pressure in the blood and, if increased, can stimulate the sensation of thirst.

Osmosis – the movement of water molecules across a semi-permeable membrane from a weak/dilute solution into a strong/concentrated solution until the concentrations of both solutions on either side of the membrane are equal. See also Diffusion.

Osmotic pressure – a measure of the strength of the osmotic draw on water provided by dissolved substances across a semi-permeable membrane. Part of the osmotic pressure is provided by the *oncotic pressure*, while the rest is provided by other dissolved substances such as sodium (Na^+) ions. For example a very strong salt solution draws water more strongly across a semi-permeable membrane (has a higher osmotic pressure) than a very weak salt solution does.

Ossification – the process by which *osteoblasts* produce new *bone* in the growing animal. See also Endochondral ossification, Intramembranous ossification.

Osteoarthritis – arthritis with some degree of bony involvement; characterised by degenerative changes to cartilage as well as bony spurs.

Osteoblast – a cell that produces the bone matrix.

Osteoclast – a cell that breaks down the bone matrix.

Osteocyte – a bone cell that recycles the minerals within the bone matrix; found within *osteons* in layers around the *Haversian canal*.

Osteoma – a fairly uncommon, benign bone tumour that is slow growing and usually affects the skull or mandible.

Osteomyelitis – inflammation of the bone and bone marrow, usually caused by bacterial infection; usually associated with open fractures, fracture repairs where implants have been placed in the bone, or secondary to tumours or soft tissue infections adjacent to the bone (eg severe periodontal disease). May be difficult to treat because many antibiotics do not penetrate the bone very well.

Osteon – the structural unit of *bone* consisting of layers of *osteocytes* around a central canal (*Haversian canal*) which contains the blood vessels supplying the bone. See also *Haversian system*.

Osteopathy – any disease process in the bone.

Osteophyte – a spur of abnormal extra bone growth in the area of a joint, usually result of injury to the joint surface (eg arthritis). Can be seen on radiography and may cause pain and restriction of movement in the affected joint.

Osteosarcoma – an extremely aggressive *malignant bone tumour*, most often seen on the *humerus*, *radius*, *femur* or *tibia*. Clinical signs include swelling, lameness and severe pain. Can be diagnosed by *radiography* and/or bone biopsy. Treatment involves removing the primary tumour, usually by limb amputation, and then *chemotherapy* to treat the *metastases*. Prognosis is poor.

Osteotome – an *orthopaedic* instrument used to make a precise cut into a bone. The tip is bevelled on both sides. See also *Chisel*.

Otitis externa – inflammation of the *external ear* canal as far as the *tympanic membrane*; caused by *parasites* (*Otodectes cynotis*), presence of a foreign body (eg grass seed), allergic skin disease or bacterial or fungal (usually *Malassezia*) infection. Breeds with very hairy, narrow ear canals or those with floppy ears are also predisposed to the condition. Clinical signs include scratching at the ear, head shaking, excess black wax in the ear, *aural haematoma* (caused by the excessive head shaking). Treatment includes administering topical antimicrobial and anti-inflammatory drugs, removal of the foreign body, antiparasite treatment and in extreme, non-responsive cases, surgery to perform *lateral wall resection*, *vertical canal ablation* or *total ear canal ablation*.

Otitis interna – inflammation of the *inner ear*; generally caused by an extension of *otitis externa* and *otitis media* but usually accompanied by vestibular symptoms such as *nystagmus*, circling and loss of balance because of infection and inflammation of the vestibular apparatus. Diagnosis can be confirmed by *radiography* of the *tympanic bulla*. Treatment is difficult and may involve medical treatment with antibiotics and anti-inflammatory drugs and/or surgical management.

Otitis media – inflammation of the *middle ear*; usually occurs as the result of the spread of *otitis externa* into the middle ear through a ruptured *tympanic membrane*. Symptoms and treatment are similar to those of otitis externa, although topical preparations should be avoided in the case of a ruptured tympanic membrane.

Otodectes cynotis – a non-burrowing parasitic mite that inhabits the external ear and causes irritation and inflammation of the ear canal in affected dogs and cats.

Otoscope – see *Auroscope*.

Out-breeding – breeding an animal with an unrelated animal; desirable because there is greater variety in the genes (increased heterozygosity) and fewer inherited diseases.

Oval window – also known as the vestibular window; an opening in the bony labyrinth in the *middle ear*. The *auditory ossicles* transmit the sound-wave vibrations across the middle ear and onto the *oval window*, which then transmits them into the inner ear.

Ovarian pedicle – the suspensory ligament of the ovary and associated blood vessels which holds the ovary in place in the abdomen. This is ligated (tied-off) and cut during ovariohysterectomy.

Ovariohysterectomy (OHT) – also called neutering or spaying; surgical removal of the uterus and ovaries, usually performed to prevent breeding, or to treat a medical condition such as pyometra.

Ovary – a pair of almond-shaped *endocrine glands* found in the abdomen of a female animal that are responsible for growing, maturing and releasing *ova* from their *follicles* (a process called *ovulation*) and for secreting the female hormones *oestrogen* and *progesterone*. See also *Testis*.

Overtransfusion (of fluids) – the patient has received too much fluid either crystalloid or colloids; signs include increased urination, coughing, noisy lung sounds and oedema (at worst pulmonary oedema). Overinfusion with a colloid could lead to right-sided heart failure.

Oviducts – see *uterine tubes*.

Oviparous – meaning to lay eggs; refers to birds and most reptiles. See also *Ovoviviparous*, *Viviparous*.

Ovoviviparous – refers to some species of reptile that retain the eggs within the body until they are ready to hatch out with live young. See also *Oviparous*, *Viviparous*.

Ovulation – the release of an ovum from an ovarian follicle under the action of various reproductive hormones.

Ovum – the female gamete (egg), produced in the ovary and released into the uterine tube during ovulation.

Oxalate crystals (calcium oxalate crystals) – a type of crystal sometimes found in urine. Low numbers may be found in normal animals but high numbers may reflect ethylene glycol (antifreeze) poisoning or elevated calcium levels in the urine.

Oxygen – required to maintain life; a colourless, odourless gas that is explosive when mixed with other anaesthetic agents. Cylinders are black with white shoulders.

Oxygen flush valve – A button that is pressed to deliver a high flow of oxygen only; found on the anaesthetic machine.

Oxygen therapy (oxygenation) – delivering oxygen only to a patient to prevent or treat hypoxia. Can be administered by: face mask, oxygen tent, nasal tubes, endotracheal tube (if unconscious or anaesthetised) or circuits (pointing the end of the circuit towards the nose and mouth).

Oxytocin – a hormone produced by the posterior *pituitary gland* that stimulates uterine contractions during parturition and milk let-down during lactation.

P

P-wave – the first part of an *electrocardiograph* trace, represents depolarisation of the atria. See *electrocardiograph*.

Packed cell volume (PCV) – the proportion of blood made up by erythrocytes (and not including leucocytes or platelets); usually expressed as a percentage. See also *Haematocrit*.

Palatability – how appealing a food or fluid is, ie if a food is not very palatable then a patient is unlikely to eat it.

Palate – the palate forms the roof of the oral cavity: the *rostral* portion is firm and immobile and is called the *hard* palate; the caudal portion is a mobile muscular flap, is involved with the swallowing mechanism and is called the *soft* palate.

Palatine – relating to the palate. See also *Hard palate*, *Soft palate*.

Palliative – a treatment that relieves the symptoms of a disease but does not cure it, eg caring for patients in organ failure or with incurable (terminal) cancer.

Palmar – an anatomical description of the area of the front paws where the pads are located; the opposite surface is known as *dorsal*. See also *Plantar*.

Palpation – using digital pressure to examine the body.

Palpebra (pl. **Palpebrae)** – also known as the eyelids. See also *Ectropion*, *Entropion*.

Palpebral reflex – blinking of the eyelids when the medial canthus is touched.

Pancreas – a mixed gland (having both *endocrine* and *exocrine* functions) located between the *stomach* and the *duodenum*. The exocrine part of the pancreas produces a watery *alkaline* secretion containing digestive enzymes, eg *amylase*, nucleotidase, *lipase* and also *bicarbonate*. The release of this secretion into the *duodenum* is stimulated by *cholecystokinin*. Within the pancreas are areas of endocrine tissue called the *islets of Langerhans*, made up of three types of cells: alpha, beta and delta cells. Alpha cells secrete *glucagon* in response to a fall in blood glucose levels, beta cells secrete *insulin* in response to a rise in *blood glucose* levels and delta cells produce *somatostatin*, which prevents dangerous swings in blood glucose levels and reduces the movement of food along the digestive tract.

Pancreatic juice – a mixture of digestive enzymes (including *amylase*, *trypsin*, *chymotrypsin* and *lipases*) and bicarbonate that is produced by the pancreas. This juice is released into the *duodenum* through the pancreatic ducts when stimulated by the hormone *cholecystokinin*. Production of pancreatic juice is an *exocrine* function of the pancreas.

Pancreatitis – inflammation of the pancreas, may be *acute* or *chronic*. Clinical signs include vomiting, diarrhoea and cranial abdominal pain. Factors that contribute to the development of pancreatitis include high-fat diet or obesity, trauma, obstruction of the pancreatic duct or *ischaemia* of the pancreas.

P

Pancytopenia – decreased numbers of all the cell lines originating from the bone marrow (ie pancytopaenia = anaemia + neutropenia + thrombocytopenia); may result from bone marrow disease or from suppression of bone marrow function with medication such as *chemotherapy*.

Pandemic – an epidemic covering a very large area, such as a hemisphere or worldwide, eg the virus that causes human influenza.

Panleucopenia – see *Feline infectious enteritis*.

Papillae – tiny fleshy nodules that cover the tongue and have a variety of functions including taste sensation (*gustation*), grooming and movement of food *boluses* caudally towards the pharynx. Most of the tongue is covered with filiform papillae. Fungiform, vallate and foliate papillae are present in lower numbers.

Papillary muscle – muscular structures on the *ventricle* walls within the *heart* onto which the *chordae tendinae* attach, preventing the *atrioventricular valves* from inverting.

Papilloma – a *benign* wart-like growth of *epithelial* cells.

Paracentesis – the draining of accumulated fluid from the *abdomen*, using a needle passed through the midline at the lowest point of the abdomen. See also *Ascites*.

Parainfluenza virus – part of the *kennel cough* complex, the *virus* targets the upper respiratory tract causing a harsh cough and a sore throat.

Parallel grid – a stationary grid with parallel lead strips.

P

Paraneoplastic disease – medical conditions caused by the presence of a tumour, or by the production of a substance by the tumour, eg *histamine* release and *eosinophilia* with *mast cell tumours* and *pseudohyperparathyroidism* (hypercalcaemia of malignancy) caused by some *lymphosarcomas* and multiple myeloma.

Paraparesis – weakness of the hindlimbs.

Paraplegia – loss of use of the hindlimbs.

Paraquat – a weedkiller; if ingested, it is highly toxic and causes vomiting, diarrhoea, collapse and convulsions and may be fatal. There is no antidote so supportive treatment is administered, such as intravenous fluid therapy, anticonvulsant drugs and oxygen therapy. See also *Veterinary Poisons Information Service* (VPIS).

Parasite – an organism that lives in or on another organism (the host), and obtains its nutrition from the host. A parasite lives at the expense of, and often causes harm to, the host, eg fleas, ticks, lice and some worms.

Parasympathetic nervous system (PNS) – part of the *autonomic nervous system* (which innervates all organs not under voluntary control) that is responsible for stimulating involuntary activities that conserve energy and lower the metabolic rate, eg lowering heart rate, *peristalsis*, pupil constriction. Predominates when the animal is in a relaxed state. See also *Sympathetic nervous system*.

Paratenic host – a host into/onto which a parasite moves, but on/in which no development of the parasite occurs. Often the parasite is waiting for the paratenic host to be eaten by its final host. See also *Intermediate host*.

Parathyroid gland – one of a pair of very small glands located close to the lobes of the *thyroid gland*; secrete *parathyroid* hormone and *calcitonin*, both of which regulate *calcium* levels in the blood. This is achieved by controlling calcium absorption from the gut, stimulating the *kidney* to reabsorb calcium in the *proximal convoluted tubule* when needed and promoting calcium movement from *bones* into the *plasma.*

Parathyroid hormone (PTH) – a hormone produced by the parathyroid glands that is involved in controlling calcium distribution in the body. PTH acts by increasing calcium absorption from the gut; increasing calcium reabsorption at the kidney, and promoting movement of calcium from the bones into the plasma when blood calcium levels are low.

Parenchyma – the cells of an organ that are actually concerned with the function of that organ (but not the supporting structures such as connective tissue or capsule).

Parenteral feeding – intravenous feeding ie providing nutrition without using the digestive tract.

Parenteral injections – injected medication avoiding the gastrointestinal tract, ie subcutaneous, intravenous, intramuscular.

Parietal cells – also called oxyntic cells; present in the stomach lining (gastric mucosa) and secrete hydrochloric acid, which aids in digestion.

Parotid salivary gland – a large saliva-producing gland located on the side of the face just in front of the ear; produces a more watery secretion than the other salivary glands.

Parturition – the act of giving birth.

P

Parvovirus – disease causing *acute* and severe *vomiting* and haemorrhagic *diarrhoea*; can be fatal in young puppies. Virus can also spread to the *heart muscle*, causing acute myocarditis and sudden death; it is resistant to many disinfectants and is therefore hard to destroy, it can be controlled by *vaccination*.

Passeriformes – order of birds that includes perching birds such as canaries and finches.

Passive drains – used when there is excessive fluid or air that must be removed, eg Penrose and Yeates. Drainage is provided by gravity, capillary action and overflow from the wound. Drains down both the outside and the inside.

Passive immunity – the short-lived *immunity* obtained from the *antibodies* a fetus or *neonate* receives from its mother, either across the *placenta* or in the *colostrum*. See also *Maternally derived antibodies*.

Passive scavenging system – removes waste gas from the expiratory limb of the anaesthetic circuit; comprises a piece of tubing attached to the expiratory valve on the circuit at one end, while the other end is placed through a hole in the wall into the outside atmosphere. Activated charcoal systems (absorptive systems) are also passive scavengers.

Patella – also known as the knee cap; a *sesamoid* bone in the *stifle joint* found in the *tendon* of the *quadriceps* muscle. *Luxation* of the patella occurs quite commonly. See also *Fabella*.

P

Patent – meaning open, free flowing, no blockages.

Patent ductus arteriosus (PDA) – a *congenital heart* defect resulting from the failure of the ductus arteriosus (a fetal blood vessel that shunts blood from the *pulmonary artery* to the *aorta*, bypassing the lungs) to close after birth, as normally happens. If left untreated, congestive heart failure occurs. The defect can be surgically corrected by ligating the vessel.

Pathogen – a disease-causing micro-organism. See also *Virulence*.

Pathological fracture – a fracture caused by a disease such as tumours or calcium deficiency.

Pathological waste – consists of pathological specimens, eg blood, cultures, tissue samples; should all be *sterilised* before placing it in *clinical waste*.

Pathologist – a vet who studies the nature, cause and progression of diseases in animals, usually within a laboratory; includes the study of *haematology*, *biochemistry*, *endocrinology*, *microbiology*, *cytology* and *histopathology*.

Pathology – the study of the nature, cause and progression of disease and the effects of disease on the body.

Patient–film distance – the distance between the radiographic film and the part of the patient being radiographed; increased distances lead to magnification, distortion and foreshortening.

Pectineus muscle – a muscle of the hindlimb, acts to *adduct* the limb.

P

Pectoral muscle – also called the flight muscles; the powerful group of muscles which attach to the keel on a bird's *sternum*.

Pedal – relating to the foot.

Pedal reflex – pulling back of the foot or limb when pressure is applied in between the digits.

Pediculosis – infestation with *lice*.

Pedigree – the record or list of full-bred dogs and cats.

Peg teeth – third pair of *incisors* found in the upper jaw of *lagomorphs*.

Pellet food – a complete diet formed in the shapes of pellets or pebbles; prevents selective eating in small furries.

Pelvis – **1.** the girdle of bones made up of two symmetrical halves, each comprising the *ilium, ischium and pubis*; connects the lumbosacral spine to the hindlimbs. It also articulates with the *femur* at the hip joint. Organs protected by the pelvic girdle include the *bladder* and *rectum*. **2.** the area at the centre of the *kidney. Urine* collects here and is funneled into the *ureter*, connecting the kidney to the *bladder*, allowing the urine to be excreted.

Pemphigus – an autoimmune condition affecting the skin and mucocutaneous junctions.

Pen torch – a torch in the shape of a pen, useful for examining the eye or areas where a direct light source is required.

Penis – the external organ of reproduction and urination in the male animal.

Pepsin – a *proteolytic enzyme* produced from the precursor *pepsinogen* in the stomach; involved in protein digestion.

Pepsinogen – the precursor for *pepsin* that is produced by peptic (or chief) cells in the stomach lining.

Peptide – two or more amino acids joined by a bond (the peptide bond); can join together to form *polypeptides*, and these in turn may join together and fold up to become *protein* molecules.

Perfusion – the supply of blood to tissues and organs.

Pericardial effusion – an increase of fluid in the *pericardium*; may be haemorrhagic, or may be transudates, modified transudates or exudates. Tumours at the base of the heart are a common cause. Pressure from the pericardial fluid makes it difficult for the heart to fill properly and the result is reduced cardiac output (this is called cardiac tamponade). Treatment involves draining the fluid and addressing the underlying cause.

Pericarditis – inflammation of the pericardium; may be caused by bacteria, viruses (such as *feline infectious peritonitis*) and *neoplasia*.

Pericardium – a closed fibrous sac surrounding the *heart*.

Perilymph – the fluid found in the tunnels of the *bony labyrinth* of the *inner ear*.

Perineal hernia – a congenital defect, failure of the rectal wall results in a flaccid pouch in the caudal rectum. See *Perineal rupture*.

Perineal rupture – as for the *perineal hernia* but the defect is acquired rather than congenital. This condition is usually seen in older male dogs and may be partly caused by excessive straining to defaecate.

Perineum – the region between the tail and the genitalia.

Perineurium – the connective tissue surrounding the bundles of nerve fibres. See also *Endoneurium*.

Periodontal ligament – the tough fibrous membrane that anchors the tooth into the tooth socket. See also Periodontitis.

Periodontal probe – a dental instrument that is inserted into the gingival sulcus (groove in the gum where it meets the tooth) next to a tooth or into any periodontal pocket to measure its depth. The tip is graduated to allow measurement of pocket depth; an assessment on how deep the pocket is determines whether the tooth needs to be extracted or not. See also *Periodontitis*.

Periodontitis – inflammation of the *periodontal ligament* caused by build-up of *plaque* and *tartar*. If left untreated, the gum will recede and the tooth will be lost.

Periosteal elevator – a double-ended dental instrument used to elevate the *gingiva* to expose the bone during tooth extractions and oral surgery.

Periosteum – a fibrous membrane covering the outer surface of *bone.*

Peripheral nervous system – system made up of all nervous tissue outside the *central nervous system*; can be divided up into two parts, the *somatic* and *autonomic nervous systems.* *Cranial* and *spinal nerves* are also classified as part of the peripheral nervous system.

Peristalsis – the rhythmical muscular contractions of the *smooth muscle* in the gastrointestinal tract that mixes up the semi-digested food and moves it along the tract; under the control of the *autonomic nervous system.*

Peritoneum – the membrane lining the inner wall of the *abdomen* (parietal peritoneum) and covering the organs (visceral peritoneum).

Peritonitis – infection and inflammation of the *peritoneum*; a painful condition often caused by penetrating wounds into the peritoneal cavity.

Perivascular – see *Extravascular.*

Permanent teeth – the second set of teeth ie in adult teeth. See also *deciduous teeth.*

Permeable – able to be penetrated, normally by a liquid.

Permission – see *Consent form.*

Peroxide – a chemical used in some environmental disinfectants, eg peroxygen compound, Virkon.

Persistent ductus arteriosus – see Patent ductus arteriosus (PDA).

Persistent right aortic arch (PRAA) – a *congenital* heart defect where the right aortic arch (which develops in the fetus but which normally degenerates before birth) does not degenerate and it forms a stricture round the *oesophagus*. Affected animals have great difficulty swallowing food and they regularly *regurgitate*. Surgery can be carried out to remove the stricture.

Pet Travel Scheme (PETS) – run by *Department for the Environment, Farming and Rural Affairs* (DEFRA); a passport scheme for pet animals allowing them to re-enter the UK without going into *quarantine*. Requirements for the scheme regularly change so it is important to check with DEFRA to get the most up-to-date information; however, as a general rule pets must be micro-chipped, they must be *vaccinated* against *rabies* and have had a blood test 30 days after the vaccination showing that sufficient *antibodies* are present and they must receive worm and *parasite* treatment from a vet in the country they are visiting before returning to the UK.

Petechia (pl. **petechiae)** – a small area of *haemorrhage*.

Peyer's patches – focal areas in the mucosa of the small intestine that are rich in lymphoid tissue and are part of the immune system.

pH – a scale that measures the acidity of a solution (measurement of the concentration of hydrogen ions in a solution). A neutral solution has a pH of 7. Acidic solutions have a pH between 0 (strongest acid) and 7, and alkaline solutions have a pH between 7 and 14 (strongest alkali).

Phagocyte – a cell that engulfs extracellular material by *phagocytosis*. Neutrophils are an example.

Phagocytosis – the engulfing of extracellular materials by a cell known as a *phagocyte*.

Phalange – meaning digit, ie finger or toe.

Pharyngeal – relating to the pharynx.

Pharyngitis – inflammation of the pharynx; may be caused by bacterial or viral infections, trauma, foreign bodies and excessive coughing.

Pharyngostomy tube feeding – a feeding tube placed into the oesophagus via the pharynx through an incision on the left side of the neck, enables artificial feeding.

Pharynx – a muscular passageway common to both the respiratory and digestive tracts; can be divided into two areas, the *oropharynx* and *nasopharynx*.

Phenobarbitone – an *anticonvulsant* drug commonly used to treat *epileptic seizures*; may cause sedation and can have adverse effects on the liver if used long term.

Phenol – an ingredient used in some environmental disinfectants, eg black phenols, Jeyes fluid.

Phenothiazines – a group of drugs that cause sedation, often to varying degrees, eg acepromazine.

Phenotype – the physical appearance and characteristics of an animal that are determined by its genes.

Pheromone – a hormone produced and excreted from the peri-anal, *anal* and tail glands that identifies the animal to others within its territory; may also play a role in courtship behaviour. Because the sense of smell is so well developed in the dog and cat, much information can be communicated between individuals through scent and pheromones.

P

Phlebitis – inflammation of a vein.

Phospholipid – a lipid molecule containing phosphorus; an important part of a *cell membrane*.

Phosphorus – an element found dissolved in the blood (called plasma inorganic phosphorus); level in the blood is commonly measured as part of an *electrolyte* panel. See also Hyperphosphataemia, Hypophosphataemia.

Photon (quanta) – bundles of energy that make up the primary beam.

Photoreceptor cell – contained within the *retina*; can be a *rod* or a *cone*, receives light and converts it to electrical impulses, which travel to the visual cortex of the brain via the *optic nerve*.

Physical examination – examination of the patient to detect any signs of ill health.

Physiology – the study of the normal functioning of the body.

Physiotherapy – helps to maintain supple flexible joints and muscle tone, also improves circulation. Types include:

❖ Active – flexion, extension and rotation of joints
❖ Passive – efflurage
❖ Assisted walking and exercises (with/without resistance)
❖ Hydrotherapy.

Phytomenadione (vitamin K) – a fat-soluble vitamin that is not stored in the body; a deficiency causes coagulation problems.

Pia mater – the innermost of the *meninges*, covering the *brain* and *spinal cord*. It is highly vascular. See also *Arachnoid layer*, *Dura mater*.

Pica – eating non-food substances, eg stones.

Piezo-electric crystal – used in ultrasound, sound-waves are produced and received by them.

Pigment – found in the skin and protects it from harmful ultraviolet light.

Pilae – small appendages on the surface of a bacterium that help it to attach to a surface. Specialised sex pilae are used to transfer genetic material from one bacterium to another during bacterial reproduction.

Pinch graft – type of free skin graft that covers part of the wound; can be full or split thickness.

Pineal gland – a small gland in the brain that produces the hormone *melatonin*; functions as a biological clock and affects reproductive cycles through the seasons.

Pinkies – bald baby mice which are used for feeding carnivorous reptiles and birds.

Pinna – the external ear flap; varies greatly in shape depending on the breed. Can often be rotated on the head to the direction from which a sound is coming. See also *Auricular cartilage*.

P

Piscivore – an animal that eats fish, eg herons and seabirds are piscivorous.

Pituitary gland – the main *endocrine* gland situated just beneath the *hypothalamus* in the *brain*. It is divided up into two lobes which secrete different *hormones*. The hormones secreted by the anterior pituitary (the front portion of the gland) influence growth, sexual development (*follicle stimulating hormone FSH* and *luteinising hormone LH*), thyroid function (*thyroid stimulating hormone TSH*), and adrenocortical function (*ACTH*). The posterior pituitary secretes the hormone *oxytocin* which increases uterine contractions and *antidiuretic hormone (ADH)* which increases reabsorption of water by the tubules of the *kidney*. See also *diabetes insipidus*.

Placenta – a temporary organ that develops during pregnancy and forms a bridge between the mother and fetus across which blood, oxygen, nutrients, immunity and waste products can pass; also secretes hormones, which maintain the pregnancy.

Plain catgut – natural, uncoated multifilament absorbable suture material, absorbed by enzymatic degradation. See also *Chromic catgut*.

Plantar – the area of the hind paws where the pads are located; the opposite surface is known as *dorsal*. See also *Palmar*.

Plaque – **1.** substance made by bacteria in the mouth and which forms a film on the teeth. An increased amount of plaque will cause *gingivitis*. Inorganic substances from saliva get deposited on the plaque and start to form *tartar*. **2.** In dermatology, a plaque is a patch of a small area of skin that appears different than the surrounding skin and is usually raised with flat top.

Plasma – the fluid part of unclotted blood (ie serum and clotting agents).

Plasma cell – cell of the immune system; a type of *B lymphocyte* that secretes *antibodies* (*immunoglobulins*) in response to the presence of a specific *antigen*.

Plasma substitutes – see *Colloid*.

Plasmid – a small loop of *DNA* found within a bacterium that is not part of its *genome*; may be transferred from one organism to another.

Plaster of Paris – a material used for casting, takes several hours to dry and is very heavy.

Plaster shears –an instrument similar to a large pair of scissors, used to remove/cut casts.

Plastron – the lower plate of a *chelonian*'s shell. See also *Carapace*.

Plate benders – an instrument used for bending plates (internal implant) to the correct angle or shape.

Platelet – a small, irregular shaped cell that helps prevent bleeding by causing blood clots to form. See also *Thrombocyte*.

Platysma – one of the superficial muscles of facial expression.

Pleura – the membranes surrounding the pleural cavity containing the *lungs*; the visceral pleura line the lungs and the parietal pleura line the pleural cavity.

P

Pleural cavity – the cavity in the *thorax* where the *lungs* are situated.

Pleural effusion – a build-up of liquid or gas in the pleural cavity (ie fluid inside the chest that is outside the lungs); *hydrothorax* is a liquid pleural effusion whereas *pneumothorax* is an effusion of air. There are many causes of pleural effusion but all prevent the lungs from expanding properly and lead to dyspnoea and eventually, if untreated, to respiratory failure.

Pleural fluid – lubricating fluid that reduces friction between the *pleural membranes* as the *lungs* inflate and deflate.

Pneumatised bone – adapted bones in the *avian skeleton* that are filled with air sacs to reduce the overall weight of the bone and allow flight to occur more easily.

Pneumocystogram – a contrast study of the bladder using negative contrast media. Often a double contrast study is performed on the bladder.

Pneumonia – inflammatory disease of the lung parenchyma (but not the bronchi) usually caused by bacteria, viruses, fungi and inhalation of irritants. Pneumonia may affect localised areas of lung, or the whole lung.

Pneumothorax – the presence of air in the *pleural cavity*, commonly caused by trauma to the chest wall. As air builds up in the pleural cavity, the pressure causes the *lungs* to collapse, causing respiratory distress; to relieve the pressure, air must be drained from the chest using a needle. See also *Thoracocentesis*.

P

PO – per os, ie administered by mouth.

Poison – a substance that is toxic to the body, or even fatal.

Pollakiuria – increased frequency and urgency of urination, usually passing small amounts of urine with each attempt; common in animals with cystitis.

Polyarthritis – inflammation of more than one joint; usually caused by immune-mediated disease but can also be caused by infectious agents. Examples include immune-mediated polyarthritis, rheumatoid arthritis and systemic lupus erythematosus.

Polyarthropathy – disease (of any type) of more than one joint, eg polyarthritis and osteoarthritis affecting more than one joint.

Polychromasia – describes the deeper colour of immature erythrocytes (*reticulocytes*) when stained in a blood smear compared to mature erythrocytes; increased polychromasia therefore indicates release of immature cells into the circulation in a *regenerative anaemia*.

Polycythaemia – increase in the proportion of circulating erythrocytes in the blood; may be a relative change, as the result of reduced fluid in the blood (dehydration) and may not be clinically significant. However, it may also occur with increased *erythropoietin* production, or with a bone marrow disorder where excessive erythrocytes are produced (known as polycythaemia vera). If it is severe, polycythaemia causes increased viscosity of the blood and may result in seizures and blood clot formation.

Polydactyly – a congenital condition that is usually hereditary where there are extra digits on the feet; occurs fairly commonly in cats and in Bernese mountain dogs.

Polydipsia (PD) – an increased thirst, drinking an increased amount of water; a common clinical sign and often associated with *polyuria*. Causes include *dehydration*, *diabetes insipidus*, *diabetes mellitus*, renal disease, *pyometra*, etc.

Polymerisation – joining together of small molecules to create a chain of molecules (a polymer), eg a polypeptide is created by polymerisation of amino acids.

Polymorphonuclear leucocytes (PMNL) – a general term for the leucocytes that have multiple lobes in their nuclei; they include the neutrophils, eosinophils and basophils.

Polymyositis – generalised inflammation of the muscles, usually caused by infectious agents, eg *Toxoplasma*, *Neospora*.

Polyp – a benign growth of tissue, often on a stalk, that grows from mucous membranes such as those in the gastrointestinal or reproductive tract. Polyps in the nasopharynx are common in cats. Some polyps may eventually become neoplastic so removal is usually recommended.

Polypeptide – a chain of peptides (amino acids joined by peptide bonds); they form proteins by joining together and folding up.

Polyphagia – increased eating.

Polyoestrous – a term used to describe animals that have a number of oestrous cycles during the breeding season if they do not become pregnant, eg cats are polyoestrous and generally have an oestrous cycle every 2–3 weeks from spring to autumn.

Polysaccharide – a large carbohydrate molecule made up of a chain of simple sugars. An example of a polysaccharide is *glycogen*.

Polyuria – an increase in the amount of urine produced; often associated with *polydipsia*. Causes include *diabetes insipidus*, *diabetes mellitus* and use of *diuretics*.

Pons – found in the *hindbrain*, it is continuous with the *medulla oblongata* and shares many of the same functions.

Popliteal lymph node – a palpable *lymph node* located behind the *stifle joint*.

Portable appliance testing (PAT) – legally required electrical testing of portable appliances to be carried out under the *Electricity at Work Regulations*. Employers are legally liable for the safety of any electrical appliances used by employees.

Porto-systemic shunt – the presence of a patent blood vessel that, in the fetus, carries blood from the gut to the vena cava but that normally closes within a few hours of birth; shunts *blood* from the *hepatic portal vein* directly into the systemic veins, by-passing the *liver*. The presence of a porto-systemic shunt causes many symptoms reflecting liver damage, including stunted growth, depression, vomiting and neurological signs, as a result of the high levels of *ammonia* in the *blood*. The condition can be surgically corrected by ligating the vessel.

Positioning aids – various props to aid with positioning during radiography, surgery or to reposition a patient in its kennel, eg rope ties, sand bags, foam wedges, rolled-up towels.

Positive contrast media – contrast media that are more radio-opaque than the surrounding tissue, eg barium sulphate, iodine compounds.

Post mortem – examination (which may involve biopsy samples of organs for histology) of a dead patient, to try and determine a cause of death.

Post-prandial – after a meal or food.

Posterior chamber – the larger of the two chambers of the *eye*, it is filled with *vitreous humour*. See also *Anterior chamber*.

Postural drainage – to aid in removal of secretions from the lungs, the patient's head is positioned lower than the body, with the affected lung uppermost.

Posture – the position of the body or the way the body is held; can give indications if a patient is in pain for example.

Potassium (K) – an element that is present as a positively charged ion (the electrolyte K⁺) in the blood, and is often measured on blood *electrolyte* panels. Has many functions and is important in acid–base balance and muscle and nerve function. See also *Hyperkalaemia, Hypokalaemia*.

Potassium bromide (KBr) – an anticonvulsant commonly used in the treatment of epileptic seizures.

Potassium hydroxide (KOH) – used to dissolve excess debris, useful in skin scrapes of deep burrowing mites.

Potter–Bucky grid – a moving grid, fitted underneath the X-ray table; eliminates parallel lines that are visible on radiographs when stationary grids are used.

PR – per rectum. Meaning via the rectum.

Precocious – describes animals which are well developed at birth and can walk shortly after birth (eg foals, guinea-pigs). See also Altricial.

Predilection site – a site at which a tumour more commonly occurs, eg for *osteosarcomas* in dogs these tend to be on the proximal *humerus* or distal *femur*, in cats *squamous cell carcinomas* tend to occur on the face and *pinnae*.

Pregnancy – the condition of female animals from the moment when an *ovum* is fertilised by a *spermatozoa* until the moment of *parturition* (birth).

Pre-medication – a drug or combination of drugs given before an anaesthetic. Drugs used include: phenothiazines, benzodiazepines, α2-antagonists, opiates, non-steroidal anti-inflammatory drugs (NSAIDs).

Premolar – tooth on the upper or lower jaw between the *canines* and the *molars*; has multiple roots which anchors it firmly to the jaw. The crown has serrated edges for cutting through flesh.

Pre-prandial – before a meal or food.

Prepuce – the sheath of haired skin which normally covers the penis.

Prescapular lymph node – palpable *lymph node* located just cranially to the *scapula*.

Preservative – agent used is sodium sulphite; when used in developer preservatives reduce oxidation and prevent staining of the radiographic film, when used in fixer, they prevent deterioration of the fixing agent.

Pressure bandage – a wad of absorbent padding placed over the wound which is then bandaged firmly in place. The pressure of the bandage on the wound helps to control the *haemorrhage*. If blood does seep through, another pressure bandage can be placed over the top of the first.

Pressure gauge – indicates gas levels.

Primary beam – see *Photon* (quanta).

Primary feathers – also known as flight feathers; provide the forward thrust during flight. Some may be clipped if an owner wants to prevent the bird from flying away. See also Secondary feathers.

Primary layer – provides padding and absorption and holds the wound dressing in place.

Primary response – a response by the *immune system* to first encountering a *pathogen*. *Lymphocytes* are produced to attack the *antigen* and memory cells are created to recognise the antigen in future.

Primary stain – the first stain in a differential stain (where more than one dye is used), eg the primary stain in the Gram's stain is crystal violet.

Primary uterine inertia – failure of the *uterus* during *parturition* to contract strongly enough to expel the fetus(es); known as *non-obstructive dystocia* and may be the result of a prolonged labour. The vet may elect to perform a *Caesarean section*.

Primary water deficit – loss of water only (not electrolytes) from the body as a result of, for example, water being unavailable, excessive panting, prolonged inappetence.

Primagravid – an animal that is pregnant for the first time.

Primaparous – an animal that has given birth for the first time.

Prion – a minute protein-like particle, smaller than a *virus*, thought to be the infectious agents for such diseases as bovine spongiform encephalopathy (BSE) and Creutzfeldt–Jakob disease (CJD).

PRN – as required, from the Latin *pro re nata*.

Proactive – attempting to prevent a situation from arising or occurring rather then reacting to the situation once it has arisen or occurred (reactive).

Proctoscopy – examination of the rectum and caudal colon using an endoscope; may be used to identify and biopsy disease colon/rectum wall, or tumours.

Professionalism – the characteristics and knowledge of a professional person.

Progesterone – a female sex *hormone* produced mainly by the *corpus luteum* after *ovulation*; important for preparation of the uterus for pregnancy and maintenance of pregnancy.

Proglottid – each segment of a *tapeworm* is called a proglottid; mature proglottids are shed from the tail of the tapeworm and are individual reproductive units, which develop into a larval tapeworm.

Prognosis – a prediction of the likely outcome of a disease, eg an animal with an advanced high-grade malignant tumour such as lymphosarcoma has a poor prognosis of recovery, which may be improved slightly by treatment with chemotherapy.

Progressive retinal atrophy – an inherited condition of the eye in which there is degeneration of the photoreceptor units in the retina; usually progresses to total blindness and affects breeds such as the Poodle, Rough collie and Irish setter more commonly than other breeds.

Prokaryote – an organism whose cells lack a membrane-bound *nucleus* and membrane-bound cell *organelles*. Bacteria and the blue-green algae are prokaryotes. See also *Eukaryote*.

Prokinetic – a drug that stimulates movement of material through the gut by enhancing muscle contractions and that is used to treat gut stasis, vomiting and constipation, eg cisapride and metoclopramide.

Prolactin – a hormone produced by the anterior *pituitary gland* which stimulates milk production (lactogenesis) during late pregnancy and lactation.

Prolapse – the slipping down or displacement of an internal organ from its normal position, eg a prolapsed *eye* where the *globe* has become displaced out of the *orbit* so that the eyelids can no longer close over it; can also be rectal, uterine, vaginal.

Promotion – a rise in your position held within the practice/company.

Pronation – a movement to rotate the paw inwards.

Pro-oestrus – the initial stage of the *oestrous cycle* during which the female animal is attractive to the male but will not allow mating; followed by *oestrus*.

Prophase – stage 1 of cell division in both *mitosis* and *meiosis*; the *chromosomes* become visible and *spindle* fibres are laid down. In meiosis, it is during this stage that *chiasmata* develop between the chromosomes and the exchange of genetic material occurs.

Prostaglandin – hormone-like molecules with many functions including roles in inflammation and muscle contraction. Prostaglandin $F_{2\alpha}$ causes regression of the corpus luteum and production of the hormone relaxin when an animal gives birth.

Prostate gland – an accessory sex gland present in some male animals, eg the dog and humans but not the cat; produces *prostatic fluid*. Older entire male dogs often suffer from *hyperplasia* and inflammation (*prostatitis*) of the prostate gland which can result in recurrent infections. *Neoplasia* of the prostate gland may also occur.

Prostatic fluid – produced by the prostate gland; contributes to *seminal fluid* and carries and nourishes the *spermatozoa*.

Prostatitis – inflammation of the prostate gland; usually occurs in entire males and may be caused by bacterial infection, *neoplasia*, *cysts*, *abscesses* or trauma. Symptoms include caudal abdominal pain, dysuria, haematuria, constipation and pyrexia. Treatment of the underlying cause and neutering are usually necessary.

Protective clothing – worn to protect personnel from infection, ionising radiation, flying objects (such as extracted teeth). Items include: gloves; aprons; goggles; lead-equivalent aprons, sleeves and gloves; thyroid protectors.

Protein – a large organic molecule formed from chains of *polypeptides* that are themselves formed from chains of *amino acids*.

Protein-losing enteropathy – chronic loss of proteins such as albumin and globulin through the gut wall into the faeces; usually occurs with severe gastrointestinal disease such as *lymphangiectasia* and may result in *hypoproteinaemia*.

Protein-losing nephropathy – chronic loss of protein such as albumin through the kidney into the urine; may result in *hypoproteinaemia* and *nephrotic syndrome*. Causes include *glomerulonephritis* as a result of chronic bacterial infection or *feline infectious peritonitis*.

Proteolytic enzymes – enzymes that break down proteins into smaller molecules (polypeptides and free amino acids) during digestion in the stomach and small intestine. Examples include *pepsin*, *trypsin* and *chymotrypsin*.

Proton – a positively charged particle found in the nucleus of the atom.

Protozoa – single-celled *eukaryotic* organisms, often parasitic and can cause disease, eg *Toxoplasma*, *Neospora*, *Encephalitozoon* and *Giardia*.

Protraction – a cranial movement of a limb. See also *Retraction*.

Proventriculus – the glandular part of the stomach in the bird.

Proximal – an anatomical description meaning near to or next to; when used to describe areas on the limbs or tail it means towards the end attached to the body.

Proximal convoluted tubule – the first part of the renal tubule between the *glomerulus* and the *Loop of Henlé*.

Pruritus – itching; a symptom of many inflammatory and parasitic conditions such as atopy and mange. (Note spelling – prur*itis* is incorrect).

Pseudocyesis – see *Pseudopregnancy*.

Pseudo-focused grid – a type of stationary grid in which the lead strips are vertical but become shorter towards the edge.

Pseudohyperparathyroidism – *hypercalcaemia* caused by some malignant tumours (such as *lymphosarcoma* and multiple myeloma) as a result of production of a protein molecule which is similar to *parathyroid hormone*. This is described as hypercalcaemia of malignancy and is a *paraneoplastic* effect.

Pseudomonas aeruginosa – a Gram-negative bacterium; a common *opportunistic pathogen* in veterinary medicine. It may be difficult to treat because it can develop *resistance* to a variety of antibiotics.

Pseudopregnancy – also known as false or phantom pregnancy, or pseudocyesis; a condition in which a female animal behaves and shows some outward signs of pregnancy when she is not pregnant. Caused by elevated *prolactin* levels following *ovulation*. Clinical signs usually develop 3–4 weeks after *oestrus* and include behaviour changes, mammary development and *lactation*. Although it usually resolves without treatment eventually, it may be distressing to the animals and can be treated medically if necessary.

Pseudostratified epithelium – a type of epithelium lining the trachea, bronchi and bronchioles.

Psittaciformes – order of birds that includes parrots.

Psittacosis – a *zoonotic* bacterial disease of *Psittaciformes* caused by *Chlamydophila psittaci*. Symptoms include ruffled feathers, diarrhoea and conjunctivitis. It can cause flu-like symptoms in humans, but it may also occasionally be fatal.

P

Psoroptes cuniculi – a parasitic mite that inhabits the ears of rabbits and causes severe irritation.

Pterygoid muscle – one of the masticatory muscles, acts to move the mandible from side to side.

Ptyalism – drooling; may be caused by *dysphagia* or *nausea*.

Puberty – the period of time during which a young animal develops into an adult through maturation of the reproductive system, and the animal becomes capable of reproducing.

Pubis – one of the three bones in each half of the *pelvis*, it lies ventrally and both sides fuse together at the pubic symphysis.

Pulex irritans – the human flea; now fortunately rare in the UK.

Pulmonary – relating to the lungs.

Pulmonary artery – an *artery* that, unusually, carries de-oxygenated *blood* from the right *ventricle* of the *heart* up to the *lungs*.

Pulmonary osteopathy – a condition secondary to a mass in the thorax, causes swelling of the forelimbs and lameness.

Pulmonary valve – the *atrioventricular valve* at the base of the *pulmonary artery* on the right side of the *heart*; prevents the *blood* from flowing back into the heart after it has been pumped towards the *lungs*.

Pulmonary vein – a *vein* that, unusually, carries oxygenated *blood*, from the *lungs* back to the left *atrium* of the *heart*.

Pulp – a soft material made from connective tissue; the pulp cavity runs down the centre of the dentine and contains nerves, blood vessels and lypmhatics.

Pulse – the pulse rate of an animal can be felt at any point where an *artery* runs close to the skin surface; each beat corresponds to the contraction of the *heart*. In the dog and cat, suitable sites for feeling the pulse include: the *femoral artery*, the digital artery, the *coccygeal artery* and the *lingual artery* (for anaesthetised patients only). The pulse can be assessed for rate (beats per minute), rhythm (regular, irregular) and character (strong, weak). Normal pulse rates for the dog range between 60 and 80 beats per minute, depending on the breed size. For the cat, the range is 110–180 beats per minute. See also *Pulse deficit, Sinus arrhythmia*.

Pulse deficit – a pulse rate lower than the heart rate; not a normal finding and may indicate dysrhythmias.

Pulse oximeter – a device that measures the oxygen saturation of *haemoglobin*; useful to have when monitoring a patient under *general anaesthesia*. A clip is applied to the animal's tongue, lip or ear and a percentage of oxygen saturation is calculated; important not to rely solely on the pulse oximeter as a monitoring device – this machine will still give a reading even if the animal has died. The device gives historical readings ie not in real time. A normal reading is 97.1 and above.

Punch biopsy – a small circular plug of tissue is removed from the mass using a handheld punch; technique is often used on superficial masses or to obtain skin *biopsy samples*. The biopsy sample is then sent for histological examination.

Punch graft – see *Pinch graft*.

Punctum lacrimale – see *Nasolacrimal duct*.

Puncture wound – a wound produced by a sharp object, eg a tooth; tends to be perpendicular to the skin, creating an entry wound only.

Pupa – the developmental stage of many insects between the larval and adult stages; often occurs with the developing insect encased in a cocoon.

Pupil – the aperture within the *iris* that controls the amount of light entering the *eye*.

Puppy party – class held by veterinary nurses and/or veterinary surgeons at the practice; young puppies (usually between 10 and 12 weeks) are invited to a course of classes to socialise and their owners can learn about care for their puppy.

Purkinje fibres – specialised fibres lining the *ventricle* walls in the *heart*, along which the *nervous impulse* from the *atrioventricular node* and the *bundle of His* passes.

Purse string sutures – a continuous circular suture that is pulled together to close or invert an opening; might be used to tighten the anal sphincter ring after replacement of a rectal prolapse.

Purulent – pus-forming, eg a purulent nasal discharge is one that contains mainly pus.

Pus – thick, yellowish liquid composed of *bacteria*, *white blood cells* and necrotic tissue debris which originates from inflamed or infected tissue. See also *Abscess*.

Pustule – an inflamed, raised skin lesion containing pus; a common feature of bacterial skin infections such as pyoderma caused by *Staphylococcus* sp.

Pyaemia – the presence of pus-forming bacteria in the blood.

Pyelonephritis – inflammation of the renal pelvis, usually associated with bacterial infection that has ascended from the lower urinary tract. Animals with a depressed immune system or glucosuria are predisposed. Can lead to acute or chronic renal failure if not treated promptly.

Pyloric sphincter – a ring of smooth muscle (*sphincter*) forming the junction between the stomach and small intestine and controlling the passage of food out of the stomach.

Pylorus – the most distal portion of the *stomach* where the *pyloric sphincter* is located.

Pyoderma – *purulent* (pus-forming) condition of the skin; usually caused by bacterial infection.

Pyometra – a serious and potentially life-threatening condition during which pus builds up inside the *uterus* (called **closed pyometra** if the cervix is closed, and **open pyometra** if the cervix is still open). Typically the dog becomes lethargic, *pyrexic* and *polydipsic* about 6 weeks after a season; older bitches are more commonly affected. There may be a vaginal discharge if the pyometra is open. Usually diagnosed by *ultrasonography* or radiography of the uterus, and treatment is almost always supportive therapy (fluids and antibiotics) and *ovariohysterectomy* as soon as possible.

Pyothorax – a type of *pleural effusion* where the fluid building up in the pleural cavity is *pus*; usually caused by bacterial infection.

Pyrexia – an abnormally elevated temperature, a fever.

Pyrexic – having an abnormally high temperature or fever.

QBC – quantitative blood count.

QID – means four times daily (from latin *quarter in die*).

QRS-complex – the part of an *electrocardiograph* trace that follows the *P-wave* and represents depolarisation of the ventricles. See *electrocardiograph* for diagram.

Quadriceps femoris – the muscle mass of the hindlimb which runs down the front of the *femur*; works to *extend* the stifle and *flex* the hip.

Quadriparesis – also known as tetraparesis; a weakness of all four limbs, although the animal can still move in a co-ordinated way if helped. See also Hemiparesis, Hemiplegia, Quadriplegia.

Quadriplegia – also known as tetraplegia; paralysis of all four limbs.

Quarantine – refers to the statutory *isolation* of an animal for a period longer than the *incubation period* of a disease to prevent the spread of an *infectious disease*; usually refers to the isolation of animals entering the UK from overseas to prevent the *rabies virus* from being brought into the country.

Quaternary ammonium compounds – a type of disinfectant used for both environment and skin, eg cetrimide (cetavlon).

Queen – a female cat of breeding age.

Rabies – a *zoonotic* and fatal *disease* caused by a *rhabdovirus*, which is spread by direct contact (biting) with infected animals. The virus replicates at the site of the bite then targets the *central nervous system* (CNS). Once the virus is in the CNS, *ataxia* develops; once it reaches the brain *hydrophobia, laryngeal spasm, dyspnoea* and fits occur. Death occurs within 5–7 days of the virus reaching the CNS. There is a *vaccine* available against rabies. Rabies is currently not found in the UK. See also *Pet Travel Scheme*.

Radial nerve – an important spinal nerve found in the forelimb.

Radiation protection advisor (RPA) – advises on protection, the controlled area and draws up the local rules; usually an external expert in radiography and either a veterinary surgeon who holds the veterinary radiography diploma or a medical physicist.

Radiation protection supervisor (RPS) – a person appointed within the practice, eg senior partner; they ensure safety and that the local rules are adhered to.

Radiation sterilisation – materials that cannot be sterilised by heat or chemicals can be sterilised with gamma radiation, eg suture material, scalpel blades.

Radiation symbol – A symbol used (usually on signs) to denote ionising radiation is used within a particular area.

Radiographic film – type of film that can be used to form an image using ionising radiation.

Radiography – the process of forming an image (of the inside of the body) using ionising radiation.

Radiolucent – cannot be seen on a radiograph following exposure.

Radio-opaque – can be seen on the radiograph following exposure.

Radius – the main bone of the forearm, it lies parallel with the *ulna* and runs from the elbow to the *carpus*.

Rampley sponge-holding forceps – an instrument with flattened pear-shaped ends used for holding sponges or swabs for skin preparation before surgery.

Ramus – an anatomical term meaning branch.

Raptor – a *bird of prey*, eg owl, kestrel.

Rare-earth screens – uses rare-earth phosphors as their fluorescent material; these are more efficient at converting light than calcium tungstate, therefore lower exposures are needed. Rare-earth phosphors emit green light. See also *Intensifying screen*.

Rat-toothed forceps – a surgical instrument (similar to a large pair of tweezers in appearance) with teeth on both ends. Used for dissecting and handling denser tissue.

Rationalisation – putting a problem or issue into context.

Reactive –see *Proactive*.

Re-breathing anaesthetic circuits – a classification of circuits. Expired gases are passed through soda lime to remove carbon dioxide and can therefore be re-breathed; these circuits include circle and to-and-fro circuits.

Receptor – a sensory nerve ending that responds to specific stimuli and triggers a *nervous impulse*. Examples include stretch receptors in the lungs, pressure, heat and pain receptors in the skin. See also *Baroreceptor*.

Recessive gene – the less dominant form of a gene in a heterozygous animal. When an animal carries two different copies of a gene (ie is *heterozygous*) the recessive gene is usually masked by the effects of the *dominant gene*, eg in dalmatians the black form of the spotting gene (**B**) is dominant over the liver-coloured spot form (**b**). A dalmation carrying **BB** or **Bb** genes will have black spots, but one carrying **bb** will have liver spots because there is no dominant gene to mask its effects.

Recipient – a patient who receives donated body tissues, blood or fluids.

Records – contains all treatment and history of the pet, can be in card form or computerised.

Recovery position – the recovery position is used as a first-aid technique for assisting people who are unconscious, or nearly so, but are still breathing. It helps the patient to breathe more easily and permits fluids (eg saliva, vomit) to drain from the nose and throat so there is no chance that they are breathed in.

Rectal prolapse – portion of the intestine (can be a few inches long) that visibly protrudes from the anus.

Rectal pull through technique – to carefully prolapse a section of rectum through the anus so that surgery may be performed on it.

Rectum – the final part of the *large intestine*; its function is to store faecal matter until it is ready to be expelled. See also *Anus*, *Defecation*.

Rectus abdominis – one of four groups of *abdominal muscles* making up the abdominal wall, they are attached from the *ribs* to the *pelvis* and cause the *spine* to flex.

Recumbency – the patient is unable to stand or get up.

Red blood cell – see *Erythrocyte*.

Red pulp – describes one type of tissue found in the *spleen*, consisting of blood vessels, stored blood products and haemopoietic tissue. See also *White pulp*.

Reducible – of a *hernia*, meaning the contents of the hernia can easily be replaced to their original position, eg small umbilical hernia.

Reducing valve – placed between the cylinder and the flowmeter, allows control of the gas flow.

Reduction – can be closed (realignment of the joint and bones by manipulation) or open (surgically realigning the joint and bones).

Reduction forceps – a surgical instrument enabling the surgeon to perform open reduction.

Referral – patient is referred to a specialist who can continue treatment and make a diagnosis.

Reflex – a response by the nervous system to a stimulus which is involuntary (not under the control of the brain), eg the patellar reflex where there is involuntary quadriceps muscle contraction in response to a tap on the patellar tendon (the stimulus). Various reflexes may be tested in a neurological examination to determine which part of the spinal cord is affected by an injury/disease.

Reflex arc – a fixed, involuntary response to a stimulus, eg if an animal stands on a sharp object, the foot is automatically withdrawn. This is a spinal reflex, involving the spinal nerves only and not the *brain.*

Refractometer – an instrument used to measure the specific gravity of a fluid (usually urine or liquid effusions).

Regenerative – describes *anaemia* when there is active proliferation and release of immature *erythrocytes* from the bone marrow into the circulation to restore the *haematocrit.* Anaemias caused by haemorrhage or haemolysis are usually regenerative. This is the response of normal bone marrow to anaemia.

Regional anaesthesia – nerves around the region of the surgical site are injected with local anaesthetic, enabling procedures such as Caesarean sections to be performed.

Regurgitation – passage of *ingesta* back up through the oesophagus and out of the mouth *before* it has entered the stomach. Regurgitation is a passive process (no abdominal contractions) and the food is undigested, and may be in a tubular form. Regurgitation may occur many hours after eating and may result simply from an animal bolting its food, or from conditions such as megaoesophagus. It should be differentiated from vomiting. The pH of regurgitated material is approximately neutral (pH 7) whereas vomited material is acidic because of the presence of stomach acid.

R

Relaxin – a *hormone* secreted by the *corpus luteum* towards the end of pregnancy that causes relaxation of the pelvic ligaments and aids dilation of the *cervix* ready for *parturition*.

Reluxation – a joint that repeatedly dislocates.

Remodelling – the process of new bone replacing the callus at the fracture site.

Renal – relating to the kidneys.

Renal corpuscle – the glomerulus and Bowman's capsule, which form the initial filtering unit of the renal tubule.

Renin – a *hormone* produced by the kidney that is important in the regulation of *blood pressure*. Renin causes production of *angiotensin I* from its precursor molecule. The system which maintains blood pressure is called the renin–angiotensin–aldosterone system (RAAS).

Replenisher – a liquid used in non-ready-to-use processing solutions, eg developer.

Replication – when a molecule (such as DNA) or organism (such as a virus or bacteria) makes a copy of itself.

Reporting of Injuries, Disease and Dangerous Occurrences Regulations 1995 (RIDDOR) – legislation laid down by the *Health and Safety Executive (HSE)* requiring practices to record details of all accidents and incidents in the *accident book* and report them directly to the HSE if appropriate.

Reptile – a cold-blooded animal with an outer covering of horny scales or plates; generally lays eggs, eg tortoise, iguana and snake.

Reservoir – a compartment where fluid from a drain is collected.

Reservoir bag – supplies a gas reservoir and is essential for intermittent positive pressure ventilation.

Residual volume – the volume of gas left in the lungs after maximal expiration.

Resistance – 1. the ability of an organism such as a bacterium or parasite to become less sensitive to a drug (antibiotic, or anti-parasitic drug) over time. Antibiotic resistance is an important problem and results in bacteria that are very difficult to kill. The bacterium methicillin-resistant *Staphylococcus aureus* (MRSA) is an example of a bacterium that is resistant to many antibiotics. **2.** also used to describe an animal's ability to fight off and avoid disease (the function of the immune system).

Resolution – the image quality on a screen, affected by the number of pixels.

Respiration – the process of gas exchange between an organism and the environment; can be internal and/or external.

Respiratory acidosis – see *Acidosis*.

Respiratory alkalosis – see *Alkalosis*.

Respiratory arrest – the cessation of respiration.

Respiratory centre – found in the medulla oblongata, it co-ordinates the actions of the respiratory muscles.

Respiratory monitors – monitors that usually involve a thermistor placed in the airway, which detect temperatures between inspired and expired gases. Depending on the type, an audible noise can be heard either as respiration is occurring or if respiration stops. These types do not measure tidal volume.

Respiratory pattern – a judgment made on the depth of each breath and rate of breathing.

Respiratory rate – the number of breaths taken per minute (count either inspirations or expirations).

❖ Dog – 10–30 breaths per minute
❖ Cat – 20–30 breaths per minute.

Smaller mammals and birds tend to have a higher respiratory rate than larger ones; reptiles may have very slow respiratory rates.

Respiratory stimulant – a drug administered to encourage respiration.

Respiratory system – the process of the body taking in oxygen and removing waste gases. See also *Respiration*.

Restraint – a means of restricting the patient from moving, for examination.

Retained spectacle – a consequence of *dysecdysis* in snakes. The transparent scale which covers the eye is retained, instead of shed. As a result, a thick layer of scales can build up over the eye. These can be very delicately removed by prolonged soaking with tear replacement solutions.

Retching – failure in attempts to vomit, the patient is seen to be 'heaving'.

Rete testis – a network of tubes that carries the *spermatozoa* from the *seminiferous tubules* to the efferent tubules which lead to the *epididymis*.

Reticulocyte – an immature *red blood cell*; remnants of the *nucleus* are often still visible in them. Often seen in the bloodstream in greater numbers at times when *erythrocytes* are being regenerated and are in short supply, eg after extensive blood loss.

Retina – the inner layer of the *eye*, composed of several layers of nervous tissue containing the *photoreceptor cells* (*rods* and *cones*); these receive light and convert it to electrical impulses that travel along the *optic nerve* to the visual cortex of the *cerebrum*. See also *Fovea*, *Tapetum lucidum*.

Retraction – a caudal movement (pulling away) of a limb.

Retroperitoneal – outside the *peritoneum*.

Retrovirus – causal agent of *feline leukaemia virus* (FeLV).

Reverse cutting needle – a surgical needle used for suturing skin, it has sharp cutting edges and in cross-section looks like an upside-down triangle.

Rhabdovirus – causal agent of rabies.

Rhinitis – infection and inflammation of the *mucous membranes* in the nasal cavity. Symptoms include sneezing and *mucopurulent* discharge; can be caused by bacterial and viral infections, *allergy* and *foreign bodies*.

Rhomboideus – muscle of the forelimb; along with the *trapezius*, it acts to elevate the limb and draw it forward.

Rib – one of 13 pairs of curved bones that attach to the spinal column and form the protective cage over the thoracic viscera; allow the *lungs* room for expansion during *inspiration*. See also *False (asternal) rib, Floating rib*.

Ribonucleic acid (RNA) – a single-stranded molecule found within the *nucleolus* and *ribosomes* of the cell, which copy the genetic code from the *deoxyribonucleic acid* (DNA) and translate it into *proteins* and *polypeptides*.

Ribosome – an organelle found within the cell on the surface of the *endoplasmic reticulum*; it is involved in protein synthesis.

Rickets – a disease resulting from dietary deficiency of vitamin D and calcium/phosphorus; the skeleton is weak and poorly mineralised. Now rare because commercial diets contain adequate nutrients.

Rigor mortis – the stiffness of muscles and joints that occurs after death.

Ringer's solution – an isotonic crystalloid fluid, used in management of primary water loss and for vomiting. It contains no lactate, unlike Hartmann's or Lactated Ringer's.

Ringworm – see *Dermatophytosis*.

Rinsing – performed between development and fixing for 20 seconds; it stops development and removes developer from the film in radiography.

Risk assessment – part of the *Control Of Substances Hazardous to Health (COSHH)* regulations; requires all practices to carry out an assessment of all the potential hazards in the workplace, eg *clinical waste*, laboratory chemicals, manual handling, etc.

Robert Jones bandage – a large bandage applied to limbs to provide support; it should be three times the diameter of the limb and on flicking should sound like a water melon.

Rodent – a small mammal with continuously erupting teeth specialised for gnawing, eg mouse, gerbil, rat.

Rodent ulcer – see *Eosinophilic ulcer.*

Rodenticide – any pest control substance used to kill rodents such as rats and mice; they are often anti-coagulants similar to *warfarin* and are often ingested accidentally by dogs (and less commonly cats). Clinical signs of rodenticide toxicity include internal and external haemorrhage, which may be fatal if untreated. If discovered quickly, treatment involves making the animals sick (using *emetics*) and then treating with the *antidote* which is *vitamin K.*

Rods – **1.** light-sensitive cells (*photoreceptors*) found in the *retina*, stimulated in dim light/dusk conditions. See also *Cone*. **2.** one of the characteristic shapes of a *bacterium*, the rod-shaped or *bacilli* bacteria. See also *Cocci*, *Spirochaete*.

Romanowsky stain – stains used to examine *haematology* and *cytology* samples that are based on methylene blue and eosin (both types of dye), eg Wright's, Giemsa and Leishman stains.

R

Rongeurs – an orthopaedic instrument with cup-like cutting tips used for nibbling away at small pieces of bone.

Root – the part of the tooth below the gum line that anchors the tooth into the bone. The root is coated in *cement* rather than *enamel*.

Rostellum – the anterior part of the *scolex* at the head end of a tapeworm (*cestode*), often covered with hooks; it anchors the tapeworm to the gut wall.

Rostral – a directional term meaning towards the nose when describing features on an animal's head, eg the nostrils are rostral to the eyes.

Rotation – the movement of a joint where the bone rotates on its longitudinal axis.

Rouleaux formation – describes erythrocytes stacking on top of one another when viewed on a blood smear. It is normal in the horse and to some extent in the cat. Increased rouleaux formation is often associated with *hyperglobulinaemia*. Rouleaux should not be confused with auto-agglutination, which occurs in *immune-mediated haemolytic anaemia*.

Round-bodied needle – a suture needle that is round in cross-section with no sharp edges, used for suturing delicate tissue, eg fat or viscera. See also *Cutting needle*.

Round window – found in the inner ear at the entrance to the *cochlea*.

Roundworm – see *Nematode*.

Royal College of Veterinary Surgeons (RCVS) – the RCVS safeguards the health and welfare of animals committed to veterinary care, through the regulation of educational, ethical and clinical standards of the veterinary profession. A certificate of membership of the RCVS is legally required to practise veterinary surgery in the UK.

Rugae – term used in anatomy to describe ridges formed by the folding of an organ wall or surface; occur in the *stomach* and on the *hard palate*.

Rush pin – an orthopaedic implant used in pairs for repairing *long bones*; has a crook at one end and is flattened at the other. See also *Intramedullary pins*.

S

Sabouraud's dextrose medium – a microbiological culture medium with a low pH and a high sugar content; used to grow fungi.

Saccule – a bony sac-like structure that is part of the *vestibular* apparatus in the ear. Its function is to detect changes in the posture of the head. See also *Utricle*.

Sacroiliac joint – attaches the pelvis to the spine.

Sacrum – three sacral vertebrae fused together to form one bone.

Saliva – a watery mucous solution in the mouth, produced by the salivary glands. It does not contain digestive enzymes in the dog or cat; has a number of functions including dissolving soluble parts of food, lubricating and softening food, heat loss (through evaporation, panting) and grooming.

Salivary glands – exocrine glands that produce saliva and deliver it into the mouth through salivary ducts. Four pairs of salivary glands: the parotids, the submandibulars, the zygomatics and the sublinguals.

Salmonella – a group of rod-shaped Gram-negative bacteria that can cause food-borne gastrointestinal disease; often associated with ingestion of uncooked poultry and eggs. *Salmonella* is potentially *zoonotic*. Septicaemia may occur (particularly in young animals). The severity of disease varies from sub-clinical to septicaemia/endotoxaemia and death.

Salter-Harris fractures – fractures of the epiphysis (growth plates); they are graded in their severity on a scale of I to V.

Saphenous vein – a vein found in the hindlimb.

Saprolegnia – a type of filamentous fungus that can cause disease in fish and amphibians.

Saprophyte – organisms that obtain their nutrition from decaying organic material; many fungi are saprophytic.

Sarcocystis – a protozoal parasite that can cause mild diarrhoea in dogs.

Sarcoma – a malignant tumour of mesenchymal origin (connective or supportive tissue such as cartilage, bone, fat, muscle and blood vessels). Common examples are haemangiopericytoma, fibrosarcoma and osteosarcoma.

Sarcoptes scabei – a parasitic burrowing mite that affects dogs and humans (but rarely cats) and causes *sarcoptic mange*. Clinical signs include intense *pruritus*, *erythema* and papule formation. Secondary bacterial infection is common. This mite is potentially *zoonotic*.

S

Scalpel – a sharp surgical sterile blade used for making incisions, is usually attached onto a scalpel handle; various sizes are available.

Scapula – flat triangular bone, with a spine in the centre. It articulates with the humerus.

Scatter radiation – created when the primary beam interacts with objects, eg X-ray table. It travels in all directions and should be considered at all times with regard to personal safety.

Scavenging system – See Active scavenging system, Passive scavenging system.

Schedule III amendment order 2002 – a correction made to the *Veterinary Surgeons Act 1966* and now includes student veterinary nurses as well as qualified and listed qualified veterinary nurses.

Schirmer tear test (STT) – a test used to diagnose *keratoconjunctivitis sicca* (dry eye); involves placing a tiny strip of absorbent paper impregnated with dye into the lower eyelid and measuring how far the dye travels as the paper soaks up the tears. This equates to the amount of tears being produced.

Schwann cells – cells that wrap around nerve *axons* creating the *myelin sheath*.

Scintigraphy – image map using gamma radiation, produced by scanning and distribution of a high-energy radiation tracer. This technique has lots of health and safety implications and is generally performed more in equine practice than in small animal practice.

Sclera – the tough white outer coat of the eye.

Scolex – the head end of a tapeworm (*cestode*).

Screen – see *intensifying screen, Rare-earth screen.*

Screw-holding sleeve – a metal sleeve that is placed over a screwdriver, holding the screw until the threads have engaged.

Scrotum – the skin-covered sac containing the *testes*, *epididymes* and the *distal* part of the *spermatic cord*. In the dog the scrotum sits between the caudal thighs; in the cat it lies beneath the anus.

Scrub suit – cotton trousers and top, solely for use in theatre.

Scruff – the excess skin found over the dorsal neck area.

Scute – the horny scales that cover the bones of the shell in *chelonians* (tortoises, terrapins and turtles).

Scutum – a shield-shaped plate made of *chitin* on the cranial dorsum of the hard *ticks*, such as *Ixodes ricinus*.

Season – see *Oestrus.*

Sebaceous adenoma – a benign tumour of the *sebaceous gland.*

Sebaceous gland – glands in the skin that produce an oily secretion called *sebum.*

Seborrhoea – excessive secretion of sebum from the sebaceous glands that results in on oily coat and skin with increased scales and crusts.

Sebum – the oily secretion produced in the sebaceous glands that provides waterproofing for the skin and coat; may also inhibit the growth of some micro-organisms.

Second gas effect – if nitrous oxide is used within the gas mixture, then the volatile agent uptake is quicker at the beginning of anaesthesia.

Second intention healing – when wound edges are not sutured together because of tissue loss or infection.

Second opinion – a client seeks another veterinary surgeon's opinion on their pet.

Secondary feathers – smaller feathers located closer to the body than the larger primary feathers; important flight feathers.

Secondary layer – used in bandaging, provides support and holds the primary layer in place.

Sedatives – see *Phenothiazines, Pre-medication*.

Sediment – heavy or solid material that sinks to the bottom of a liquid solution, eg when a urine sample is placed in the *centrifuge* any cells, crystals and casts will sink to the bottom to form a sediment. Sediment examination is useful in the diagnosis of urinary tract disease.

Seizure – also called a convulsion or fit; a temporary alteration in the electrical activity in the brain which results in altered mental status, and often involves unco-ordinated, unconscious muscle movements (see *Tonic–clonic movement*). May occur in the normal brain as a result of *metabolic* or *toxic* abnormalities, as a result of disease within the brain (such as tumour or inflammation) or may be *idiopathic*.

Selective eating – the patient selects a particular food within the diet offered; often results in ill-health because the patient does not receive a complete diet. Rabbits are very prone to selective eating; it is a major cause of malnutrition because of lack of fibre intake. Rabbits selectively ingest tasty carbohydrate-rich pellets over grass and hay, which are crucial for normal functioning of their digestive tract.

Selectively permeable – see *Semi-permeable membrane*.

Self-conforming dressing – a dressing material that sticks to itself, used in the tertiary layer of bandages.

Self-interference – patients interfering/attacking their own wounds and/or bandages.

Self-tapping screw – a screw that does not require tapping because it cuts its own thread when inserted with a screwdriver.

Semen – a milky liquid consisting of sperm from the *epididymis* and *seminal fluid* from the accessory sex glands which passes out through the *urethra* during ejaculation.

Semi-circular canals – the main part of the *vestibular system* in the ear. The semi-circular canals are three loop-shaped canals arranged at right angles to one another. They detect rotational acceleration and deceleration (turning) of the head in any plane.

Semi-lunar valve – see *Aortic valve*, *Pulmonary valve*.

Semi-membranosus – one of the hamstring muscles in the caudal thigh; extends the hip.

Semi-permeable adhesive dressing – a dressing material (often a spray) suitable for wounds that have little or no exudates.

Semi-permeable membrane – a membrane that allows the passage of small molecules only.

Seminal fluid – liquid produced by the accessory sex glands (prostate in the dog and both prostate and bulbourethral gland in the cat); weakly alkaline to neutralise the acidity of the female reproductive tract, and contains sugars to provide energy for the spermatozoa.

Seminiferous tubule – tiny tubes within the *testes* that contain the germ cells and are the site of *spermatogenesis*.

Semitendinosus – one of the hamstring muscles in the caudal thigh; extends the hip, flexes the stifle and extends the hock.

Senior health clinic – clinic held by veterinary nurses or veterinary surgeons to provide health checks to cats and dogs, usually aged 8 years and over or aged 5 years and over if a large-breed dog.

Sensible water losses – the fluid losses over which the body has some control, eg 10–20 ml/kg per day in faeces and 20 ml kg per day in urine.

Sensory neurone – a nerve cell that carries information from the organs, skin, bones, muscles and joints to the spinal cord or brain.

Sepsis, septic – infection in the blood or tissues.

Septicaemia – blood poisoning; the presence of rapidly multiplying bacteria in the blood, often with production of bacterial toxins. Usually there is a widespread inflammatory response and the animal is seriously ill.

S

Septum (pl. **septa)** – a wall that divides a cavity in two. Septa occur in many places: the nasal septum divides the nasal cavity into two nostrils; there is a septum which divides the scrotum into two compartments, each containing a testis. Some fungi have septa along their length.

Serology – analysis of the serum to measure *antibodies* and *antigens* for specific diseases. Used widely in veterinary medicine to test animals for diseases including feline leukaemia virus, feline infectious peritonitis, leptospirosis, *Encephalitozoon cuniculi* and many more; also used to assess levels of immunity following vaccinations.

Seroma – a collection of fluid within the tissues; large seromas may require surgical draining.

Serosa – the outer lining of internal organs, such as the gastrointestinal and reproductive tracts. The serosa secretes serous fluid, which lubricates the organs so they slide against one another without friction.

Serous membrane – see *Serosa*.

Sertoli cells – the cells that make up the walls of the seminiferous tubules in the testes. They support the developing spermatozoa and also secrete hormones.

Serum – the fluid that remains when blood has clotted; comprises basically *plasma* without the *coagulation* (clotting) factors and *fibrinogen*. Used widely in *biochemistry*, *endocrinology* and *serology* tests.

Serum protein electrophoresis (SPE) – a laboratory test in which the proteins in serum are separated out into *albumin* and the various *globulins*; can be used to detect abnormalities in the globulins which occur in some diseases such as some types of lymphoma, and multiple myeloma.

Sesamoid bone – a bone that is found within a *tendon*, usually close to a joint. Their function is to protect the tendon from pressure or friction, and to alter the angle of pull of the tendon. The patella is a sesamoid bone.

Sex hormones – a group of steroid hormones made mainly by the reproductive organs (testes and ovaries) and important for the development of the reproductive organs and in control of reproductive cycles. The main ones are testosterone, oestrogen and progesterone.

Sexing – examining the patient to determine if they are male or female.

Sexual dimorphism – differences between male and female animals.

Sharpness – the clarity of the visible structures on the radiograph.

Sharps – refers to any sharp instrument, eg needles, scalpel blades. Sharps must be safely disposed of in a specially designated container.

Shearing wound – tearing or peeling of the skin, may also involve joints or bones.

Sheet graft (meshed or unmeshed) – a type of free skin graft that covers the whole of the wound; can be full or split thickness.

Shell rot – a general term for any bacterial or fungal infection affecting the shell of *chelonians*; often results from shell damage. Treatment involves thorough cleaning and debridement, meticulous attention to hygiene, and antimicrobial medications.

Sherman compression plate – a plate used for internal fixation, it is narrowed between the screw holes but its design is considered to weaken the plate.

Shock – a group of symptoms resulting from a severe deterioration in the animal's clinical signs; occurs when there is inadequate perfusion of all the body tissues with blood resulting in widespread cell damage. There are different types of shock: *hypovolaemic* shock, *cardiogenic* shock, *anaphylactic* shock, *endotoxic* shock and *neurogenic* shock.

Sick euthyroid syndrome – a reduced circulating level of *thyroid* hormones, such as *thyroxine*, which is *not* the result of thyroid function problems. Many diseases and medications cause a reduction in thyroxine levels, such as *hyperadrenocorticism*, steroid or phenobarbitone therapy, *diabetes mellitus*. For this reason the results of thyroid tests must be interpreted very carefully.

SID – once daily (from Latin *semel in die*).

Side-effect – an unintended effect of a drug on the body; usually inconvenient (eg polydipsia, pruritus, diarrhoea), but may occasionally be seriously harmful (eg bone marrow suppression, gastrointestinal ulceration).

Silk – a non-absorbable suture material; it is natural, has good knot security and is multifilamentous; however, it does have a high tissue reaction. Used in ligatures, skin sutures and in ophthalmology.

Silver halide (bromide) crystals – a compound of silver and bromine, the tiny crystals are suspended in the gelatin layer of radiographic film.

Simple continuous suture pattern – a running stitch that is rapidly placed; used in fascia, midline and viscera.

Simple fracture – the bone is fractured across one line without damage to the surrounding areas. Can be spiral, oblique or transverse depending on the direction of the line.

Simple interrupted suture pattern – a standard pattern of individual sutures; provides more security than a simple continuous pattern. Used for skin closure, midline and viscera.

Sino-atrial node (SA-node) – a group of cells in the wall of the right *atrium* that controls the rhythmic beating of the heart (the pacemaker).

Sinus – a cavity or indentation. There are sinuses in the skull called the frontal and maxillary sinuses. Function of sinuses is not fully understood.

Sinus arrhythmia – a normal variation in the heart rhythm where the heart rate increases slightly during inspiration (breathing in) and slows again on expiration (breathing out).

Sinusitis – inflammation of the sinuses, usually caused by bacterial, viral or fungal infection.

Sire – the male parent.

Skeletal muscle – also called striated muscle; contractile tissue that is responsible for virtually all *voluntary* movement. Skeletal muscle is attached at one or both ends to a bone so that, when stimulated by its nerve, it can pull on the bone and alter its position.

Skeleton – a bony framework providing support.

Skin – the outer covering of the body; provides protection, insulation and an aid to manufacturing vitamin D, and prevents excessive water loss.

Skin graft – providing skin to an area so a wound can heal.

- ❧ Pedicle skin graft – an area of skin is rotated from part of the body to another part including its blood supply
- ❧ Free skin graft – an area of skin is transferred from part of the body to another part without a blood supply
- ❧ Autogenous graft – skin is taken from a separate area on the same patient
- ❧ Full thickness graft – contains all dermal structures.

Skull – the bony skeleton of the head of vertebrates which encases and protects the brain; and provides support for features such as the ears and face.

Slander – falsely spoken or defamatory information.

Slough – necrotic tissue that peels away from the underlying structures or tissues.

Small intestinal bacterial overgrowth (SIBO) – the presence of abnormally high numbers of bacteria in the small intestine; may be caused by motility disorders, inflammatory bowel disease, foreign body, or tumour. Treatment involves correcting the underlying problem, and careful antibiotic use to reduce the number of bacteria.

Small intestine – the part of the digestive system that extends from the *stomach* to the *ileocaecocolic junction.* It is in three parts: the *duodenum*, the *jejunum* and the *ileum.* The functions of the small intestine are further *digestion* of material that leaves the stomach, and *absorption* of the products of digestion.

Smooth muscle – contractile tissue that moves in an *involuntary* manner; found in the walls of the blood vessels, gut, respiratory and urogenital tracts. Carries out automatic tasks such as constriction of the blood vessels and *peristaltic* movement.

Snake hook – a long metal hook used to handle snakes gently while keeping them at a safe distance from the operator.

Socket – a hollow in a bone where a structure fits, eg the *acetabulum*, which provides the socket part of the *ball and socket* hip joint (with the head of the femur being the 'ball' part); the *alveolus*, which is the socket into which each tooth is anchored.

Soda lime – used for absorbing carbon dioxide from anaesthetic circuits. It is the chemical calcium hydroxide within the soda lime that absorbs the carbon dioxide.

Sodium (Na) – an element that is present as a positively charged ion (the electrolyte Na^+) in the blood, and is often measured on blood *electrolyte* panels; has many functions and is important in the body's water balance. See also *Hypernatraemia, Hyponatraemia*.

Sodium chloride (NaCl) – an isotonic crystalloid fluid, used for water loss eg vomiting. See also *Glucose saline (fluid therapy)*.

Soft palate – the caudal portion of the *palate*; a mobile muscular flap involved with the *deglutition* (swallowing) mechanism.

Softbills – birds that eat soft food such as fleshy fruit, insects or pollen and nectar (as opposed to seed-eating or hardbill birds).

Solubility – the amount of a substance that can be dissolved in an amount of water, or in blood when volatile agents are used.

Solution – fluid or water containing a substance dissolved within it.

Solvent – a fluid capable of dissolving other substances.

Somatic cell – any cell in the body with the exception of the gametes (ova and spermatozoa).

Somatostatin – an inhibitory hormone produced by the *hypothalamus* and also in the *stomach* and the delta cells of the *pancreas*. It reduces gut motility and inhibits secretion of pancreatic and gastric fluids, also suppresses release of *growth hormone* and *thyroid-stimulating hormone*.

Somatotrophin – see *Growth hormone (GH)*.

Spasm – involuntary contraction of a muscle.

Spay – see *Ovariohysterectomy*.

Spay hook – a surgical instrument that has a blunt hook at one end. It is used for drawing the uterine horns out of the abdomen during ovariohysytectomy.

Spaying – performing an ovariohysterectomy in female dogs and cats; surgically removing the ovaries and uterus.

Specific gravity – **1.** concentration of urine. **2.** the ability of tissues to absorb X-rays, generally the higher the specific gravity of the tissue (eg bone has a high specific gravity) the more X-rays are absorbed.

Spectacle – the transparent scale that covers the eye of a snake; usually shed each time the snake sheds its skin (*ecdysis*), but if the *humidity* is incorrect the animals does not shed properly (*dysecdysis*) and the spectacle may be retained.

Speculum – an instrument used for examining cavities, eg the ear.

Spencer Wells artery forceps – an instrument used to provide haemostasis.

Spermatic cord – a bundle of tubular structures and tissues that attaches the testicle to the body; contains the deferent duct, the cremaster muscle and the blood and lymph supply to the testis. It also contains autonomic nerves.

Spermatogenesis – the production of *spermatozoa* from germ cells within the *seminiferous tubules*, in the testes.

Spermatozoon (pl. **spermatozoa**) – the male *gamete* or sex cell that is produced in the *seminiferous tubule* in the *testis*.

Sphenoid – a bone at the base of the skull.

Sphincter – a ring of muscle that opens and closes to control the movement of a substance out of an organ, eg the *pyloric sphincter* and the *external anal sphincter*.

Sphygmomanometer – an indirect method of monitoring blood pressure; involves the placing of a cuff on a limb and inflating it to occlude the artery, then detecting the return of blood flow as the cuff is released.

Spigot – a type of adaptor used to connect syringes to certain tubing.

Spinal cord – the posterior section of the central nervous system (ie caudal to the brain) that extends from the *foramen magnum* to the *cauda equina*; located within the vertebral canal. It is a long tube of nervous tissue that receives information from the body and relays it to the brain. It also relays information from the brain back to the body.

Spinal reflex – a reflex involving the spinal cord but not the brain, and therefore allowing a very quick response to the stimulus, eg the patellar reflex.

Spindle – the microtubules (tiny fibres) that are laid down in a cell by the *centrioles* during cell division (*mitosis* and *meiosis*). Chromosomes line up along the spindle and become attached by their *centromeres*.

Spindle cell tumour – a tumour of mesenchymal origin (connective or supportive tissue such as cartilage, bone, fat, muscle and blood vessels). Common examples are lipoma, haemangiopericytoma, fibrosarcoma and osteosarcoma. See also *Sarcoma*.

Spinous process – provides a site for muscle attachment along the vertebrae; they vary in size.

S

Spirochaete – a spiral-shaped Gram-negative bacterium such as *Leptospira* (which causes leptospirosis) and *Treponema* (which causes syphilis in rabbits).

Splanchnic – relating to the internal organs, as opposed to the supportive structure of the body. See also *Viscera*.

Splanchnic skeleton – a part of the skeleton that is connected with an organ, eg the *os penis* bone is part of the splanchnic skeleton.

Spleen – an abdominal organ that stores blood; removes old and damaged erythrocytes and cellular particles from the blood; produces lymphocytes and monocytes; and is a site of haematopoiesis in the fetus (and can regain this function in the adult if needed). Animals can survive without the spleen although they may be more susceptible to infections.

Splenectomy – surgical removal of the spleen, often performed in animals with splenic tumours such as haemangiosarcoma.

Splenic – relating to the spleen.

Splenomegaly – enlargement of the spleen; may be associated with tumour, or increased splenic activity (eg in animals with haemolytic anaemia). Some anaesthetic agents such as thiopentone may cause splenomegaly on induction.

Split thickness graft – a type of free skin graft that contains the epidermis and part of the dermis.

Spoon feeding – feeding a patient with a spoon or fork to encourage eating.

Spore – a resting or dormant form of a bacterium (*Clostridia*, or *Bacillus*) which is very resistant to heat, desiccation, cold, radiation and chemical treatment (which would kill the normal growing form of the bacterium). Spores can survive in the environment for extended periods and are difficult to kill using the usual cleaning techniques.

Spore test – strips of paper impregnated with bacterial spores, usually *Bacillus stearothermophilus*. The strip is placed in the centre of the load to be sterilised and is then cultured for 72 hours after sterilisation. If sterilisation has been successful there will be no growth.

Sprain – an injury resulting from excessive force on a joint. See also *strain*.

Spruell's needle – an instrument with an opening down the centre, used when flushing ears.

Squamous cell carcinoma (SCC) – malignant tumour of squamous epithelium; often associated with solar radiation and more commonly seen in animals with less pigment (eg on the tips of the ears or face of white cats). Can occur wherever there is squamous epithelium, such as in the lung, mouth or oesophagus.

Squamous epithelium – a type of *epithelium* made from layers of flat cells. Simple squamous epithelium is found in *capillary* walls, and lining the *alveoli* and *Bowman's capsule*. Stratified squamous epithelium consists of more layers, and is found in places where there is more wear and tear, such as on the skin (where the surface contains *keratin* for extra protection) and in the lining of the mouth and oesophagus, and the rectum and vagina.

Stage – the horizontal platform on a microscope where the slide or sample is placed.

Stainless-steel wire – see *Cerclage wire*.

Stamp graft – a type of free skin graft that covers part of the wound; can be full or split thickness.

Stance – how a patient stands and holds itself.

Stapes – the stirrup; one of the three tiny bones within the ear (the *auditory ossicles*) which transmit sounds across the middle ear onto the *vestibular (oval) window.*

Staphylococcus – *Gram-positive* bacteria that are usually arranged in bunches. Most species are harmless but can cause infection opportunistically (eg if they get into a wound). Species commonly encountered in veterinary medicine include *Staphylococcus intermedius* and *Staphylococcus aureus*. See also *Methicillin-resistant Staphylococcus aureus*.

Staple – a metal clip that is placed with an applicator; an alternative to sutures.

Starvation – a severe state of hunger, emaciation can sometimes be present.

Static electricity – artefact seen on a developed radiograph, looks like lightning; occurs either because the radiographic film was pulled out of the box too quickly or was brushed against nylon clothing/material.

Status epilepticus – a potentially life-threatening condition where the patient has a very prolonged seizure, or has a cluster of seizures without time for recovery in between.

Steam sterilisation – achieving sterility through moist heat. Autoclaves may be upward displacement, downward displacement or vacuum assisted.

Steatorrhoea – faeces containing excessive fat.

Steinmann pin – see *Intramedullary pins*.

Stenosis – narrowing or stricture of any vessel or passageway.

Stercoraceous vomiting – vomit containing faeces, eg in severe constipation.

Sterile – an object/item that is free from all micro-organisms including bacterial spores.

Sterilisation – the process of destroying all micro-organisms including bacterial spores.

Sternal recumbency – describes a patient who is lying down, but resting on the sternum compared to lateral recumbency.

Sternebra (pl. **sternebrae)** – the eight bones that make up the sternum. They articulate with each other through the intersternebral cartilage.

S

Sternotomy – a surgical incision into the sternum.

Sternum – bony structure made of 8 sternebrae and which the ribs attach.

Steroid – a family of molecules which all have a similar structure. Most naturally occurring steroids are hormones such as the corticosteroids (*glucocorticoids* and *mineralocorticoids*) and sex hormones. *Cholesterol* is also a steroid. Synthetic steroids, such as prednisolone and dexamethasone, are used widely as drugs to treat inflammation, immune-mediated conditions and some types of tumours.

Stethoscope – an instrument used to listen to low-level sounds such as the heart beat or noises within the abdomen.

Stifle joint – a synovial joint that possesses two menisci between the femur and tibia. The collateral ligaments and cruciate ligaments prevent lateral and cranial/caudal movement respectively. Movement of the stifle is flexion and extension only.

Stirrups (RJ bandage) – long pieces of a sticky tape, eg Leukpore, are applied to the cranial and caudal ends of the limb, before the tertiary layer is applied. These strips are pulled back up and over the dressing and stuck down. This is to help prevent the bandage from slipping. See also Robert Jones bandage.

Stock rotation – newly purchased items are placed at the rear of the stock, any items with short sell-by-dates or soon to expire are placed to the front.

Stoma – the site where a tube exits onto the skin.

Stomach – a dilated portion of the gastrointestinal tract between the oesophagus and small intestine; the site of the first stage of chemical digestion in dogs and cats. The wall is muscular so that the stomach can churn and grind the ingesta, it also acts as a storage vat and controls the rate of delivery of ingesta to the small intestine.

Stomatitis – inflammation of the mucous membranes within the mouth; may be associated with dental disease, ingestion of irritants, or with viral infections such as feline immunodeficiency virus or calicivirus in cats. Animals in advanced renal failure may develop uraemic stomatitis.

Strain – tearing of a muscle or tendon. See also *sprain*.

Strangulated hernia – type of hernia where the blood supply to the herniated tissue has become compromised; very painful and can be life-threatening if an organ is involved.

Stranguria – painful urination because of spasms in the bladder and/or the urethra.

Streptococcus – *Gram-positive* bacteria that are usually arranged in chains. Species commonly encountered in veterinary medicine include *Streptococcus equi* and *Streptococcus zooepidemicus*, which are important pathogens in horses, and *Streptococcus canis*, which may be seen in dogs and cats.

Striated muscle – see *Skeletal muscle*.

Stridor – an abnormal, high-pitched noise during respiration.

Strip graft – a type of free skin graft that covers part of the wound; can be full or split thickness.

S

Strobila – the chain of reproductive units (*proglottids*) which makes up the body of *cestodes* (tapeworms).

Stroke volume – the volume of blood ejected from the heart with each heart beat.

Struvite crystals – sometimes called triple phosphate crystals; found in small numbers in the urine of normal animals but can cause disease when present in large numbers. Bacterial infection and alkaline urine may predispose an animal to develop struvite crystalluria.

Stud – a male animal used for breeding.

Stylet – a metal insert used to strengthen some tubes that is later discarded.

Stylohyoid bones – the most cranial bones of the *hyoid apparatus* which articulate with the mastoid process on the *temporal bone* of the skull.

Subarachnoid space – the space surrounding the brain and spinal cord; contains cerebrospinal fluid. It widens at the *cisterna magna* and lumbar cistern where cerebrospinal fluid samples may be taken.

Subclinical – the early part of a condition before signs or symptoms are seen.

Subconjunctival injection – injection just beneath the conjunctiva of the eye.

Subcutaneous – meaning under the skin.

Subcutaneous injection – method of administering drugs under the skin by an injection.

Subdural space – a virtual space within the vertebral column that can become enlarged following injury, eg subdural haemorrhage.

Subgingival – below the gum line.

Sublingual pulse – a pulse found underneath the tongue.

Sublingual salivary glands – a chain of saliva-producing glands running just beneath the floor of the mouth; secrete a saliva that is mainly mucous in character.

Subluxation – partial displacement of the articular surfaces in a joint.

Submandibular lymph nodes – a pair of lymph nodes just ventral to the angle of the jaw; become enlarged when there is inflammation in the oral cavity, nasal cavity or on the face. May also be enlarged as a result of the presence of tumour cells (such as lymphoma).

Submandibular salivary glands – paired saliva-producing glands found under the chin adjacent to the submandibular lymph nodes; produce a mixture of watery and mucous secretions.

Submucosa – the layer beneath the mucosa in organs such as the gastrointestinal tract, reproductive tract, respiratory tract; contains blood vessels, lymphatics, nerves and occasionally glands.

Suckling – the mouth action of neonates when feeding either from their mothers or from bottles.

Sucrose – a disaccharide made from one glucose molecule and one fructose molecule.

Sudiferous/sudorific gland – see *Sweat gland*.

Supernatant – the fluid that sits on top of the sediment when a sample has been centrifuged.

Supination – a term used to describe outward rotation of the paw (think – thumbs up!).

Supplement – extra nutrients added to an animals's diet.

Supraspinatus – a muscle on the cranial part of the *scapula* which inserts on the *humerus* and causes extension of the shoulder.

Supravital stain – also called supervital stains; used to detect inclusions in blood cells such as *Babesia* or *Leishmania*.

Suspensory ligament – also known as the ovarian ligament; holds the ovary in position in the abdomen. It is part of the *ovarian pedicle* which is cut during *ovariohysterectomy*. There are also suspensory ligaments in the eye which hold the *lens* in place.

Suture – a stitch, placed in wounds to aid healing.

Swab – **1.** a surgical swab is a piece of gauze material used to soak up any haemorrhage during surgical procedures; must be sterile and of a suitable ply. **2.** a swab for microbiology, involves placing the swab (like a large cotton bud) directly in contact with the wound, it is then placed into transport medium (usually provided by the laboratory) and sent to the laboratory for culture.

Sweat gland – also called sudorific gland; a type of gland found mainly on the skin of the feet in cats and dogs and a minor route of heat loss in these species.

Swim bladder – an internal sac of gas in the dorsal part of the coelom in fish which helps them to remain neutrally buoyant (ie they do not sink or float). Disorders involving the swim bladder cause fish to have buoyancy problems.

Symbiont – an organism that lives in symbiosis with another.

Symbiosis – a close association between two organisms of different species; a symbiotic relationship can be *parasitic*, *commensal* or *mutualistic*.

Sympathetic nervous system – a division of the *autonomic nervous system* that prepares the body for action (fight or flight). *Adrenaline* and *noradrenaline* are responsible for the effects of the sympathetic nervous system, such as dilation of the pupil, increased *cardiac output*, increased blood flow to the muscles and decreased blood flow to the gut.

Symphysis – a cartilaginous joint between two bones such as the pubic symphysis in the pelvis, and the mandibular symphysis.

Symptom – a sign or evidence of illness or disease.

Symptomatic – a patient who is demonstrating symptoms.

Synapse – a junction where an impulse is passed from one nerve to another.

Synchondroses – cartilaginous joints between two bones that allow a small amount of movement, such as the mandibular symphysis.

Syncope – fainting or a temporary loss of consciousness.

Syndesmoses – when two bones are joined by ligaments such as the radius and ulna.

Synovial fluid – lubricating fluid found within the synovial joint.

Synovial joint – a type of joint where a fluid-filled space (the synovial cavity) separates the articulating bones, eg the stifle joint.

Synthesis – the production of a new compound from two or more different elements.

Syringe feeding – feeding a patient a liquid-type diet via a syringe; can only be performed if they are conscious and swallowing.

Systemic – a condition that affects the whole body. See also Generalised.

Systemic lupus erythematosus (SLE) – a serious autoimmune condition where antibodies are created against the animal's own DNA. Symptoms include polyarthritis, skin lesions, lethargy and many others.

Systole – the phase of the cardiac cycle where the ventricles contract and blood is ejected from the heart.

T-lymphocyte – a type of *lymphocyte* that originates from the *thymus* and is important in the cell-mediated immune response; recognises foreign *antigens* and causes destruction of foreign cells. Special memory T-lymphocytes remember the antigen so that a similar response can be mounted more quickly if the antigen is encountered in the future.

T-wave – the part of an *electrocardiograph* trace that follows the *QRS-complex* and represents repolarisation of the ventricles during *diastole*.

Tachycardia – increased heart rate.

Tachypnoea – increased respiratory rate.

***Taenia* spp.** – a group of cestodes (tapeworms) that affect dogs including *Taenia hydatigena*, *Taenia pisiformis*, *Taenia multiceps*, *Taenia serialis* and *Taenia ovis*. *Taenia taeniformis* affects the cat. The adult worms rarely cause clinical disease although the *metacestode* may cause disease in the *intermediate host*.

Tail gland – oval area of skin on dorsal part of tail, produces pheromones.

Talus – a large bone of the *tarsus* (hock) which articulates with the *tibia* and *fibula*, the *calcaneus* and the more *distal* tarsal bones.

Tamponade – a condition affecting the heart where a build-up of fluid outside the heart (*pericardial effusion*) prevents the heart from filling properly, and results in reduced *cardiac output*.

Tap – a surgical instrument for cutting a thread in a pre-drilled hole.

Tapetum lucidum – a reflective layer in the retina that reflects light onto the photoreceptor cells and improves vision in low light conditions.

Tapeworm – see *Cestode*.

Tapping screws – screws that provide a snug fit and prevent micro-fractures, require the bone to be tapped first. Identified by their hexagonal head.

Target – see *Anode*.

Target organ – an organ, cell or gland where a hormone has an action, eg *thyroid-stimulating hormone* (TSH) has an action (stimulates production of thyroid hormones) on its target gland (the *thyroid gland*).

Tarsal gland – also called *meibomian gland*; a type of sebaceous gland that lines the edge of the eyelid and produces secretions that contribute to the tear film.

Tarsus – also called the hock; joint of the lower hindlimb that equates to the ankle in humans. Consists of two large bones – the *talus* and *calcaneus*, and a number of smaller tarsal bones. There are joints between the bones of the tarsal joint.

Tartar – a build-up of plaque on the teeth that becomes calcified and cannot be removed by brushing.

Taurine – an extra essential amino acid required by the cat. One sign of taurine deficiency is retinal degeneration, leading to blindness. Taurine is often added to cat food.

Teat canal – the tube that extends from the teat sinus (where milk is stored) to the orifice (opening) in the mammary gland, through which milk travels.

Teat orifice – the opening on the surface of the teat through which milk is secreted. In the dog there are between 8 and 20 orifices per teat, whereas in the cat there are between 4 and 7.

Telogen – the resting phase in the hair cycle.

Telophase – a phase towards the end of cell division when a new nuclear membrane forms around each group of chromatids and the nucleolus re-forms.

Temperature – a thermometer is used to take a core temperature reading using either a rectal thermometer or an ear thermometer. Normal readings for core temperatures are:

1. Dog: 38.3–38.7°C (100.9–101.7°F)
2. Cat: 38.0–38.5°C (100.4–101.6°F)

Temporal bone – a bone that forms part of the skull and is located caudally and laterally; articulates with the jaw and houses the inner ear.

Temporal lobe – one of the lobes of the cerebrum in the brain; located caudally and laterally and has functions involving hearing.

Temporalis muscle – a large masticatory (chewing) muscle located caudally and laterally on the head; function is to close the jaw.

Temporomandibular joint (TMJ) – the synovial joint between the lower jaw (*mandible*) and the skull. The condylar process of the mandible articulates with the mandibular fossa of the *temporal bone* of the skull.

Tendon – band of connective tissue that attaches muscle to the bone. See also *ligament*.

Tendonitis – inflammation of a tendon.

Tenesmus – also known as *dyschezia*; difficulty in passing faeces, usually involving excessive straining.

Tension band wiring – see *Cerclage wiring*.

Terrapin – an aquatic or semi-aquatic *chelonian* living in fresh water, eg the red-eared terrapin. They have complex husbandry requirements (diet, lighting, heating, water hygiene, etc) and often suffer from diseases related to poor husbandry.

Terrestrial – belonging to or living on land.

Tertiary amine – an ingredient used in environmental disinfectants, eg trigene.

Tertiary layer – the third layer of a bandage, provides protection from the environment.

Testis (pl. **testes**) – also called the testicle; one of the paired male gonads, oval organs suspended in a sac (the *scrotum*). They produce the male *gametes* (*spermatozoa*) and also have an *endocrine* function secreting *hormones* such as *testosterone*.

Testosterone – a *steroid hormone* that is the male sex hormone; produced in the *testes* and has a number of functions including growth and development of the reproductive organs; body composition and growth rate; *libido*, and aggression.

Tetralogy of Fallot – a complex *congenital* heart condition comprising pulmonic *stenosis*, a *ventricular septal defect*, an over-riding aorta, and right ventricular *hypertrophy*. Treatment is *palliative*.

Tetraparesis – see *Quadriparesis*.

Tetraplegia – see *Quadriplegia*.

Thalamus – part of the brain that receives sensory information (except *olfaction*) and relays it to the relevant part of the brain (usually the *cerebrum*).

Therapeutic effect – the intended effect which the medication has on the patient either in the management of disease or the manipulation of physiological function.

Thermionic emission – 'Boiling off of electrons', the cloud of electrons at the cathode are released.

Thermocautery – see *Diathermy*.

Thermoluminescent dosemeter (TLD) – used to monitor the amount of radiation a person receives during radiography; contains fine crystals that are sensitive to radiation. The crystals are heated and emit light proportional to the amount of radiation absorbed. Sent off for readings every 1–3 months; they are usually yellow or orange.

Thermoplastic casts – a material used for casting; very lightweight and dries within minutes.

Thermoregulation – control and maintenance of the body temperature (part of homeostasis). Many things contribute to thermoregulation such as the skin and hair coat, subcutaneous fat, blood flow to the skin, sweating, panting and behaviour (lying in the shade, or seeking heat).

Thermostatic heaters – a thermostatically controlled heating system used in automatic processors in radiography.

Thiamine (vitamin B1) – a water-soluble vitamin, part of the B-complex vitamins.

Third eyelid – see *Nictitating membrane*.

Thoracic duct – the vessel in the cranial thorax that delivers *lymph* from the *lymphatic system* into the blood. Damage to or obstruction of the thoracic duct can cause *chylothorax*.

Thoracic inlet – the cranial opening into the thoracic cavity through which the oesophagus, trachea and blood vessels and nerves pass. The boundaries are created by the thoracic vertebrae dorsally, the first ribs laterally and the manubrium ventrally.

Thoracocentesis – the procedure of aseptically obtaining a sample of thoracic fluid by inserting a needle through the thoracic wall into the thoracic cavity; often used to drain or sample a pleural effusion.

Thoracotomy – a surgical incision into the thoracic cavity.

Thorax, thoracic – a cavity enclosed by the thoracic vertebrae, sternum, ribs and caudally by the diaphragm; contains the heart, lungs, thoracic portions of the oesophagus and trachea and the pleural cavity.

Thread – the helical rib around a screw.

Thrombocyte – see *Platelet*.

Thrombocytopaenia – a decrease in the number of circulating *platelets* which, if severe, can result in bleeding. Causes include reduced production in the bone marrow, increased consumption (haemorrhage, *disseminated intravascular coagulation*), or immune-mediated destruction (see *Immune-mediated thrombocytopaenia*).

Thrombocytosis – an increase in the number of circulating platelets; may result from inflammation, splenectomy, or excitement and is not usually clinically significant.

Thromboembolism – a blood clot occluding a blood vessel.

Thrombophlebitis – a blood clot causing inflammation in a blood vessel.

Thrombus – a blood clot. See also *Thromboembolism*.

Thymus gland – a lymphoid organ in the cranial thorax that is larger in young animals; produces T-lymphocytes.

Thyroid gland – one of a pair of glands adjacent to the trachea in the neck; secretes thyroid hormones, *thyroxine* (T_4) and *tri-iodothyronine* (T_3) under the action of *thyroid-stimulating hormone*. The thyroid hormones are important for maintenance of the *basal metabolic rate*, and for growth and development of some tissues.

Thyroid protector – see *Protective clothing*.

Thyroid-stimulating hormone (TSH) – a hormone released from the anterior *pituitary gland* which stimulates the *thyroid gland* to produce and release thyroid hormones.

Thyroxine (T_4) – one of the thyroid hormones produced by the thyroid gland. Thyroid hormones are important for maintenance of the *basal metabolic rate*, and for growth and development of some tissues. See also *Hyperthyroidism*, *Hypothyroidism*.

Tibia – the larger bone of the lower leg which articulates proximally with the *femur* in the *stifle*, and distally with the *talus* in the *tarsus* (hock).

Tibialis cranialis – see *Cranial tibial muscle*.

Tick – parasitic wingless arachnids (possessing eight legs) which ingest the blood of their host. *Ixodes ricinus* is common in the UK. The hedgehog tick (*Ixodes hexagonus*) is seen less commonly. Ticks may act as a *vector* for some diseases such as Lyme's disease.

TID – means three times daily (from Latin – *ter in die*).

Tidal volume – the volume of gas inspired with each breath during normal respiration.

Tie – during mating in dogs the *bulbus glandis* in the dog's penis swells up and becomes locked in position in the bitch's vagina; the dogs are locked together or 'tied' until the swelling subsides (usually about 20 minutes). *Ejaculation* continues during the tie.

Tieman's catheter – a type of urinary catheter.

Tissue – a group of cells with a common origin with some specialised structure and a common function, eg epithelial tissue, connective tissue, adipose (fat) tissue, muscle, cartilage, bone, neurones and vessels. Tissues are often further organised into organs.

Tissue culture – *viruses* can only multiply within cells and so cannot be grown on conventional culture material. Instead they are grown on sheets of specially grown living animal's cells. This is called tissue culture.

Tissue glue – a method of repairing a wound; an alternative to sutures.

Tissue perfusion – see *Perfusion*.

Titre – a way of expressing how high the levels of *antibody/ antigen* are in a *serology* sample; a high titre means that a sample has to be diluted more times before the results become negative (ie it contains a larger amount of antibody or antigen).

To-and-fro anaesthetic circuits – a re-breathing anaesthetic circuit, used to deliver and maintain anaesthesia and also to remove waste gases; uses soda lime to absorb carbon dioxide housed in a Water's canister (a plastic canister fitted within the to and fro circuit to house soda lime), which is placed between the patient and the reservoir bag. Nitrous oxide should not be used with this circuit. Use in patients under 10 kg.

Tongue – a muscular organ in the mouth that is suspended from the skull by the *hyoid apparatus* and has a freely mobile tip. It has a variety of functions including taste (*gustation*), lapping liquid, manipulating food in the mouth, grooming, vocalisation and heat loss. Attached to the floor of the oral cavity by a *frenulum*, and the dorsal surface is covered with *papillae.*

Tonic-clonic movement – the type of movement that often accompanies an epileptic seizure. Tonic describes the stiffening of the body as a result of muscle contraction and clonic describes the jerky movement of the limbs as a result of repeated contraction and relaxation of the muscles.

Tonsil – a collection of lymphoid tissue in the palatoglossal arch at the back of the oral cavity; provides protection against infection with micro-organisms entering the oral cavity.

Tonsillitis – inflammation of the *tonsils,* usually caused by bacterial or viral infection, or neoplasia.

Topical – treatments applied to the surface of the body.

Topical anaesthesia – local anaesthesia applied to the skin or mucous membranes, eg EMLA cream.

Total ear canal ablation (TECA) – the surgical removal of both the vertical and horizontal ear canals.

Total lung capacity – the total amount of air in the lungs after maximal inspiration.

Total protein (TP) – a measure of all the protein within a sample; measured in blood profiles, and also in urine samples, effusions, joint fluid and cerebrospinal fluid. The main components of total protein are albumin and globulin (and fibrinogen in a sample that has not clotted, ie plasma). See also Hyperproteinaemia, Hypoproteinaemia.

Tourniquet – a tight cuff applied proximal to a wound, occluding blood vessels; can only be used on the limbs and tail and should not be left on for more than 10 minutes. Used to stop haemorrhage and for raising veins for blood samples.

Toxaemia – the presence of toxins in the blood.

Toxascaris leonina – a parasitic *nematode* that inhabits the small intestine of cats and dogs; not as common as *Toxocara* in the UK. This parasite is potentially zoonotic.

Toxic, toxicity – see *Toxin*.

Toxigenicity – the ability to produce toxins which cause further damage.

Toxin – a poisonous or harmful substance.

Toxocara – *Toxocara canis* and *T. cati*; parasitic *nematodes* that inhabit the small intestine of dogs and cats, respectively. The commonest parasitic nematodes in dogs and cats in the UK; can be passed to offspring via the *transplacental* and *transmammary* routes so that puppies and kittens can be born with an infestation. Potentially *zoonotic* and can result in *ocular* and *visceral larval migrans*.

Toxoid – a toxin that has been treated, either physically or chemically, to make it non-toxic.

Toxoplasma gondii – a tissue-cyst-forming *protozoan parasite* that causes disease in a number of species including humans. The *final host* is the cat. The *intermediate host* may be any warm-blooded animal. Cats often become infected by ingesting infected birds or rodents. Most cats show no clinical signs when infected but occasionally there may be neurological or muscular disorders, hepatitis, or respiratory disease. Pregnant women and people with a suppressed immune system are at greater risk of toxoplasmosis.

T-plate – a special plate used for repairing fractures of the distal radius.

Trabecula (pl. **trabeculae)** – a fine mesh of bone found in cancellous bone.

Trachea – an open tube made up of incomplete rings of hyaline cartilage, fibrous connective tissue and smooth muscle fibres. Carries air from the larynx to the lower respiratory tract.

Tracheal collapse – common in certain toy breeds, eg Yorkshire terriers, either the thoracic part of the trachea can collapse or all of it, because the hyaline cartilage rings are weakened.

Tracheitis – inflammation of the trachea.

Tracheostomy – a surgical opening into the trachea that is permanent, to aid respiration.

Tracheotomy – a temporary surgical opening into the trachea to aid with respiration; a tracheotomy tube can be fitted.

Tranquilliser – a drug that causes calm and tranquillity but not sedation, eg diazepam.

Trans – prefix meaning the opposite side.

Transcellular fluid – extracellular fluid that is separated from the normal fluid compartments by cellular barriers, eg *synovial fluid* and *cerebrospinal fluid*.

Transdermal – entering through unbroken skin.

Transducer – a device used in ultrasound, it is placed over the area to be scanned. There are three types:

❖ Linear and curved array transducers – crystals are arranged in a line; produces a rectangular view
❖ Mechanical sector transducer – one crystal that oscillates back and forth or three to five crystals mounted on a rotating wheel; produces a pie-shaped view
❖ Phased array sector transducer – approximately 60 piezo-elements that do not move; produces a pie-shaped view.

Transformer – can be a step-up or a step-down transformer, alters the voltage so that it becomes higher or lower, respectively.

Transfusion – the transfer of blood from one patient to another.

Transfusion reaction – patient reactions to blood transfusions can be immediate or delayed. Can occur if the blood was not cross-matched first, meaning the patient receives blood of the wrong blood group.

Transitional epithelium – a type of epithelium that consists of layers of cells and is capable of stretching out until it is one or two cells thick, and that is able to recoil back to its original form. It lines the bladder and ureters.

Transmammary – passage of a substance from the mother to the offspring through the mammary gland, eg *Toxocara canis* infection can occur when a puppy ingests milk containing the larvae.

Transmission – passage of a disease or infectious agent from one organism to another; may be *direct* or *indirect*, or through *fomites*, *vectors*, *intermediate hosts*, *aerosols*, *faeces*, body fluids or contaminated food or water.

Transplacental – passage of a substance from the mother to the offspring through the placenta, eg *Toxocara canis* infection can occur when larvae cross the placenta from the mother and infect the fetus.

Transport host – term used in parasitology to describe the host that carries the parasite from one area to another, or one animal to another.

Transport medium – a substance used to transport microbiological samples (bacteria, viruses and fungi) from the animal to the laboratory, protecting the organism from desiccation and damage.

Transudate – a type of effusion that contains very few cells and very little protein; often results from *hypoproteinaemia* because the *oncotic pressure* of the blood is too low to hold water in, and it leaks into the body cavities.

Transverse process – provides sites for muscle attachment along the vertebrae; they vary in size.

Trapezius muscle – a muscle found in the neck that elevates and abducts the forelimb.

Trauma – a wound or physical injury, usually caused by an external force.

Travers retractors – self-retaining retractors, used to hold wound edges open.

Trematode – a parasitic flatworm commonly known as a fluke; the liver fluke *Fasciola hepatica* can cause disease in ruminants and humans.

Trephine biopsy – a hollow trephine biopsy needle used to penetrate bone and obtain a core sample.

Triceps – a muscle of the upper forelimb and shoulder that extends the elbow and flexes the shoulder.

Trichodectes canis – a biting *louse* that occurs on the dog and may be a *vector* for the tapeworm *Dipylidium caninum*.

Trichoepithelioma – benign skin tumour previously known as a Basal Cell tumour.

Trichophyton mentagrophytes – a fungal pathogen that is a common cause of *dermatophytosis* (ringworm) in dogs, but less commonly in cats.

Trichuris vulpis – the whipworm; a parasitic *nematode* inhabiting the *caecum* of dogs. Infestations cause intermittent diarrhoea.

Tricuspid valve – see *Atrioventricular valves*.

Trigeminal nerve V – the fifth pair of cranial nerves, their sensory function is most facial structures and their motor function is the masticatory muscles.

Trigone – the triangle formed by the two *ureteral* openings and the *urethra* in the bladder wall. This area is more sensitive to expansion and informs the brain when the bladder is filling.

Tri-iodothyronine (T_3) – a *thyroid hormone*; the active form of the hormone. The thyroid hormones are important for maintenance of the *basal metabolic rate*, and for growth and development of some tissues. See also *Hyperthyroidism*, *Hypothyroidism*.

Tripod unit – a unit or stand with three legs.

Trixacarus caviae – a burrowing *mite* similar to *Sarcoptes* causing mange in guinea-pigs.

Trochlear nerve IV – the fourth pair of cranial nerves; their sensory and motor functions are the eyeball muscles.

Trolley unit – a unit or stand with four legs.

Trombicula autumnalis – the harvest mite; bright orange and hairy. It is only parasitic in the larval stage and causes irritation and hypersensitivity in any animal including humans.

Trophoblast – a layer of cells in the developing *zygote* that develops into part of the *placenta*.

Trypsin – a *proteolytic enzyme* found in the *pancreatic juice* which is involved in protein digestion in the small intestine.

Trypsin-like immunoreactivity (TLI) – a diagnostic test used to assess the production of digestive enzymes (namely *trypsinogen*) in the *pancreas*. Increased TLI can be caused by *pancreatitis*; decreased TLI reflects *exocrine pancreatic insufficiency* (EPI).

TST indicator strips – paper strips with an indicator spot; used as sterility indicator and are sensitive to time, steam and temperature. Can be used in autoclaves and with ethylene oxide.

Tube feeding – feeding a patient their full nutritional requirements via a tube. Also known as assisted feeding and enteral feeding. See also *Parenteral feeding*.

Tube head – the device that houses the cathode and anode.

Tumour – literally means 'swelling' but is used to describe the abnormal purposeless proliferation of cells; may be *benign* or *malignant* (cancerous).

Tungsten carbide – an insert that can be placed on the tips of instruments that are used for cutting or gripping, increasing their life span. Instruments that have tungsten carbide inserts have gold handles to distinguish them.

Tunica vaginalis – see *Vaginal tunic*.

Turbidity – a term used to describe the cloudiness of a solution. A highly turbid solution contains many suspended particles, which reduce the amount of light that passes through. Increased turbidity may be caused by crystals, cells and cellular debris, bacteria and secretions (semen, mucus, prostatic fluid and pus).

Turbinate bones – delicate scrolls of bone found in the caudal nasal cavity; covered with mucous membrane and their function is to moisten and warm the air before it travels to the lower airways, and also to trap small particles to prevent them from travelling further into the airway. See also *Ethmoid bones*.

Turgor – the elasticity of skin; related to the hydration status of skin.

Tympanic bulla – the bony case surrounding the middle ear.

Tympanic membrane – a thin membrane separating the external and middle ears. Also known as the eardrum.

U

Ulcer – the loss of tissue on the surface of the *skin* or on a *mucous membrane* to form an open sore; types include: *corneal, gastric, decubitus,* ulcers of the gingiva or mouth and *rodent ulcers* (*eosinophilic granulomas*). May be caused by chemical damage, irritation, neoplasia or infection.

Ulna – *bone* of the forelimb, lies side by side with the *radius*; the *olecranon* is the bony projection on its proximal end, which helps to stabilise it against the *humerus*.

Ultrasound – an imaging method in which sound waves are used to create an image on a screen.

Ultraviolet light (UV) – part of the electromagnetic spectrum, its wavelengths are shorter than those of visible light.

Umbilical cord – connects the placenta to the fetus; contains the umbilical artery and vein and the urachus.

Umbilical hernia – a defect in the *ventral midline* where the *umbilical cord* attached to the fetus and which has not closed over completely. The contents of this type of *hernia* can normally be easily replaced.

Umbilicus – the point where the umbilical cord enters the fetus.

Uncinaria stenocephala – the hookworm; uncommon parasitic *nematodes* affecting dog and cats. The *larvae* penetrate the skin and migrate to the small intestine. Clinical signs include diarrhoea and weight loss; seen more commonly in racing greyhounds and hunt kennels.

Unconsciousness – a comatose state where the animal is unaware of its surroundings and does not respond to external stimuli; can be caused by poisoning, *epilepsy*, head trauma or *anaesthesia*.

Unicellular – made up of or containing one cell; include *bacteria* and *protozoa*.

Unilateral – meaning one side of the body.

Unipolar – a rare type of *neurone* with the cell body lying to one side of the *axon*. See also *Bipolar, Multipolar*.

Urachus – a vessel that is present in the fetus and carries nitrogenous waste (urine) from the fetal bladder to the *umbilicus*. It normally closes at birth but occasionally can persist, resulting in leakage of urine from the umbilicus in *neonates*.

Uraemia – clinical signs associated with severe *renal failure*; include halitosis (ammonia smell to breath), ulceration of the mucous membranes, lethargy, vomiting, diarrhoea and coma.

Urate crystals – a type of crystal made from ammonium urate found in the urine; may be associated with bacterial infections, *portosystemic shunt*, acidic urine. Also frequently seen in the urine of Dalmations and English bulldogs.

Urea – the end-product of *protein* metabolism that is formed in the *liver* from the breakdown of *amino acids* and other compounds containing nitrogen and is excreted in the *urine*. Measurements of blood urea/nitrogen (BUN) levels can be used in the laboratory as an indication of how well the *kidneys* are functioning. An increase in the BUN level is known as *azotaemia* and can indicate *dehydration*, decreased *renal perfusion*, renal failure, or obstruction to the flow of urine; low urea may reflect liver dysfunction. See also *Creatinine*.

Ureter – a pair of tubes that connect the *renal pelvis* to the neck of the *bladder*. They enter the bladder at a site called the *trigone* and their role is to carry *urine* from the *kidneys* to the bladder. Each ureter is lined with *transitional epithelium*; *smooth muscle* in the ureter walls allows waves of *peristalsis* to propel the urine along the tube towards the bladder. Do not confuse with Urethra.

Urethra – a tube running from the *bladder* to the exterior of the body. In the male it runs to the tip of the *penis*; in the female it opens into the *vestibule*. *Smooth muscle* in the urethral wall acts as an internal *sphincter* (under involuntary control), while *striated muscle* surrounding the urethra acts as an external sphincter (under voluntary control). For *urination* to occur, the internal sphincter is forced open, once a certain volume of urine has collected in the bladder. This then causes the external sphincter to relax, allowing urination to occur. See also *Incontinence*.

Urethrostomy – a surgical procedure to create an opening from the urethra to the outside of the body.

Urethrotomy – a surgical procedure to create a temporary opening into the urethra.

Uric acid – nitrogenous waste excreted by birds and reptiles in urine. See also *Urate crystals*.

Urinalysis – physical and chemical analysis of urine; very useful for diagnosing, localising and monitoring disease. Involves visual and chemical assessment of the liquid portion; and separation (by centrifuge) and examination of the urine deposit (material suspended in the urine).

Urinary retention – accumulation of urine in the bladder because of an inability to urinate.

Urinary system – comprises the *kidneys, ureters, bladder* and *urethra*; functions are to excrete waste products (*urea*) and to maintain *homeostasis* (regulation by the *kidney* of the acid–base balance in the body).

Urinary tract infection – a bacterial, viral or fungal infection anywhere in the urinary tract from the kidneys to the bladder and urethra. Urinalysis and imaging of the urinary tract may help localise the disorder. Culture and identification of the organism involved allows treatment to be directed more efficiently.

Urination – also known as *micturition*; the act of periodically passing *urine* from the *bladder*, along the *urethra* and out of the body. In adults it is under both voluntary and involuntary control. Young puppies and kittens lack voluntary control over urination but this develops with age and with suitable training. An average dog will pass between 20 and 40 ml urine per kg bodyweight each day, a cat between 18 and 25 ml/kg per day. See also *Incontinence*.

Urine – a pale yellow fluid produced by the *kidneys* containing waste products from the *blood* (urea); stored in the *bladder* until it is expelled from the body via the *urethra*. Normal reference ranges for the *specific gravity* of urine are: dog 1.015–1.045 and cat 1.020–1.040 and the pH for both dogs and cats is between 5.5 and 7. Microscopic analysis of urine will also show the presence of *epithelial cells, leucocytes, erythrocytes, bacteria, spermatozoa, calculi* and *casts*. See also *Urate crystals, Urinalysis*.

Urine protein : creatinine ratio (UP : Cr) – a diagnostic test used to determine the amount of protein being lost in the urine; performed as a ratio to creatinine so that the dilution of the urine sample does not affect the results.

Urine protein electrophoresis (UPE) – a laboratory test where the proteins in urine are separated out into *albumin* and the various *globulins*; can be used to characterise the proteins being lost in the urine and to detect abnormalities in the globulins, which occur in some diseases such as some types of lymphoma and multiple myeloma.

Urine scald – skin damaged by urine soaking. Skin damaged by being soaked for a long time in urine. Eg an incontinent recumbent dog may get urine scalding if not frequently bathed and if soiled bedding is not frequently replaced.

Urobilinogen – a product from degradation of *bilirubin* in the liver; some is excreted in the urine. Increased levels in the urine may reflect *haemolytic* disease, and hepatic or biliary disease; however, this is not consistent and this test is not usually diagnostically useful.

Urolith – a stone made from mineralised material in the urinary tract; presence of uroliths is always abnormal. May be composed of aggregates of crystals such as struvite, oxalate, urate or cysteine. Cause irritation to the urinary tract, predispose the animal to *urinary tract infection*, and may cause urinary tract obstuction.

Urolithiasis – disease caused by the presence of *uroliths* in the urinary tract.

Urticaria – an allergic response that appears suddenly as raised swellings or wheals on the skin. The skin may also appear reddened and be *pruritic*.

Uterine inertia – lack of contraction of the uterine muscles during *parturition* causing maternal *dystocia*.

Uterine tubes – also known as oviducts or, in humans, the Fallopian tubes; the tubes which collect the *ovum* at *ovulation* and transport it to the uterus. *Fertilisation* takes place in the uterine tubes.

Uterus – a hollow muscular organ in female animals where the fertilised *ovum* implants and develops throughout pregnancy. In cat and dog the uterus consists of a short body and a pair of elongated horns. The inner surface of the uterus is called the *endometrium*, the muscular layer is the *myometrium*. Uterus is suspended from the dorsal surface of the *abdominal* cavity by the *broad ligament*; it is capable of great expansion during *pregnancy*. See also *Parturition, Primigravid*.

Utricle – bony sac-like structure in the *inner ear* containing sensory receptors to detect the changes in head position. These sensory cells transmit this information via *cranial nerve VIII* (*vestibulocochlear nerve*) to the *cerebellum* where balance and movement are controlled.

Uvea – the middle, vascular layer of the *eye* consisting of the *choroid, ciliary body* and *iris*.

Uveitis – inflammation of the uveal tract.

V

Vaccination – a process by which a harmless form of the pathogen is given to the animal (usually by injection or inhalation) to stimulate the *immune system* into making *antibodies* against the *pathogen*. If the animal is then exposed to a harmful form of the pathogen, the immune system can quickly mount an effective response to it.

Vacuole – a cavity in the *cytoplasm* of a cell that may contain water, waste products or may store products such as lipid, carbohydrate or protein.

Vacutainer – a tube made of glass and sealed with a rubber bung; there is a vacuum in the tube and the tubes are used for collecting blood.

Vacuum-assisted autoclave – machine used to sterilise equipment by using steam under pressure; by incorporating a vacuum pump, higher temperatures can be reached more quickly. See also *Autoclave*.

Vagina – part of the *female reproductive tract*; a muscular tube extending from the *cervix* to the *vulva*, the caudal part is called the *vestibule*. Has both *reproductive* and *urinary* functions: reproductive functions are to receive the *sperm* during *mating*, and to expand, forming part of the birth canal, during *parturition*; the *urethra* opens into the floor of the vestibule, allowing *urine* to pass out of the body.

Vaginal tunic – a layer of connective tissue surrounding the *testis*, *epididymis* and *spermatic cord* in the *scrotum*.

Vagus nerve – *cranial nerve X*; supplies *parasympathetic* nerve fibres to most of the viscera of the *respiratory* and *digestive* tracts.

Valsava manoeuvre – expiration (trying to breathe out) against a closed *glottis*, which increases the pressure in the thorax; occurs during *emesis* (vomiting), or when an animal is straining, eg to defecate, or during parturition.

Valve – a small flap in a hollow organ that controls the flow and direction of blood or fluid; eg valves in *veins* and *lymphatic vessels* and the valves in the *heart*, preventing the back-flow of blood.

Vaporiser – a piece of equipment that allows a volatile agent to be used; can be calibrated and non-calibrated and used in or out of circuit.

Vas deferens – see *Deferent duct*.

Vascular – having a blood supply. See also *Avascular, Ischaemia*.

Vasectomy – the surgical section (cutting) and ligation of the *deferent duct* (vas deferens) to prevent sperm passing out of the body. Because the male hormones are still produced a vasectomised animal will still mate with females but will not make them pregnant. Vasectomy is useful in species such as the ferret where the females must be mated to end oestrus.

Vasoconstriction – the narrowing of blood vessels as a result of the smooth muscle in the vessel wall contracting; occurs when *blood pressure* drops – the *medulla oblongata* co-ordinates a response to increase blood pressure by various means, including constricting the blood vessels. See also Vasodilation.

Vasodilation – the widening of the blood vessels as a result of the *smooth muscle* in the vessel wall relaxing; occurs when *blood pressure* increases – the *medulla oblongata* co-ordinates a response to reduce blood pressure by various means, including dilating the blood vessels. See also *Vasoconstriction*.

Vasopressin – see *Antidiuretic hormone (ADH)*.

VAT – a tax added to the cost of most purchases.

VDS – Veterinary Defence Society; an organisation that advises on ethics and legal issues within veterinary practices and for veterinary surgeons.

Vector – an insect such as a *tick* or *flea* that carries a *parasite* from one *host* to another, eg the flea that acts as a vector for *Dipylidium caninum*.

Vein – a type of large *blood vessel* that carries de-oxygenated *blood* (except in the *pulmonary vein*) back to the *heart*. Veins have *valves* to prevent the back-flow of blood and the flow is helped along by the movement of body muscles around the veins.

Velpeau sling – a bandage used to support the shoulder.

Vena cava (pl. **venae cavae)** – the 'great veins', carry *blood* from the body back to the *right atrium* of the *heart*. See also Aorta.

Venables compression plate – an orthopaedic implant used for fracture fixation; available in various lengths and distinguishable from other plates by having a rectangular shape with round screw holes. See also *Dynamic compression plate*, *Sherman plate*.

Venepuncture – an *aseptic* procedure by which a hypodermic needle or *catheter* is inserted into a *vein*. See also *Intravenous (IV)*.

Venodilator – a drug that causes dilation of veins; used to treat cardiac disease, eg glyceryl trinitrate.

Venomous – an animal that is poisonous or produces poison.

Venous – referring to veins.

Venous pooling – collection of blood in the veins, usually in the distal limbs.

Ventilate – to manually 'breathe' for a patient while they are anaesthetised.

Ventilator – a piece of equipment that mechanically 'breathes' for the patient, factors such as rate and volume can be altered.

Ventral – anatomical description meaning towards or near the belly or lower body surface; also used to describe the underside of the neck and tail. See also *Dorsal*.

Ventricle – **1.** one of four fluid-filled chambers in the *brain*. **2.** one of two blood-filled chambers in the *heart*.

Ventricular septal defect – a congenital heart defect in which the septum between the ventricles has not formed properly, leaving a defect so that blood can pass from one ventricle to the other. Size of the defect determines how severe the clinical signs are, ie a small defect might mean an animal is asymptomatic, whereas a large defect can cause *congestive heart failure* (CHF). A heart murmur can be heart on *auscultation*.

Ventriculus – see *Gizzard*.

Ventrodorsal (VD) – term used in radiography to describe the view, the beam enters the ventral surface and leaves through the dorsal surface.

Ventroflexion – flexion of the neck so that the chin rests close to the sternum; may be associated with *hypokalaemia* in cats.

Venule – a small blood vessel that collects de-oxygenated blood from the *capillary* network and feeds it back to the *veins*.

Vernier scales – a scale for measuring small objects accurately, present on the stage of many microscopes.

Vertebra (pl. **vertebrae)** – one of the bony segments of the *vertebral column*. Each vertebra provides points for attachment of muscles. See also *Spinous process*, *Transverse process*.

Vertebral column – also known as the spinal column; extends from the skull to the tip of the tail and is made up of *vertebrae* separated by *intervertebral discs* and connected by *ligaments*. Can be divided into segments, namely *cervical*, *thoracic*, *lumbar*, *sacral* and *coccygeal*. Provides support for the body, attachments for many muscles, and houses and protects the *spinal cord* and *meninges*. See also *Intervertebral disc*.

Vertebrate – an animal that possesses a bony or cartilaginous backbone (*vertebral column*). Mammals, birds, reptiles, amphibians and fish are all vertebrates. Insects, worms and arachnids are *invertebrates* (without a backbone).

Vertical canal ablation (VCA) – the surgical removal of the vertical ear canal, which is carried out in cases of recurrent and non-responsive *otitis externa*. See also *Lateral wall resection*, *Total ear canal ablation*.

Vestibular syndrome – a disease affecting the balance mechanisms that occurs most commonly in elderly animals. Symptoms include a head tilt, circling, *ataxia*, *nystagmus* and often *nausea* and *vomiting*. Cause is often *idiopathic* but it can sometimes be related to an inner ear infection (*otitis interna*). First-aid treatment is limited but involves settling the patient in a comfortable kennel so that injury through falling is prevented.

Vestibular system – a system within the ear that informs the *central nervous system* of the movement and position of the head; very important for balance. It consists of the *semicircular canals*, the *utricle* and the *saccule*. Impulses travel from the vestibular system through the *vestibulocochlear nerve* (*cranial nerve VIII*) to the *cerebellum* in the brain, where balance and movement are controlled.

Vestibular window – see *Oval window*.

Vestibule – a body cavity that leads to another cavity, eg in the vagina and in the ear.

Vestibulocochlear nerve – *cranial nerve VIII*; concerned with the senses of hearing and balance.

Veterinary Poisons Information Service (VPIS) – a telephone service that provides emergency 24-hour information for veterinary surgeons on the clinical effect of most poisons, along with advice on suitable antidotes and treatment methods.

Veterinary Surgeon's Act 1966 – professional legislation governing the veterinary profession and restricts the right to practise veterinary surgery to listed members of the *Royal College of Veterinary Surgeons* (RCVS).

Vial – a small glass bottle that can be opened by breaking it at the neck; some have a red dot on the neck and placing your thumb over this area enables easier breaking. Also called *ampoule*.

Vibrissa (pl. **vibrissae)** – whiskers, large sensory hairs on the *muzzle* of many animals, used to help detect head position in relation to objects in the environment.

Villus (pl. **villi)** – a finger-like projection on the *mucosa* of the small intestine that serves to increase the surface area to allow greater absorption of nutrients.

Viraemia – describes the presence of viruses in the *blood*.

Viral haemorrhagic disease (VHD) – also known as haemorrhagic viral disease (HVD); frequently fatal viral infection affecting rabbits and often causing sudden death. There is a vaccine available to prevent this infection.

Virulence – the measure of a *pathogen*'s ability to cause disease; its virulence depends on its invasiveness and its toxigenicity.

Virus – a microscopic infectious agent that requires a host cell in which to reproduce and develop; smaller than a *bacterium* and contains within a *capsid* either *RNA* or *DNA* but not both; some also have an outer *envelope* around the capsid. Reproduce by replication within the host cell; very difficult to treat because it is hard to produce a drug that can gain entry into a cell and kill the virus within but not also kill the host cell. Important viral diseases include *canine parvovirus, canine distemper, feline leukaemia virus* and *feline immunodeficiency virus.*

Viscera – the internal organs of the body.

Visceral larval migrans (VLM) – *nematode* larvae that migrate to the tissues. *Toxocara canis* is a potentially *zoonotic* nematode parasite that can have this effect in humans.

Viscosity – the thickness of a fluid.

Vision – another term for eyesight.

Vital capacity – the maximum volume of gas that can be expired after a maximal *inspiration*.

Vital signs – signs of life, eg *pulse, respiration,* eye position, pupil size, *corneal reflex* and movement.

Vitamin A – a fat-soluble vitamin, required to maintain skin, vision and hearing. Excesses are toxic.

Vitamin B-complex – water-soluble vitamins, the group contains thiamine (B1), riboflavin (B2), pyridoxine (B6), cobalamin (B12), folic acid, pantothenic acid, niacin and biotin. All are required for growth and metabolism.

Vitamin C – water-soluble vitamin, required to maintain healing properties and prevent conditions such as scurvy.

Vitamin D – a fat-soluble vitamin, required for growth and maintenance of bones and teeth. Excesses are toxic.

Vitamin E – a fat-soluble vitamin, required for maintenance of skin and reproductive ability.

Vitamin K – a fat-soluble vitamin, required to maintain coagulation properties. Used to treat warfarin poisoning. See *Warfarin.*

Vitreous humour – the viscous, jelly-like liquid that fills the *posterior chamber* of the eye. See also *Aqueous humour.*

Vivarium – an area in which live animals are kept in conditions as close to their natural environment as possible, eg reptiles are kept in an environment with the correct temperature, humidity, substrate and feeding regimens.

Viviparous – giving birth to live young. See also *Oviparous, Ovoviviparous*.

Vocal folds – found in the *larynx*; membranous folds that vibrate to produce sound as air passes over them.

Vocalisation – the act of making a sound via the vocal folds.

Volatile anaesthetic agent – gaseous agent used to induce or, more commonly, maintain anaesthesia, eg isoflurane, sevoflurane and halothane.

Volkmann curette – a double-ended surgical instrument used for scraping out bone cavities; one end has a round cup, the other an oval cup.

Volkmann retractor – a hand-held retractor with a tip that looks like a rake; used to retract tendons and muscles during surgery to expose the structures underneath.

Volvulus – a twist of the stomach or small intestine that cuts off the blood supply, resulting in ischaemia and necrosis of the affected part. See also *Gastric dilatation/volvulus (GDV)*.

Vomiting – also known as emesis; an active process by which the *abdominal* muscles contract and food and liquid pass out of the *stomach*, up the *oesophagus* and out of the mouth. The vomited material is usually partially digested and has an acidic *pH*; can sometimes be confused with *regurgitation*. See also Haematemesis.

Von Willebrand's disease – a hereditary disease affecting Doberman pinschers and Weimaraners in which there is a defect in platelet function in the blood; *haemorrhage* may spontaneously occur, eg *epistaxis*, or it may occur following surgery.

Von Willebrand's factor (vWF) – a protein which is important for platelets to perform their haemostatic function. Hereditary deficiency of this factor is called Von Willebrand's disease.

Voracious appetite – eating large volumes of food.

Vulva – the most caudal part of the female genital tract, the vulval opening is surrounded by the labia.

'Walking dandruff' – See *Cheyletiella*.

Warfarin – an *anticoagulant* used as a rat bait or *rodenticide*. Accidental ingestion of rat bait by a pet should be treated as an emergency. Induce *emesis* if the poison was ingested within the last hour. The antidote to warfarin poisoning is *vitamin K* (Konakion).

Warning light systems – red lights or an illuminated sign at any entrance point into the X-ray room.

Washing – performed in wet development of radiographic film. Washing the film (after fixing) for 15–30 minutes removes any processing chemicals.

Water deprivation test – a test used to diagnose *diabetes insipidus* that involves withholding water from an animal until it has lost 5% of its bodyweight and measuring the specific gravity of urine throughout the test period. Normal animals will concentrate their urine as they become dehydrated. Animals with diabetes insipidus are incapable of concentrating their urine. This test should be used with great care and *never* in animals with renal dysfunction.

'Water hammer' pulse – a strong and jerky pulse, associated with congenital heart defects.

Water intake – to maintain hydration levels, an adult animal needs an intake of water of 50–60 ml/kg bodyweight per day.

Water-soluble vitamins – vitamins B and C; a daily intake is required because excess is not stored in the body.

Water's canister – See *To-and-fro anaesthetic circuit*.

Weaning – the process of young animals beginning to eat solid food rather than drinking their mother's milk.

Weil's disease – also known as leptospirosis; the causal agent of this *zoonotic* disease is *Leptospira icterohaemorrhagiae* (a *bacterium*). Spread by direct contact with the *urine* of infected dogs and rats. Clinical signs include *haemorrhagic diarrhoea, jaundice* and *pyrexia*.

Wet-dry dressing – used in infected wounds secreting moderate to large amounts of exudates, eg swabs soaked in Hartmann's solution are placed in or over the wound and bandaged in place. The dressing would be removed 24 hours later, removing infected and necrotic tissue.

Whelping – a term used to describe *parturition* in the bitch.

Whipworm – see *Trichuris vulpis*.

White blood cell – see *Leucocyte*.

White matter – area of the brain and spinal cord containing the myelinated nerve fibres. See also *Grey matter*.

White pulp – one of two types of tissue found in the *spleen*, consisting of *lymph nodes*. See also Red pulp.

Wobbler syndrome – also known as cervical vertebral spondylopathy; an abnormality in the *vertebrae* in the neck that puts pressure on the spinal cord in the affected area leading to *ataxia*. Large-breed dogs, such as Doberman pinschers, and horses are more commonly affected.

Wood's lamp – a hand-held ultraviolet light that causes some *dermatophytes* (such as *Microsporum canis*) to glow bright green, and is used to diagnose *dermatophytosis* (ringworm). However, many dermatophytes do not fluoresce under a Wood's lamp, so a negative result does not rule out dermatophytosis.

Wound – trauma creating a break in the skin.

Xenograft – skin is taken from a patient of another species.

Xiphoid process – also known as the xiphisternum; the most caudal and the longest of the eight bones (*sternebrae*) in the *sternum*. A cartilage plate is attached to the xiphoid process and the abdominal muscles attach here. See also Manubrium.

X-ray machine – there are three types of X-ray machine:

❀ Portable – have low outputs, can be used for field radiography
❀ Mobile – more powerful than portables but can only be moved between rooms
❀ Fixed – the most powerful machine and cannot be moved.

Xylazine – an α2 agonist, used as an analgesic and sedative.

Y

Yeast – a fungus; examples that can cause disease in animals are *Candida albicans* and *Malassezia pachydermatis*.

Z

Ziehl-Neelsen stain – a stain used to distinguish acid fast bacteria.

Zoonosis (pl. **zoonoses)** – a zoonotic disease is one which can be passed between animals and humans. Extreme care must be taken and scrupulous hygiene must be observed when dealing with an animal with a zoonotic disease. Examples of zoonoses include *sarcoptic mange*, *ringworm* and *toxoplasmosis*. See also *Barrier nursing*, *Isolation*, *Rabies*, *Weil's disease*.

Zygomatic arch – the cheekbone.

Zygomatic salivary gland – paired saliva-producing gland found in the cheek area close to the *zygomatic arch*.

Zygote – the fused male and female *gametes* (ie the *spermatozoon* and the *ovum*); when fertilisation occurs the zygote starts to divide and becomes an *embryo*.

Prefixes and suffixes

Prefixes

Prefix	Meaning	Example
A-, an-	without, lack of	Anuria (no urine produced)
Ab-	away from	Abduction(move away from body)
Ad-	towards, to, near	Adrenal (near the kidney)
Ante-	before, in front of	Antenatal (before birth)
Anti-	against, opposing	Antiseptic (against sepsis)
De-	remove, reverse	Dehydrate (remove water)
Dys-	difficult, painful, abnormal	Dysuria (difficulty passing urine)
Ecto-	outside	Ectoparasite (parasite living outside body)
Endo-	inside, inner	Endometrium (lining of uterus)
Extra-	outside of, beyond	Extracellular (outside the cell)
Hemi-	half	Hemiplegia (paralysis on one half of body)
Hyper-	excessive, above	Hyperthermia (high body temperature)
Hypo-	deficient, below	Hypothyroidism (deficient thyroid activity)
Infra-	below, beneath	Infraspinatus (muscles below the spine)
Inter-	between	Intercostal (between the ribs)
Intra-	within, into	Intramuscular (into the muscle)

Prefix	Meaning	Example
Neo-	new, recent	Neonate (newborn)
Peri-	around	Periosteum (around the bone)
Poly-	much,excessive,many	Polyphagia (excessive appetite)
Post-	after	Postoperative (after surgery)
Pre-	before	Prenatal (before birth)
Pseudo-	false	Pseudocyesis (false pregnancy)
Retro-	behind, backward	Retroperitoneal (behind the peritoneum)
Semi-	half, partial	Semi permeable (partly permeable)
Sub-	under, beneath	Subcutaneous (under the skin)
Super-	above, superior, excess	Supernumerary (excessive number)
Supra-	above, higher	Supraspinatous (muscle above spine)
Trans-	across, through	Transplacental (passing across the placenta)
Ultra-	beyond, excess	Ultrasonic (beyond upper limit of hearing)

Suffixes

Suffix	Meaning	Example
-algia	pain	neuralgia (nerve pain)
-centesis	surgical puncture	cystocentesis (from bladder) to remove fluid
-cyte	cell	leukocyte (white blood cell) erythrocyte (red blood cell)
-ectomy	cutting out	appendectomy (appendix removal)
-emesis	vomit	haematemesis (vomiting blood)
-itis	inflammation	otitis (inflammation of ear) cystitis (bladder inflammation)
-logy	science, study of	biology (study of life)
-oma	tumour	lipoma (benign tumour of adipose tissue)
-paenia	lack of, deficiency	lymphopaenia (lack of lymphocytes)
-pexy	fixation	gastropexy (fixation of stomach)
-phobia	abnormal fear, intolerance	photophobia (intolerance of light)
-plasia	growing, changing	neoplasia (new growth, tumour)
-pnoea	breathing	apnoea (absence of breathing)
-scopy	act of examining	endoscopy (using an endoscope)
-stomy	surgical opening	gastrostomy (surgical opening into stomach)
-tomy	cutting, incision	cystotomy (incision into bladder)

Reference ranges

Reference Ranges
(Courtesy of IDEXX Laboratories, Wetherby, UK)

Haematology ranges

Haematology	Canine	Feline
Red blood cells (RBC; $\times 10^{12}$/l)	5.5–8.5	5.0–10.0
Haemoglobin (Hb; g/dl)	12.0–18.0	9.0–15.0
Haematocrit (Hct)	0.38–0.57	0.26–0.47
Mean corpuscular haemoglobin (MCH; pg)	20.0–26.0	13.0–17.5
Mean corpuscular volume (MCV; fl)	61.0–80.0	42.0–57.0
Mean corpuscular haemoglobin concentration (MCHC; g/dl)	30.0–36.0	28.0–36.0
White blood cells (WBC; $\times 10^{9}$/l)	6.0–15.0	6.0–15.0
Neutrophils ($\times 10^{9}$/l)	2.5–12.5	2.5–12.5
Band neutrophils ($\times 10^{9}$/l)	0.0–0.4	0.0–0.2
Lymphocytes ($\times 10^{9}$/l)	0.5–4.8	2.0–7.0
Monocytes ($\times 10^{9}$/l)	< 0.8	< 0.6
Eosinophils ($\times 10^{9}$/l)	0.05–0.8	0.05–0.7
Platelets ($\times 10^{9}$/l)	150–450	150–550

Notes: There are a number of breed variations affecting haematology parameters. For example: sighthounds, such as greyhounds, have a higher packed cell volume than other breeds; about half of all clinically normal Cavalier King Charles Spaniels have low platelet counts with enlarged platelet forms (macroplatelets).

Biochemistry ranges

Biochemistry	Canine	Feline
Total protein (TP; g/l)	55–75	60–80
Albumin (g/l)	25–41	25–45
Globulin (g/l)	20–45	25–45
Urea (mmol/l)	2.5–6.7	2.5–9.9
Creatinine (µmol/l)	20–150	20–177
Alanine aminotransferase (ALT; IU/l)	5–60	5–60
Alkaline phosphatase (ALKP; IU/l)	< 130	< 60
Total bilirubin (µmol/l)	0.1–5.1	0.1–5.1
Amylase (IU/l)	100–1200	100–1200
Lipase (IU/l)	0.1–200	0.1–250
Glucose (mmol/l)	3.3–5.8	3.3–5.8
Creatine kinase (CK; IU/l)	20–225	20–225
Cholesterol (mmol/l)	3.2–6.2	2.2–4.0
Fasting bile acids (µmol/l)	0.1–5.0	0.1–5.0
Triglycerides (mmol/l)	0.3–1.2	0.3–1.2
Sodium (mmol/l)	135–155	145–157
Potassium (mmol/l)	3.6–5.6	3.5–5.5
Sodium : Potassium ratio	28.8–40.0	28.0–40.0
Inorganic phosphorus (mmol/l)	0.8–1.6	0.9–2.2
Calcium (mmol/l)	2.45–3.10	2.00–2.50
Chloride (mmol/l)	100–116	100–124

Note that reference ranges vary depending on the machine and analytical method used.